W9-DGX-548

Serial Murderers and Their Victims

Contemporary Issues in Crime and Justice Series
Roy Roberg, San Jose State University: Series Editor

Crime and Justice: Issues and Ideas (1984)
Philip Jenkins, Pennsylvania State University

Hard Time: Understanding and Reforming the Prison (1987)
Robert Johnson, The American University

The Myth of a Racist Criminal Justice System (1987)
William Wilbanks, Florida International University

Gambling without Guilt: The Legitimation of an American Pastime (1988)
John Rosecrance, University of Nevada at Reno

Ethics in Crime and Justice: Decisions and Dilemmas (1989)
Joycelyn M. Pollock-Byrne, University of Houston

Sense and Nonsense about Crime: A Policy Guide, Second Edition (1989)
Samuel Walker, University of Nebraska at Omaha

Crime Victims: An Introduction to Victimology, Second Edition (1990)
Andrew Karmen, John Jay College of Criminal Justice

Death Work: A Study of the Modern Execution Process (1990)
Robert Johnson, The American University

Lawlessness and Reform: The FBI in Transition (1990)
Tony G. Poveda, State University of New York at Plattsburg

Women, Prison, and Crime (1990)
Joycelyn M. Pollock-Byrne, University of Houston

Perspectives on Terrorism (1991)
Harold J. Vetter, Portland State University
Gary R. Perlstein, Portland State University

Serial Murderers and Their Victims (1991)
Eric W. Hickey, California State University, Fresno

Serial Murderers and Their Victims

Eric W. Hickey
California State University, Fresno

Brooks/Cole Publishing Company
Pacific Grove, California

Consulting Editor: Roy R. Roberg

Brooks/Cole Publishing Company
A Division of Wadsworth, Inc.

© 1991 by Wadsworth, Inc., Belmont, California 94002.
All rights reserved. No part of this book may be reproduced, stored in a retrieval system,
or transcribed, in any form or by any means—electronic, mechanical, photocopying,
recording or otherwise—without the prior written permission of the publisher, Brooks/
Cole Publishing Company, Pacific Grove, California 93950, a division of Wadsworth, Inc.

Printed in the United States of America

10 9 8 7 6 5 4 3

Library of Congress Cataloging-in-Publication Data

Hickey, Eric W.
    Serial murderers and their victims / Eric W. Hickey.
      p. cm.
    Includes bibliographical references and index.
    ISBN 0-534-15414-X
    1. Serial murders—United States. I. Title.
HV6529.H53 1991
364.1'523'0973—dc20   90-21988
                                      CIP

Sponsoring Editor: *Cynthia C. Stormer*
Editorial Assistant: *Cathleen S. Collins*
Production Coordinator: *Fiorella Ljunggren*
Production: *Stacey Sawyer, Sawyer & Williams*
Manuscript Editor: *Stacey Sawyer*
Permissions Editor: *Marie Dubois*
Interior Design: *Adriane Bosworth*
Cover Design: *Sharon L. Kinghan*
Art Coordinator: *Stacey Sawyer*
Interior Illustration: *Anne Eldridge, HieroGraphics*
Typesetting: *Harrison Typesetting, Inc.*
Cover Printing: *Phoenix Color Corporation*
Printing and Binding: *The Maple-Vail Book Manufacturing Group*

TO THE VICTIMS, BOTH THE LIVING AND THE DEAD. MAY THEIR SUFFERING NOT BE IGNORED OR FORGOTTEN.

AND TO THE MEMORY OF HAROLD E. SMITH, MY FRIEND AND COLLEAGUE.

About the Author

Eric W. Hickey earned a Ph.D. in sociology from Brigham Young University and taught sociology and criminology courses at West Georgia College and at Ball State University. In 1990 he became a member of the criminology department at California State University, Fresno, where he currently teaches courses in psychology of crime, juvenile delinquency, victimology, and corrections.

Dr. Hickey has had considerable field experience. For nearly three years he worked with psychopaths, sex offenders, psychotics, and the criminally insane in the forensic unit of the Utah State Mental Hospital. He has published articles and book chapters on female offenders, missing and murdered children, and victimization. He also continues to conduct extensive research on violent offenders, victims, and deviant behavior.

Foreword

The Contemporary Issues in Crime and Justice Series introduces important topics that until now have been neglected or inadequately covered to students and professionals in criminal justice, criminology, law, psychology, and sociology.

The volumes cover philosophical and theoretical issues and analyze the most recent research findings and their implications for practice. Consequently, each volume will stimulate further thinking and debate on the issues it covers, in addition to providing direction for policy formulation and implementation.

The phenomenon of serial murder has become a very serious social problem; yet there is very little understanding about those who commit these heinous acts or the impact such acts have on survivors of the victims. This empirical examination of the lives of 203 serial offenders by Eric Hickey significantly adds to our understanding of these topics.

The book examines the cultural, historical, and religious influences that have, over time, contributed to the stereotyping of and myths about serial killers. It also offers a theoretical foundation for the violent behavior of serial murderers by discussing biological, psychological, structural, and social process theories. In addition, it presents the author's trauma-control model for understanding serial murder behavior—a model that suggests that violent behavior, fueled by facilitators (such as fantasies, alcohol, and pornography) and reinforced by the "routine" traumas of day-to-day living, keeps the serial killer caught up in a self-perpetuating cycle of violence.

Hickey has chosen to classify serial offenders into three groupings—female, male, and team killers—which allows for a more precise examination and understanding of each class of offender. Profiles of the various types of serial killers are provided in an effort to understand their personal histories and patterns of killing. For example, case studies of offenders such as Nancy Hazel Doss (the "Giggling Grandma"), Theodore Robert Bundy, David Richard Berkowitz ("Son of Sam"), and Kenneth Bianchi and Angelo Buono (the "Hillside Stranglers"), although gruesome and often macabre, offer insight into their personalities and behavior. In line with this approach, an in-depth interview with a serial murderer, recounting his crimes and describing his emotions, is included. The book also examines empirically the victims of serial killers, with speical attention focused on missing and murdered children.

The subject of the growing number of unsolved killings in the United States is addressed, along with that of serial killing in foreign countries. Finally, the role of law enforcement in dealing with serial murderers, the final disposition of cases, and future issues and research agendas are discussed. Until now, little research has been done and serious thought given to this topic; this work, however, will change all that. Because of its empirical and comprehensive nature, *Serial Murderers and Their Victims* will make a major contribution to the understanding of this topic and its impact on society.

Roy Roberg

Preface

Serial Murderers and Their Victims is the first comprehensive, empirical examination of serial murder in the United States. It provides a thorough analysis of the lives of serial killers through the examination of individual cases, typology construction, and models. The extensive data included not only provide insights into individual killers but reveal factors common to more than 200 serial killers—including male solo offenders, female offenders, and those who murder with accomplices.

Serial Murderers debunks the myths and stereotypes that have evolved from public efforts to find easy explanations for the relatively rare yet horrifying phenomenon of serial murder. It also raises many questions about serial killers and their behavior. The research for this book has included visits to prisons, police departments, and numerous university libraries across the United States, as well as interviews with several serial murderers, their spouses, ex-spouses, lovers, and one-time friends. I explored the lives of dead victims and victims who survived the attacks, and I communicated with families and relatives of the victims. The social, psychological, physiological, and financial devastation inflicted by serial murderers on their victims and the victims' families belies the fact that victims are often reduced to little more than crime statistics. The etiology of victimization and the continued suffering of survivors must not be forgotten or neglected.

Organization

This book explores five aspects of serial murder. First, Chapter 1 examines the emergence of serial killing in the United States and the many problems involved in adequately defining the phenomenon. Chapters 2, 3, and 4 explore cultural, biological, psychological, and sociological frameworks as explanations for serial murder and present a model for understanding serial killing as a *process*. Chapter 5 examines the victims and prospective victims of serial murderers: young women, childen, and the elderly. Chapters 6, 7, 8, and 9 sort out the demographic, social, and behavioral characteristics of male and female offenders and those who murder with accomplices; they also include an indepth interview with an incarcerated serial killer. Finally, Chapter 10 addresses current issues faced by law enforcement officials, such as the detection and the apprehension of offenders using psychological profiling, sentencing, punishment, treatment, and prevention of serial murder.

This book is intended for students interested in understanding the nature of serial killing, the offenders, and their victims. It is designed to supplement a variety of college and university courses—including criminology, criminal justice, deviant behavior, victimology, abnormal psychology, and penology. Students using this book will be exposed to concepts and information that will help prepare them to understand society's most dangerous criminals. For those currently working in law enforcement, this book should serve as a useful reference and inservice tool.

Acknowledgments

I wish to recognize and thank many people who helped during the course of my research and its publication. I have deeply appreciated the counsel and encouragement of my colleagues John R. Fuller, John D. Hewitt, Ted Simon, and Candice Skrapec. I also wish to thank Scott Berning, Sally Clark, Paige Martin, and Allison Riley for their assistance in data collection, as well as Gena Herring, Amy McClellan, Kathy Downs, and Mike Elliott for their secretarial support. I especially want to thank Sue Sergott for her thoroughness, thoughtfulness, and extra hours donated to ensure the timely completion of this manuscript. My gratitude also goes to my special friend Thom O. Garg for his willingness to assist me in locating materials pertinent to this research.

A special thanks to Ball State University for their financial support in helping me complete this project and to Roberta Roper of the Stephanie Roper Committee and Ruth and John Kuzmaak of Victim's Voices United for their willingness to share their personal tragedies and their efforts to be more than mere survivors. I also want to thank those who reviewed the manuscript for their helpful comments. They are Terry C. Cox of Eastern Kentucky University, Ron Holmes of the University of Louisville, Chester McLaughlin of the University of Texas at El Paso, and Marc Riedel of Southern Illinois University. In addition, my appreciation goes to the entire Brooks/Cole team, especially editors Cindy Stormer, Claire Verduin, and Roy Roberg, for their support and guidance, and to editorial assistant Cathy Collins and production services manager Fiorella Ljunggren, for their enthusiasm and assistance in producing this book. I also want to sincerely thank Stacey C. Sawyer, who deserves much credit for her insightful and timely editing of this book. Never could an author expect to find a more competent, professional team of editors than those provided by Brooks/Cole.

Finally, and most importantly, I want to thank my lovely wife, Margo, for her encouragement and sacrifice on my behalf, and our four children Trevor, Erin, Alicen, and Chad, who missed their Dad when he "had to work on his book."

Eric W. Hickey

Contents

CHAPTER 1

Introduction: The Phenomenon of Serial Murder

The apparent increase in modern serial, or multiple, murders has incited interest among social scientists in several areas. Researchers have begun to explore the social, psychological, and biological makeup of the offenders in order to establish accurate profiles. In spite of their efforts, the body of knowledge about serial murders remains small compared to the number of unanswered questions—especially about the extent of the phenomenon. Law enforcement personnel and academicians have only begun to understand the dynamics of serial killing and its etiology, or causation.

The pure sensationalism and horror of serial murder has also spawned a plethora of novels about such murders, and the figure of the "cold-blooded, senseless" serial killer has been exploited by the media: for example, in television documentaries and prime-time shows—such as those that depicted California's Hillside Strangler case and the infamous Ted Bundy (*The Deliberate Stranger*)—and in various box office thrillers. Because of the wide publicity given to serial murderers, a stereotype of this type of killer has formed in the mind of American society. The offender is a ruthless, bloodthirsty sex monster who lives a Jekyll-and-Hyde existence—probably next door to you. In his book *The Red Dragon*, Harris (1987) gave a fictional account of a serial killer who took great pleasure in annihilating entire families. Later his work was made into the movie *Manhunter*, a terrifying drama of psychopathology, blood, and carnage.

The fictional accounts of serial killing, however, often fail to surpass the horror described in nonfictional accounts of serial murder by writers such as Ann Rule—former acquaintance of Ted Bundy, who was executed in January, 1989. Besides her work on Bundy (*The Stranger Beside Me*, 1980), she has written about Randy Woodfield (*The I-5 Killer*, 1984), Jerry Brudos (*Lust Killer*, 1983), and Harvey Carignan (*The Want-Ad Killer*, 1988). Recently, female serial killers have been given increased attention—for instance, by R. Robin McDonald (*Black Widow*, 1986).

The researchers who have been examining the phenomenon of serial murder to promote greater understanding—and, they hope, develop intervention strategies—have also been busy. Case study analysis of serial murder has begun to provide researchers with insightful information, however tenuous. For example, Elliot Leyton (1986) in his books *Hunting Humans* and

Compulsive Killers provides in-depth examinations into the lives and minds of a few contemporary U.S. serial killers and their relationships with their victims. In *Mass Murder: The Growing Menace* (1985), Jack Levin and Jamie Fox assess some of the dynamics of serial and mass murder. Ronald Holmes and James DeBurger, in their work *Serial Murder* (1988), formulate typologies and include material gathered from interviews with serial murderers. Holmes's second work, *Profiling Violent Crimes* (1990), has become a useful tool in the investigation of serial murder. Steve Egger's work, *Serial Murder: An Elusive Phenomenon* (1990), underscores several critical problems encountered by researchers of serial murder. Robert Keppel, who as a law enforcement officer investigated several cases of serial killing, published his observations in *Serial Murder: Future Implications for Police Investigations* (1989).

Many other people associated with research on serial murder have also contributed to the body of knowledge on the subject. For instance, Harold Smith, editor for *Criminal Justice International* at the University of Chicago, has collected data on transnational serial killers—that is, killers whose victims are from different countries. Philip Jenkins, at Pennsylvania State University, has explored the social environments of serial murderers, whereas Candice Skrapec, a psychologist at John Jay College of Criminal Justice, has gathered data on the psychogenic status of serial offenders. Al Carlisle, a psychologist at the Utah State Prison and Provo Canyon Boys School, has explored dissociative states and other forces that may affect the mind of a serial killer.

People in law enforcement have been dealing with serial murders for many, many years. Recently, however, the nature and sophistication of investigation techniques have changed. Computer technology has expedited data collection and analysis. During the mid-1980s, the Federal Bureau of Investigation established, at their Behavioral Science Unit in Quantico, Virginia, the Violent Criminal Apprehension Program (VI-CAP). The VI-CAP program is designed to collect detailed information on homicides throughout the United States. Investigators like FBI Agent Robert Ressler, who has probably interviewed more serial killers than anyone else in the United States, have made considerable progress in understanding certain types of serial offenders. Ressler and colleagues published their findings in *Sexual Homicide* (1988). In addition, the U.S. government continues to develop programs such as the National Center for the Analysis of Violent Crime (NCAVC) to focus specifically on repetitive offenders, including serial murderers.

Numbers and Types of Mass Murders and Serial Killings in the United States

The number of murders in the United States currently fluctuates around 20,000 per year. Over the past 20 years we have seen the murder and best way to lash out against a cold, forbidding society is to destroy its children. Gunning down children on a schoolyard not only provides the needed sense of power and control but is also a way of wreaking vengeance where it hurts the community the most.

The social impact of mass murders tends to be restricted to the communities in which they occurred. Increased security at schools, office buildings, and shopping malls is the usual response, including improved social services to better identify potentially dangerous individuals. However, the track record at predicting criminal behavior thus far has been dismal. Recognizing potential mass murderers is usually a matter of hindsight; we are quick to attach motivating factors and personality defects to offenders once they have vented themselves on their victims. The fact remains, however, that mass murders, in relation to other crimes—even other forms of homicide—are relatively rare, and they appear to occur as randomly as serial killings do.

Differences Between Mass Murderers and Serial Killers

In both mass and serial murder cases, victims die as the offender momentarily gains control of his or her life by controlling others. But the differences between these two types of offenders far outweigh the similarities. First, mass murderers are generally apprehended or killed by police, commit suicide, or turn themselves in to authorities. Serial killers, by contrast, usually make special efforts to elude detection. Indeed, they may continue to kill for weeks, months, and often years before they are found and stopped—if they are found at all. In the case of the California Zodiac killer, the homicides appeared to have stopped, but an offender was never apprehended for those crimes. Perhaps the offender was incarcerated for only one murder and never linked to the others, or perhaps he or she was imprisoned for other crimes. Or the Zodiac killer may have just decided to stop killing or to move to a new location and kill under a new *modus operandi*, or method of committing the crime. The killer may even have become immobilized because of an accident or an illness or have died without his or her story ever being told. Speculation currently exists that the Zodiac killer is stalking victims in the New York City area. The Zodiac case is only one example of unsolved serial murders, many of which will never be solved.

Second, although both types of killers evoke fear and anxiety in the community, the reaction to a mass murder will be much more focused and locally limited than that to serial killing. People generally perceive the mass killer as one suffering from mental illnesses. This immediately creates a "they"/"us" dichotomy in which "they" are different from "us" because of mental problems. We can somehow accept the fact that a few people go "crazy" sometimes and start shooting others. However, it is more disconcerting to learn that some of the "nicest" people one meets lead a Dr. Jekyll and Mr. Hyde life: a student by day, a killer of co-eds by night; a caring, attentive nurse who secretly murders sick children, the handicapped, or the elderly; a building contractor and politician who enjoys sexually torturing and killing young men and burying them under his home. When we discover that people exist who are not considered to be insane or crazy but who enjoy killing others for "recreation," this indeed gives new meaning to the word "stranger." Although the mass murderer is viewed as a deranged soul, a product of a stressful environment who is just going to "explode" now and then (but of course somewhere else), the serial murder is seen as much more sinister and is more capable of producing fear.

● Third, the mass murderer kills groups of people at once, whereas the serial killer individualizes his or her murders. The serial killer continues to hurt and murder victims, whereas the mass murderer makes his or her "final statement" in or about life through the medium of abrupt and final violence. We rarely if ever hear of a mass murderer who has the opportunity to enact a second mass murder or to become a serial killer. Similarly, we rarely if ever hear of a serial killer who also enacts a mass murder.

The mass murderer and the serial killer are quantitatively and qualitatively different, and disagreement continues about their characteristics just as it does about the types of mass and serial offenders that appear to have emerged in recent years. Perhaps the single most critical stumbling block that today stands in the way of understanding serial murder is the disagreement among researchers and law enforcement about how to define the phenomenon.

Defining Serial Murder

In February, 1989, the Associated Press released a story about a serial killer who preyed on prostitutes in the same area of Los Angeles that harbored the Southside Slayer.* He was believed to have killed at least 12 women, all with a small handgun. The news story referred to the victims as "strawberries"—young women who sold sex for drugs. Farther north, the Green River Task Force in Seattle, Washington, investigated a series of murders of at least 45 young women over the past eight years. When the corpses of boys and young men began appearing along the banks of the Chattahoochee River in Atlanta, Georgia, during the early 1980s, police became convinced a serial killer was at work in the area.

The preceding cases are typical of homicides one might envision when characterizing victims of serial killers. The media quickly and eagerly focus attention on serial killings because they appear to be so bizarre and extraordinary. They engender the kind of headline that sell newspapers: "The Atlanta Child Killer," "The Stocking Strangler," "The Hillside Strangler,"

---

*Identity unknown; killed 12–20 victims between September 1983 and May 1987. Offender believed to be black and to have enjoyed mutilating his young female victims.

"The Sunday Morning Slasher," "The Boston Strangler," ad infinitum. The media focus not only on how many victims were killed but on how they died. Thus they feed morbid curiosity and at the same time create a stereotype of the typical serial killer: Ted Bundy, Ed Kemper, Albert DeSalvo, and a host of other young white males attacking unsuspecting women powerless to defend themselves from the savage sexual attacks and degradations by these monsters.

But what is the reality? For those in law enforcement, serial killing generally means the sexual attack and murder of young women, men, and children by a male who follows a pattern, physical or psychological. However, this definition fails to include many offenders and victims. For example, in 1988 in Sacramento, California, several bodies of older or handicapped adults were exhumed from the backyard of a house where they were supposed to have been living. Investigators discovered the victims had been killed for their Social Security checks. It was apparent the killer had premeditated the murders, had selected the victims, and had killed at least six over a period of several months. Most law enforcement agencies would naturally classify this case as a serial killing—except for the fact that the killer was female. Because of rather narrow definitions of serial killing females are generally not classified as serial killers even though they meet the requirements for such a label. One explanation may simply be that we rarely if ever hear of a female "Jack the Ripper." Women who kill serially generally use poisons to dispose of their victims and are not associated with the sexual attacks, tortures, and violence of their male counterparts.

Although many offenders actually fall into the serial killer classification, they are excluded because they fail to meet law enforcement definitions or media-generated stereotypes of brutal, blood-thirsty monsters. The "angels of death" who work in hospitals and kill patients, or nursing home staff who kill the elderly, or the "black widows" who kill their family and relatives also meet the general criteria for serial killing except for the stereotypic element of violence. These men and women do not slash and torture their victims nor do they sexually attack them; they are the quiet killers. They are also the kinds of people who could be married, hold steady jobs, or simply be the nice man or woman who lives next door. They are rare among serial killers, just as serial murders are rare compared with other types of homicide.

To include all types of serial killers, the definition of serial murder must clearly be as broad as possible. For instance, Hickey (1986), by simply including all offenders who through premeditation killed three or more victims over a period of days, weeks, months, or years, was able to identify several women as serial killers. However, there exists such confusion in defining serial killing that findings can also easily be distorted. In addition, current research presents some narrow operational definitions of serial murder without any documented assurances that the focus does not exclude pertinent data. To suggest, for example, that all victims of serial murder are strangers, that the killers operate primarily in pairs, or that they do not kill for financial gain is derived more from speculation than verifiable evidence, given the current state of serial murder research.

In essence *serial murderers* should include any offenders, male or female, who kill over time. Most researchers agree that serial killers have a minimum of 3–4 victims. Usually there is a pattern in their killing that may be associated with the types of victims selected or the method or motives for the killing. This includes murderers who, on a repeated basis, kill within the confines of their own home, such as a woman who poisons several husbands, children, or elderly people in order to collect insurance. In addition, serial murderers include those men and women who operate within the confines of a city or a state or even travel through several states as they seek out victims. Consequently, some victims have a personal relationship with their killers and others do not, and some victims are killed for pleasure and some merely for gain. Of greatest importance from a research perspective is the linkage of common factors among the victims—for example, as Egger (1985) observed, "victims' place or status within their immediate surroundings (such as vagrants, prostitutes, migrant workers, homosexuals, missing children, and single and often elderly women)" (p. 3). Commonality among those murdered may include several factors, any of which can prove heuristic in better understanding victimization.

Typologies of Murder

Much of our information and misinformation about criminal offenders is based on taxonomies, or classification systems. Megargee and Bohn (1979) noted that researchers usually created typologies based on the criminal offense. This invariably became problematic because often the offense comprised one or more subgroups. Researchers then examined repetitive crime patterns, which in turn created new complexities and problems. Megargee and Bohn further noted that, depending on the authority one chooses to read, one will find between two and eleven different types of murderers (pp. 29–32). Although serial murder is believed to represent a relatively small portion of all homicides in the United States, already researchers have begun the difficult task of classifying serial killers. Consequently, various typologies of serial killers and patterns of homicides have emerged. Not surprisingly, some of these typologies and patterns conflict with one another. Some are descriptions of causation, whereas others are diagnostic in nature. In addition, some researchers focus primarily on individual case studies of serial killers, whereas others create group taxonomies that accommodate several kinds of murderers.

● Wille (1974) identified ten different types of murderers covering a broad range of bio-socio-psychological categories:

1. depressive
2. psychotic
3. afflicted with organic brain disorder

4. psychopathic

5. passive aggressive

6. alcoholic

7. hysterical

8. juvenile (the child was the killer)

9. mentally retarded

10. sex killers

Lee (1988) also created a variety of labels to differentiate killers according to motive, including:

1. profit

2. passion

3. hatred

4. power or domination

5. revenge

6. opportunism

7. fear

8. contract killing

9. desperation

10. compassion

11. ritual

Even before American society became aware, in the early 1980s, of serial murder as anything more than an anomaly, researchers had begun to classify multiple killers and assign particular characteristics and labels to them. Guttmacher (1973) described the sadistic serial murderer as one who derives sexual gratification from killing and who often establishes a pattern, such as the manner in which they kill or the types of victims they select, such as prostitutes, children, or the elderly. Motivated by fantasies, the offender appears to derive pleasure from dehumanizing his or her victims. Lunde (1976) recognized and noted distinctions between the mass killer and the serial killer, notably that the mass killer appears to suffer from psychosis and should be considered insane. By contrast he found little evidence of mental illness among serial killers. Danto (1982) noted that most serial murderers may be described as obsessive-compulsive because they normally kill according to a particular style and pattern.

Researchers have been attempting to create profiles of the "typical" serial killer from the rapidly accumulating statistics on offenders and victims in the United States. The most stereotypical of all serial murderers are those who in some way are involved sexually with their victims. It is this type of killer who generates such public interest and alarm. Stories of young women being abducted, raped, tortured, and strangled appear more and more frequently in the newspapers.

Sexual Homicides

Most serial killers known widely to the public have usually been involved sexually with their victims. This may include rape, sodomy, and an array of sexual tortures and deviations. Indeed it is a shared belief among most law enforcement officials and many clinicians that most serial murders are sexual in nature (Lunde, 1976; Ressler et al., 1985, 1988; Revitch, 1965). There have been serial killings that appear to have no sexual connotations; however, not all sex murders *overtly* express sexual needs. In other words, some serial killing that may appear to be motivated by factors such as financial gain or cult-related goals may actually have sexual motives. In one instance a multiple murderer who had been killing patients for financial gain later admitted she also became aroused watching her victims die.

Some researchers differentiate sex murderers from lust murderers. The sex murderer kills often out of fear and a desire to silence his victim, whereas the lust murderer appears to harbor deep-seated fantasies. This certainly does not exclude the possibility that some rapists may also premeditate their killings *and* experience deep-seated fantasies. For killers such as Albert DeSalvo, the Boston Strangler, rapes are only a continuation of progressive sexual fantasies and behaviors that finally lead to murder. Revitch and Schlesinger (1981) also noted that women, although in fewer numbers than men, also are capable of developing homicidal fantasies and being involved in sadistic murders and mass killings.

In recent years researchers have continued to note differences between rape murders and lust killings (Prentky et al., 1986; Ressler et al., 1985; Scully & Marolla, 1985). Special agents from the FBI examined a sample of 36 sexual murderers, 29 of whom were convicted of killing several victims. Specifically they were interested in the general characteristics of sexual murderers across the United States. They explored the dynamics of offenders' sexual fantasies, sadistic behaviors, and rape and mutilation murders. These investigators noted several deviant sexual behaviors practiced before, during, or after the victim has been killed. The act of rape, whether it be the actual physical act or a symbolic rape during which an object is inserted into the vagina, was found to be common among serial killers in this study. For some offenders the act of rape served as only one form of sexual assault; they engaged in a variety of mutilations, sexual perversions, and desecrations of the victim's corpse (Ressler et al., 1988, pp. 33–44).

Of course, these and other sexual deviations have influenced our perceptions and definitions of those who kill. "Sex maniac" becomes the layman's term for anyone capable of performing acts of sexual perversion on his or her victims. Each of the following categories describes a type of sexual behavior engaged in by one or more serial killers in this study that was believed to be in some way linked to the killings. The list is not exhaustive nor does it imply cause and effect. What is important to understand is how these categories of sexual behavior influence the typecasting of offenders.

1. *Animal torture:* Stabbing or chopping animals to death, especially cats, and dissecting them. One offender admitted killing several puppies in order to relive the experience of killing his first child victim.

2. *Anthropophagy:* Eating the victim's flesh or slicing off parts of flesh from the body. Several offenders practiced this form of cannibalism. Some are known to have eaten the breasts of victims, another cooked portions of his victim's thighs in casseroles, whereas another delighted in a main diet of children.

3. *Coprophilia:* An interest in feces whereby the offender may receive some sexual gratification from touching or eating excrement and/or urine. Although rare among serial killers, at least one is known to have eaten his own excrement.

4. *Fetishisms:* Finding sexual gratification by substituting objects for the sexual partner. In one case a person (although not a serial killer) had been breaking into several homes in a city in Georgia. A voyeur, this person also enjoyed collecting women's underwear, and on his arrest police discovered over 400 pairs of women's underwear in his possession. In October of 1988 in Riverside, California, a man known as the "panty bandit" was arrested after a series of robberies. During the course of his robberies this man would often order the female clerks to remove their underwear and then would engage in sexual acts in front of his captive audience.

Serial killers have also been known to engage in a variety of fetishes. Some offenders have been known to remove the breasts of their victims for later use, another saved sex organs by placing them in containers, and yet another removed the skin of his victims, out of which he fashioned articles of clothing, ornaments, and even purses. Others have saved victims' teeth or hair as part of their "souvenir fetish." In one case the offender enjoyed decapitating his victims. Later, after shampooing their hair and applying makeup, including lipstick, he would have sex with the heads, sometimes while showering. A final example was the offender who cut off the foot of at least one of his victims. He kept the foot in his refrigerator so he could dress it up in red spiked heels for his personal gratification.

5. *Gerontophilia:* Seeking out elderly persons of the opposite sex for sexual purposes. Those serial killers who seek out elderly persons are often believed to harbor hatred toward them. Some of these offenders reported sexual gratification from raping elderly women, some of whom have been in their eighties and nineties. One offender raped and killed several elderly tenants of an apartment complex, whereas another sought out elderly widows who lived alone.

6. *Lust murder:* Murdering sadistically and brutally, including the mutilation of body parts, especially the genitalia. One offender who chopped off

the penis of a young boy with a pair of wire cutters still expresses a strong desire to mutilate sexual organs. Another would sometimes shoot his victims in the head while they performed oral sex, and another enjoyed crushing his victims' nipples with pliers and mutilating their breasts. Others have torn off the nipples of their victims with their teeth. On several occasions offenders have completely dismembered their victims' bodies, then tossed the parts onto highways or into wooded areas, shallow graves, or sometimes left them for animals to consume. One offender was discovered with several pounds of body parts stashed in his refrigerator. A few offenders drank the blood of their victims. Sex murderers may perform similar acts but often are more spontaneous and react more out of fear of detection than lust murderers do.

7. *Mixoscopia:* Sometimes referred to as *triolism;* experiencing sexual pleasure from watching two other persons engaged in sexual relations. The extent of this behavior is still unknown, but in cases in which serial killers had accomplices or partners, offenders (both male and female) have admitted to watching while another offender raped or sodomized a victim. One female offender voluntarily watched while her male counterpart raped a child.

8. *Necrofetishism:* Having a fetish for dead bodies. Some offenders actually enjoyed keeping cadavers in their homes. In one case police found six decomposing corpses in the bedroom of one offender. Another offender liked to share his bed with various corpses, some of which had been decapitated.

9. *Necrophilia:* Having sexual relations with dead bodies. This form of deviation is common among offenders who are involved sexually with their victims. Generally necrophilia is thought to be practiced only by males, but Gallagher (1987) noted that in 1983 a California woman confessed to having sex with dead people. This woman, a mortuary employee, said she would often climb into coffins to have sex with the corpse or drive corpses in a hearse up to the mountains where her "love making" would not be disturbed. Apparently she had been sexually "involved" with at least 40 corpses. In another case of serial killing, the offender had sex with the corpse of a child, then placed her body under his bed so that he could repeat the experience.

10. *Pedophilia:* Having sexual relations with children. A 16-year-old boy who had been arrested for sexual assault on children admitted to me that his favorite places to pick up children were the toy centers in department stores. Knowing that some parents are willing to leave their small children to look at toys while they go shopping for a few minutes, he easily found victims. He would simply select the youngest or most vulnerable-looking children and take them to the washrooms, where he would molest them. It was not uncommon for this young man to find three or four victims in one evening. Although most pedophiles have no intention of violence toward their victims, some serial killers destroy their victims as a way of destroying the

evidence against them. One serial killer who sexually assaulted several young boys admitted he killed them to cover up his sexual misconduct.

11. *Pederasty:* Adults having anal intercourse with children (anal intercourse in general is called *sodomy*). This is a common act among serial killers who target children as victims. In some cases various "instruments" were used to sodomize the child.

12. *Using photographs/recordings:* Taking pictures or making video recordings of victims. One offender took snapshots of his nude victims, then enlarged the photographs and mounted them on his bedroom walls. Another offender took photographs of victims performing oral sex on his partner. Still other offenders used tape recorders to reproduce the screams and terror of dying victims as they were sexually mutilated.

13. *Using pornography:* Using sexually explicit literature and photographs. Even among serial killers pornography tends to be used only by certain types of offenders. However, trying to determine how much and to what degree pornography affects an offender is nearly impossible to measure. Some offenders admit to occasional or frequent use of pornography, sometimes violent material involving bondage and the torture of women.

14. *Rape:* Having forced sexual intercourse with another person. This appears to be the most common of all sexual behavior among serial killers in this study. Often the rapes involved beatings and torture. One offender enjoyed taking his victims out into the desert, where he would lash them to the front of his car, tear off their clothing, rape them, and then strangle them to death.

15. *Torture:* Resorting to a large variety of sadistic acts including burning victims' breasts, dismembering living victims, placing victims in water and electrocuting them, and touching bare electrical wires to victims' arms, face, breasts, or genitals. Often those who engage in these acts will also be involved in other "lust murder" behaviors.

16. *Sadomasochism:* Inflicting mental/physical pain on others (sadism) or oneself (masochism). Although masochism is not particularly common among serial killers, one offender over the years had inserted dozens of needles into his genital area, occasionally burned himself, and eagerly anticipated the experience of his own execution.

17. *Voyeurism:* Receiving sexual gratification by peeping through windows and so forth to watch people. Several offenders in this study had at one time or another peeped through windows. One offender explained how he first began as a voyeur, then graduated to raping women, and finally practiced necrophilia. The connection between voyeurism and homicide is not automatic. Most "peeping Toms" never progress past this deviant stage, whereas some may later attempt rape or other violent sexual behaviors.

Serial Murder Typologies

Creating sexual taxonomies to categorize serial killers represents one of several ways by which offenders have been classified by researchers. For some investigators, the sexual nature of the crime may be viewed as a subtype of one or more general taxonomies. In certain serial killings the sexual attack is an integral part of the murder both psychologically and physiologically for the offender. For other offenders the sexual attack may represent the best way to degrade, subjugate, and ultimately destroy their victim but have little connection to the actual motive(s) for the killing.

Holmes and DeBurger (1988, pp. 55–60) characterized four types of serial murderers and examined the motives reported to have influenced the offenders. The formation of these typologies was based on specific assumptions about the phenomenon of serial killers. These assumptions included the belief that such crimes were nearly always psychogenic, meaning that such behavior is usually stimulated not by insanity or economic circumstances but by "behavioral rewards and penalties." The "patterns of learning" are in some way related to "significant others" who in some way reinforce homicidal behavior. A second assumption involved an "intrinsic locus of motives" whereby motives were explained as something only the offender could appreciate because they exist entirely in his or her own mind. Most "normal" people have great difficulty in fathoming why someone would want to kill other people. However, in the mind of the killer the motivations are often very meaningful. In a final assumption, Holmes and DeBurger explained that the reward for killing is generally psychological even though some killers may benefit materially from their crimes. According to these "core characteristics" Holmes and DeBurger identified the following four types of serial killers:

1. *Visionary type:* Such murderers kill in response to the commands of voices or visions usually emanating from the forces of good or evil. These offenders are often believed to be suffering from some form of psychosis.

2. *Mission-oriented type:* These offenders believe it is their mission in life to rid the community or society of certain groups of people. Some killers may target the elderly, whereas others may seek out prostitutes, children, or a particular racial/ethnic group.

3. *Hedonistic type:* Offenders in this category are usually stereotyped as "thrill seekers," those who derive some form of satisfaction from the murders. Holmes and DeBurger also identified subcategories in this typology, including those who kill for "creature comforts" or "pleasure of life." This would include individuals such as Dorothea Montalvo Picente of Sacramento, California, who was arrested in November, 1988, for allegedly poisoning to death at least seven destitute elderly victims in order to cash their Social Security checks. Another subcategory Holmes and DeBurger referred to was "lust murderers," which included offenders who become sexually involved with the victims and often perform postmortem mutilations.

4. *Power/control-oriented type:* In this typology Holmes contends "the fundamental source of pleasure is not sexual, it is the killer's ability to control and exert power over his helpless victim" (1985, p. 32). Some offenders enjoy watching their victims cower, cringe, and beg for mercy. In one case an offender killed his young victims only after he had been able to break their will to survive. Once the victim had acquiesced, the offender would complete his task and slaughter him or her.

These general classifications of serial killers are useful in organizing existing data. Such motivational taxonomies help us to understand why certain offenders take the lives of their victims. Levin and Fox (1985) also constructed types of serial murders including sexual or sadistic killings that appear to mirror Holmes's and DeBurger's subcategory of "lust murders." Another typology similar to Holmes's and DeBurger's hedonistic subtypes was described by Levin and Fox as murders of expediency or for profit (1985, pp. 99–105). Their third typology identifies "family slayings" as a major category of murder. This "type" does not appear to be particularly consistent with their prior two categories, which are constructed from motivational dynamics. Although family killers could be motivated by sadism or expediency, with few exceptions they are generally blood related to their victims and kill them all in a relatively short period of time. However, the noting of this inconsistency should not be viewed as a criticism of Levin's and Fox's work.* Instead we are obliged to recognize the need for other typologies that may not be constructed solely on the basis of apparent motivations.

The Federal Bureau of Investigation, through extensive application of profiling techniques, identified the characteristics of "organized" and "disorganized" murders (Ressler et al., 1988, Chapter 8). Using information gathered at the scene of the crime and examining the nature of the crime itself, agents constructed profiles of the offenders, which in turn were categorized as "organized" or "disorganized." For example, an organized murderer is often profiled as having good intelligence and being socially competent, whereas the disorganized offender is viewed as being of average intelligence and socially immature. Similarly, some crime investigators often find that organized offenders plan their murders, target strangers, and demand victims to be submissive, whereas disorganized killers may know their victims, inflict sudden violence on them, and spontaneously carry out their killings (pp. 121–123).

In a quest for understanding why serial murderers treat the lives of others so callously, research usually focuses on the perceived overt motivations of the offenders. Did they kill for money? Thrills? Were they focusing

---

*In the data set constructed by Levin and Fox, 33 cases were identified involving 42 offenders, including those who had been involved in simultaneous incidents of murder and cases of serial killing. Little differentiation was noted between simultaneous and serial murder.

on hatred, revenge, sexual pleasures, or other likely motivations? We erroneously assume that if we stare long and intently enough at a perceived motivation for homicidal behavior we will be able to comprehend the dynamics of its etiology. What we must not forget is that the amount of research to date in the area of multiple homicide is limited. Recognizing this handicap, researchers, whether they are involved with the technical forensics of a case or responsible for classifying/typing offenders, must be willing to explore other factors that may contribute to motivations or to the construction of typologies.

To say a serial killer murdered as a result of greed, hatred, or fantasy may easily obscure other important variables. For example, the types of victims or the methods used to kill may point to other reasons why the murders occurred.

Figure 1.1 illustrates just one of the many possible combinations of factors that may assist researchers in the construction of typologies. Since we have only begun to explore serial murder in an organized manner we may find that matching variables may generate new ways of conceptualizing offenders' behavior or victimization patterns. In Figure 1.1 each cell refers to victims and methods of killing victims. Theodore Bundy, for example, sought out young, attractive females whom he bludgeoned and tortured to death. He was particularly specific in both victim selection and method of killing. David Bullock of New York was suspected in 1982 of killing at least six victims, including a prostitute, his roommate, and several strangers, by shooting each one. In this case the killer sought out a variety of victims but used a specific method to kill them. In the case of Richard Cottingham, also known as "The Ripper," the killer hunted prostitutes in New Jersey and New York. While he went after specific targets, he varied his methods of killing. Finally, Herbert Mullin, of California, is believed to have killed 13 victims including campers, hitchhikers, friends, and people in their homes using a

FIGURE 1.1 Factors for Constructing Typologies

	A	B
	Specific victims Specific methods	Variety of victims Specific methods
	Specific victims Variety of methods	Variety of victims Variety of methods
	C	D

variety of methods. Why is it that some offenders have no specific victims as targets while others are extremely particular in whom they choose to murder? And why do some offenders always follow a ritualistic pattern of killing while others use different methods of killing their victims?

Some serial killers such as Ted Bundy always go hunting for their victims and, once they find a suitable person, kill and dispose of the body in remote areas. Conversely, some serial killers wait at home for their victims to walk into their traps, similar to the spider awaiting the fly. In some cases the victims are killed and buried on the offender's property. John Wayne Gacy is believed to have killed 33 young males, most of whom became buried trophies under the offender's home. In other cases offenders advertise in the newspapers for offers of employment, marriage, and so on, waiting for unsuspecting victims to ring their doorbell. Each of these modus operandi may be useful in generating particular typologies of serial killers.

Hickey (1986) noted specific variations in the degree of mobility exercised by offenders. Three distinct groups of offenders were delineated: (1) traveling serial killers, who often cover many thousands of miles each year, murdering victims in several states as they go; (2) local serial killers, who never leave the state in which they start killing in order to find additional victims (Wayne Williams, for example, operated in several different law-enforcement jurisdictions in and around Atlanta, Georgia, but never had a need to move elsewhere); and (3) serial killers who never leave their homes or places of employment. The victims already reside in the same physical structure, or they are lured each time to the same location. These "place-specific" killers include nurses (male and female), housewives, offenders who are self-employed, and other individuals or accomplices who prefer to stay at home rather than go out hunting.

Each new typology raises the issues of motivation and etiology. We may find sometimes that typologies may overlap one another or that one generates more explanations and understanding than do others. For the present, researchers continue to examine the phenomenon from a multitude of perspectives. Different perspectives will continue to generate a variety of typologies and operational definitions of serial murder. Which typologies are the most appropriate depends on who is making the determination. What is important to remember is that the limited research done so far on serial murder leaves considerable room for new ideas.

Methodology Used in This Book

The data for this study were gathered through biographical case-study analysis of serial murderers and their victims. Glaser and Strauss (1967) convincingly argued that there are systematic methods in conducting qualitative research that may point toward theoretical explanations for social behavior. Their notion of "grounded" theory as a methodology included what Glaser and Strauss refer to as "constant comparisons." By examining different groups or individuals experiencing the same process we learn to identify structural uniformities. Grounded theory stresses a systematic, qualitative field method for research. In this research, I sought out cases of serial murder within a specified time frame. These cases were identified through as many avenues as possible, including interviews, newspapers, journals, bibliographies, biographies, and computer searches of social science abstracts, until the process became repetitive or redundant and new information ceased to be found.

Unfortunately, one can never be sure of the precise moment when the data collection should be halted. I was confident that systematic searches of several different sources of information would generally yield most of the existing data. Using other definitions of serial murder, a researcher might envision a variety of serial-related killings that technically could be included in this type of research. These killings could include those committed by individuals who work as enforcers within the realm of organized crime, political and/or religious terrorists who kill repeatedly, and members of street gangs. One might also include those who repeatedly tampered with food and medicinal products bringing death to persons who ingest them, those who practice euthanasia, or—for some people—those who carry out abortions in clinics. From an historical perspective one might also include the gunslingers of the old West who frequently killed in order to promote themselves and their lifestyles. Other definitional considerations for cases to be included in or excluded from a study of serial murder may be generated from a variety of taxonomies including motives, methods, or specific numbers of victims.

Although each of these typologies and perspectives may be worth attention, this study excludes them from its overall operational definition of serial murder. Instead, each time a case appeared in a text or a news report in which an offender had been charged with killing three or more individuals over a period of days, weeks, months, or years, it was included in the study.

A few exceptional cases were also included in which offenders were reported to have killed only two victims but were suspect in other slayings or in which evidence indicated their intent to kill others. To justify inclusion, the homicides had to be deliberate, premeditated acts whereby the offender selected his or her own victims and acted under his or her own volition. Often a distinct pattern emerged in the method of killing or in the apparent motives for the murders. Usually the murders were to some degree motivated by sex, money, vengeance, hatred, or an unidentifiable impulse to kill. Each case was analyzed for specific data, including the time frame and the geographic locations of the criminal behavior, the number of victims, the relationship of victim to offender, age and gender of particular victims, and the degree of victim facilitation (responsibility of the victim for his or her own death).

Spanning the time frame between 1795 and 1988, the findings from these data represent the victims of thirty-four women and one hundred sixty-nine men in the United States. They are responsible for a minimum of

1,483 homicides and a maximum of 2,161 homicides. This victim range is specified because a few serial murderers killed so many people that only close approximations of the actual number can be ascertained. Difficulty occurs in accurately determining the number of victims of serial murderers, especially when one is dealing with a few offenders who have allegedly killed over one hundred people. The problem is compounded when the majority of these particular cases occurred in the nineteenth century when record keeping was not as accurate or efficient as it is today. Often data sources are not consistent in reporting figures for these "super" serial killers. In addition, some of the victim data may have been exaggerated because of the sensational nature of the crimes. Consequently, the killers in these cases were excluded from our study as were the killers in unsolved cases of homicide in which serial murder was suspect. Although I recognize that the data do not represent an exhaustive study of serial murderers, I do believe them to include (with the exception of the Federal Bureau of Investigations records) statistics on one of the largest and most varied assortments of multiple killers ever studied. (The total number of serial murders will, in all probability, never be known.) In tandem with the increasing number of serial murder typologies is the expanding literature that attempts to sort out and explain why such a phenomenon occurs with such regularity. Indeed, I will examine a plethora of literature in the following two chapters, including perspectives from medical, biological, psychological, sociological, structural, philosophical, religious, and environmental viewpoints.

CHAPTER 2

Cultural Development of Monsters, Demons, and Evil

Halloween, *Friday the 13th*, *Nightmare on Elm Street*, and other "splatter" movies remind us that there are evil, dangerous beings in our communities. The notion of evil monsters, demons, ghouls, vampires, werewolves, and zombies roaming the earth can be traced back to early civilization. In the past, explanations for mass and serial murders were often derived from demonology or the belief that life events were controlled by external forces or spirits. The notion that life on earth was primarily controlled by forces of good and evil has its origins in the belief in the existence of gods and devils.

In many past cultures—and in some modern ones—mental illness was generally viewed as a distinct form of possession, the controlling of a human by an evil spirit. The Gospel of St. Matthew in the Bible refers to two persons possessed with devils who were "exceedingly fierce," and when Christ bade them come out they went immediately and entered the bodies of swine. In turn the "swine ran violently" to the sea and perished in the waters (Matthew 8:28–32). In the Gospel of St. Mark a similar experience occurs except the man was described as a lunatic possessed with a devil. The devil was discovered to be many devils and thus were called Legion and were consequently cast out into a herd of swine. In turn, the swine again "ran violently" into the sea and perished (Mark 5:1–14). In the modern-day world, David Richard Berkowitz, the "Son of Sam" or "44-Caliber Killer," who hunted 13 victims over a period of 13 months in New York City, first claimed he did the killings because his neighbor's demonically possessed dogs commanded him to do so. Later he admitted he concocted the story to get back at his neighbor and his noisy dogs.

There seems to have been some confusion in the past in separating insane persons from those who were "possessed." Sometimes those who were mentally ill were defined as being possessed and vice versa, at least in the Middle East, and sometimes mentally ill or possessed people were revered as oracles for a deity or a soothsayer. In other times and places, similarly afflicted people were stoned to death or subjected to trephining, an early form of treatment of illnesses whereby holes were drilled in the skull to allow the evil spirits to leave (Suinn, 1984, p. 32).

Some cultures also believed that a person could be "invaded" by more than one spirit at a time. In modern days we might call such a manifestation a case of "multiple personalities," as described in Thigpen's and Cleckley's *The Three Faces of Eve* (1957) and Flora Schreiber's *Sybil* (1973). The notion of multiple personalities has been sometimes used as a defense by serial killers. For example, Kenneth Bianchi, one of the "Hillside Stranglers" in California and also Washington state claimed he was involved in killing 12 women because he was controlled by multiple personalities. Convincing for a while, Bianchi's defense finally came apart under close scrutiny by psychiatric experts.

People have also believed that evil spirits can inhabit the bodies of animals, causing them to act wildly. Because many cultures have long entertained the notion that criminals can be possessed by demons, it was not difficult for them to identify particular animals that were most likely to be possessed. In many legends and much folklore wolves were singled out as being the most likely animal to have dealings with the devil. The natural enmity between wolf and man has existed for centuries, and consequently wolves have been hunted relentlessly. If one believes that humans and animals can be demonically possessed, then it is not surprising that one might also believe that a possessed human could become a wolf. A person able to command such a metamorphosis became known as a werewolf (*were* was an old English term for *man*). The belief in "lycanthropy," or transformation of persons into wolves, can be traced back to at least 600 B.C., when King Nebuchadnezzar believed he suffered from such an affliction. Jean Fernal (1497–1558) of France, a physician, believed lycanthropy to be a valid medical phenomenon. Many societies around the world have a term for "werewolf": France, *loup-garou*; Germany, *Werwolf*; Portugal, *lob omen*; Italy, *Lupo mannaro*. In Africa stories abound of were-leopards and were-jackals, whereas were-tigers are common in India (Hill & Williams, 1967, p. 185).

To those living in the sixteenth and seventeenth centuries witches were similar to werewolves in that one was able to experience the transformation only if a pact was made with the Prince of Darkness, or Satan. In the sixteenth century, Paracelsus wrote that violent, wicked men may have the opportunity to return after death as an animal, usually a wolf. The purpose of this human-to-wolf transformation was the inevitable killing of humans, particularly children, in order to eat their flesh. Recurrent throughout werewolf literature is the theme of anthropophagy, or the enjoyment of eating human flesh. Jean Grenier, a young seventeenth-century Frenchman, claimed to be a werewolf and confessed that he had devoured the flesh of many young girls. Another notorious werewolf was Germany's Peter Stubb, or Stump, of the sixteenth century. After completing a "pact" with the devil he simply donned a wolf skin belt and was able to transform himself whenever he had the urge to kill. Naturally he murdered those who offended him along with several women and girls whom he raped and sexually tortured before cannibalizing. Stubb, who fathered a child by his daughter and then ate his own son, managed to murder 13 young children and two expectant mothers by some of the most perverse and cruel methods (Hill & Williams, 1967, pp. 189–190).

Lycanthropy was also viewed as a form of madness in which a person believed him- or herself to be an animal, usually a wolf, and expressed a desire to eat raw meat, experienced a change in voice, and had a desire to run on all fours. To ensure the perpetuation of werewolf lore, stories of those possessed usually included reminders of how difficult it was to destroy such monsters. The werewolves were believed to be extraordinarily powerful creatures who could change back to human form at will or at the break of day. Belief in these terrifying creatures was often fueled by the occasional discovery of a mutilated corpse along a highway or brought in with the tide. Consider the story of the Sawney Beane family and how their behavior may have reinforced the belief in werewolves and other similar monsters.

Born under the reign of James I of Scotland, in east Lothian near Edinburgh, Sawney Beane, described as idle and vicious, took up with a woman of equally disreputable character. They relocated to a large cave that was difficult to detect because the sea tide covered the entrance. Sawney and his wife took shelter in this cave and began robbing and murdering unsuspecting travelers. To avoid detection they murdered every person they robbed, and to satisfy their need for food they resorted to cannibalism. Each time they killed someone they carried him or her to their den, quartered the victim, and salted the limbs and dried them for later consumption. Each family member played a specific role in capturing and killing their victims. To ensure that no one escaped, precautions were taken to attack no more than six people on foot or two on horses. This arrangement lasted several years during which time they sired six sons and six daughters, eighteen grandsons and fourteen granddaughters, most the offspring of incest.

Frequently the Beane family would dispose of surplus legs and arms by throwing them into the sea. In due course many of these body parts were carried by the tides to other shores, where they were discovered by townspeople. Search parties failed to uncover any new information; they just cast suspicion on innocent travelers and innkeepers. Although dozens of persons were arrested, people continued to disappear regularly. Following several years of searching, soldiers finally discovered the cave, but they were not prepared for what they found inside. Aside from many boxes of jewels and other valuables, arms, legs, and thighs of men, women, and children hung in rows while other body parts were soaking in pickling. The family was arrested and executed without trial, the men suffering death by extreme mutilation and the women burned at the stake [Kerman, 1962, pp. 11–15].

Vampires also took their place in the showcase of horror but not until they received the attention of writers in the nineteenth century. Bram Stoker's *Dracula* (1897) was modeled on the fifteenth-century Wallachian nobleman Vlad Tepes, also known as "Vlad the Impaler" and "Drakul" (Dragon). He was particularly known to be a "vicious and depraved sadist" who enjoyed torturing and murdering peasants who lived within his jurisdiction. Stories circulated about the horror chambers secreted in the depths of his castle and how he was believed to be the Devil or at least one of his emissaries (Hill & Williams, 1967, p. 195). Tales evolved suggesting that some vampires could also transform themselves into werewolves. However, vampires usually had but one goal—to drink human blood—whereas werewolves mutilated and cannibalized. Vampires were also believed to be sexually involved with their victims, albeit discreetly, because of (for some people) the erotic nature of sucking human blood. One cannot discount the repeated implications of sexual mania in the role-creation of the vampire (pp. 200–202). In his book *Man Into Wolf* (1951), Robert Eisler described a British "vampire" who in 1949 murdered nine victims and drank blood from each of them.

Werewolves and vampires are joined by a host of other sinister monsters all bent on the destruction of mankind, especially young women and children. Among them are zombies, or walking "corpses," and ghouls who reportedly feast on both live and dead bodies. The sexual connotation of these acts is pervasive.

Some of the early European serial killers who were thought to have been vampires or other "creatures of the night" in reality were nothing more than depraved murderers. Following are brief descriptions of two such people:

> *Gilles de Rais*, born in 1404, became heir to the greatest fortune in the whole of France. After fighting alongside Joan of Arc and being awarded the title Marshall of France, his beloved Joan of Arc was captured and put to death. Apparently he never recovered from the loss and soon lost his great wealth. Convinced that he needed to make a pact with the Devil himself in order to regain his fortunes, he murdered a young boy by slitting his throat, severing his wrist, cutting out his heart, and ripping out his eyes from their sockets. He then saved the boy's blood to write out his pact with the Devil. Having discovered his enjoyment for torturing and killing children, he began to recruit them in large numbers for his own murdering pleasure. Although documentation is not available, it is believed he killed several hundred children, drinking their blood and engaging in necrophilia. One of his many perverted pleasures was to have the heads of his child victims stuck on upright rods. De Rais would then have their hair curled by a professional beautician and have their lips and cheeks made up with rouge. A beauty contest was then held, and the "winner" was used for sexual purposes.

> *Countess Elizabeth Bathory* of fifteenth-century Hungary became heavily involved in sorcery, witchcraft, and devil worship. Although she married and bore children, she maintained a predilection for young girls. With her husband off to the wars, she began to indulge herself in the torture and slaying of young girls and women. Stimulated by sado-eroticism, the countess bathed in the blood of her victims in order to maintain her fair complexion. She was believed to have been responsible for the deaths of more than a hundred victims.

Such people appear to be the forerunners to the modern serial killer.

Their acts are no more disgusting or cruel than those of their twentieth-century counterparts. We have kept their legends alive by scapegoating the wolf and perpetuating the tales of vampires, witches, ghouls, and zombies.

A function of the early European church was to find ways to eradicate the problems attributed to witchcraft and sorcery. Under guidance from Pope Innocent VIII, two Dominicans, Heinrich Institor (Kramer) and Jakob Sprenger produced the first encyclopedia of demonology, the *Malleus Malefi-carum (Witch's Hammer)*, in 1486. This compendium of mythology would be used for centuries to identify and destroy witches, wizards, and sorcerers. Thousands of people were "identified" through torturous means and then promptly burned at the stake (Marwick, 1970, pp. 369–377). The latent or unintended function of the great witch hunt, or the Grand Inquisition, was the creation of a witch "craze" that cost many innocent lives. Sanctioned by government, the witch hunt took on new meaning, and practically overnight witches were to be found everywhere. The efforts of the church and state probably did more to perpetuate the belief in sorcerers, werewolves, vampires, witches, and so on than any other single force in society.

One more type of historical "monster" bears mentioning: In Jewish medieval legend a *golem* was a robot, or an artificial person. (*Golem* means a "clay figure supernaturally brought to life.") Golems were given "life" by means of a charm; occasionally they ran amok and had to be destroyed. Dr. Joshua Bierer (1976) used the term *golem* to describe a case in which a man and his wife were having serious marital problems due primarily to his inability to develop any kind of meaningful relationship. His extramarital affairs were frequent, always in search of something he could not find. His mistresses did not sense that he was actually without love, commitment, or a desire for meaningful relationships. In reality he hated all women and wanted to kill them. To avoid this he moved quickly from one affair to another. Dr. Bierer explained that this client had had a difficult childhood during which his mother was incapable of showing him any affection. Both parents were absent for long periods of time leaving him to the whims of a cruel nanny who apparently forced him into frequent, emotionally stressful situations. Dr. Bierer concluded that everybody needs love, affection, and attention. Without these one can become emotionally truncated and run the risk of developing into a golem (1976, pp. 197–199).

Although we cannot assume that people suffering from the "golem syndrome" will become murderers, the golem profile does appear to capture the essence of many serial killers. A person who can orchestrate the destruction of another human being and have no remorse, no feeling for his or her victim or external need to defend his or her actions exemplifies the term *golem.*

For example, I had the opportunity of working with a patient during the late 1970s who was confined to a state mental hospital for the criminally insane. As a young man, rather alienated from others, he had dropped out of school but was still living with other students. His feelings of inferiority and fear of others fueled his journey into loneliness. Fantasy replaced reality, and soon he began indulging himself in morbid literature while his disdain intensified for those around him. He began reading a work by Dr. David Abrahamsen, *The Murdering Mind*, and quickly identified with the main character. He also began to fantasize about death and how it might feel to kill another person. One night after quarreling with a roommate over a box of detergent, this young man drifted into his fantasy world. He decided it was now time to realize his fantasy. He went to a closet and removed and loaded a shotgun and then went into his roommate's bedroom. He carefully placed the shotgun next to the head of his intended victim, and a moment later another roommate across the hall was jolted awake by the blast. The killer calmly propped the shotgun against the wall, called the police, and informed them that he had just killed his roommate and that he would be waiting for them to come and get him. People were appalled by his "coolness," his lack of remorse, his lack of feeling for what had taken place. He appeared to be void of emotions entirely. He was finally found guilty but mentally ill and confined to the state hospital.

Although the monsters we have discussed have their origins in demonology, witchcraft, belief in the supernatural, and folklore, modern "monsters," of course, are no longer attributed to such causes. The mutilated and dissected corpses strewn about private residences in Wisconsin and the bodies left to rot in secluded wooded areas of Washington state or secreted under the floorboards of someone's home in Chicago are not the victims of fictional monsters. Instead, they are the victims of the Jeffrey Dahmers, the Ted Bundys, and the John Gacys of our society. Monsters in their own right, but the monster lives within and is unleashed only when the intended victim has entered their area of control. Are the men and women who commit such atrocities today possessed of the devil or are they simply evil people, devils unto themselves who make their conscious choice for evil, just as others choose good? The answer may become difficult and complicated as we explore the possible explanations for serial murder.

Serial Murder, Cults, and the Occult

Closely tied to the notions of evil and demonology are cult-related activities. In the United States it is not a crime to belong to a cult—the term means "a system of religious worship; devotion or homage to person or thing." Nor is it a crime to practice beliefs of the occult—things that are "kept secret, esoteric, mysterious, beyond the range of ordinary knowledge; involving the supernatural, mystical, magical" (Sykes, 1976, pp. 249 and 755)—provided those practices occur within an accepted legal framework.

Satanic cults in the United States appear to have attracted a growing number of followers interested in the worship of Satan. The problem does not stem from the fact that people join satanic organizations but from the growing body of evidence that such cults practice human sacrifices. Anton La Vey, a one-time rock musician and actor consultant for the movie *Rosemary's Baby* founded the Church of Satan on the witches' feast day of Walpurgis Night (Walpurgisnacht), April 30, 1966, which reportedly has a membership of 20,000 (Holmes, 1990). According to the Satanic Bible written by La Vey, members worship the trinity of the devil—Lucifer, Satan, and the Devil—including the nine pronouncements of the devil:

1. Satan represents indulgence, instead of abstinence!
2. Satan represents vital existence, instead of spiritual pipe dreams!
3. Satan represents undefiled wisdom instead of hypocritical self-deceit!
4. Satan represents kindness to those who deserve it, instead of love wasted on ingrates!
5. Satan represents vengeance, instead of turning the other cheek!
6. Satan represents responsibility, instead of concern for the psychic vampires!
7. Satan represents man as just another animal, sometimes better, more often worse, than those who walk on all fours, who because of his divine and intellectual development has become the most vicious of all!
8. Satan represents all of the so-called sins, as they lead to physical, mental or emotional gratification.
9. Satan has been the best friend the church has ever had, as he has kept it in business all these years! [La Vey, 1969, p. 25]

Holmes (1990), who interviewed two high priests and several coven members of satanic cults, noted that members are encouraged to fulfill their potential by advancing through different levels of "actualization" via magic, spells, rituals and so on. They progress by holding membership in the Church of Satan and participating in traditional worship services similar to the rituals, hierarchy, and organization of other churches. They may then progress to other levels within the church. Members learn from their Satanic Bible various "invocations," including the Invocations Employed Toward the Conjuration of Lust and Destruction. One chapter carries the title "On the Choice of a Human Sacrifice." Those who are proven devotees and have advanced in the levels of "personal affiliation" are invited to participate in human and animal sacrifices that include the use of various devices and rituals. It is important to understand that membership involvement in satanic churches depends on factors common to any church, including loyalty, knowledge, and understanding of doctrines and oaths and the degree of commitment to these covenants. Indeed, many satanic cults operate independent of the main church.

In the late 1960s, Charlie Manson and his followers gave new meaning to the word *cult*. Each member was believed to have paid homage to Manson and to have carried out his death sentences. In the late 1980s a voodoo cult in Matamoros, Mexico, heavily involved in drug smuggling into the United States, was believed to have killed 15–20 victims, executing them with machetes, guns, and knives. The group had come to believe that through certain forms of witchcraft the drug smugglers could gain protection from police, bullets, and other threats to their drug trade. By cutting out and burning the brains of a victim and then mixing them with blood, herbs, rooster feet, goat heads, and turtles, the cult members believed they could operate with impunity.

Voodooism predates La Vey's Church of Satan by hundreds if not thousands of years and varies considerably in rituals, spells, and hoaxes. Rather than a formal organization, voodoo is the use of or belief in religious witchcraft. Persons trained in practice of voodoo cast spells on or bewitch others as a means of protection, vengeance, and so forth. In this particular case the secret charms and hoaxes of voodoo were practiced to meet the "special" needs of the smugglers. The group, led by a "godfather" and a female witch, killed and mutilated anyone for their own reasons, including greed and vengeance.

Most serial murderers who are involved in cult-related homicides do not appear to be particularly advanced in satan worship. Several appear to be self-styled satanists who dabble in the occult, but the extent of their involvement is difficult to measure. Donald Harvey, believed to have methodically murdered 58 victims in at least three different hospitals, had books on satan worship in his possession but refused to comment about the material. Richard Ramirez, the Night Stalker in California, ardently proclaimed his ties to satanism and displayed his pentagram* tattooed on his left palm. Henry Lucas, a serial killer who roamed the southern states and killed hitchhikers, confessed his involvement with satan worship. Allegedly he and his partner Otis Toole were paid to kidnap children to be used for human sacrifices, prostitution, and black market sales. Robin Gecht and three other young men terrorized Chicago in the early 1980s by abducting, mutilating, and killing several young women. In a form of satan worship they were believed to have cut up animal and human body parts for sacrifice on a makeshift altar. Robert Berdella of Kansas City publicly admitted in 1989 to the ritual tortures and homosexual murders of several young men but denied any connection to satan worship even though evidence indicated otherwise.

Assessing the degree of influence of satanic worship among serial killers has begun to attract both law-enforcement and academic researchers. It is premature to state that serial killers in general have ties to satanic cults. The fact remains that many serial killers have had no ties to satan worship before or during their murder careers. Perhaps offenders mention satanism when

---

*A five-pointed star formed by intersecting lines, used as a mystical symbol.

they are captured simply to add to the already sensational nature of the homicides. Perhaps the police and the media overreact and refer to satanism when they are confronted by the work of a serial killer. Perhaps there are certain types of serial killers who can be described as cult-driven, whereas others are influenced only superficially by satanism. In the cases of those who do become involved in satanic worship and serial killing, we should determine which behavior started first. Does satanic worship stimulate individuals or groups of people to kill, or were they already murderers when they found satanism to be attractive? For whatever reasons, it appears that reports of cult-related homicides are increasing—which may provide researchers with useful research data.

The Notion of Evil

Levin and Fox (1985) refer to multiple murderers as evil people (p. 210). In the "hard sciences" such as chemistry and physics, exactness and quantification are necessary requirements; however, the notion of evil is intangible and unmeasurable, and it is often used as a misnomer for inappropriate behavior. In Western culture the closest we come to quantifying good or evil is by observing that someone is a really good person or a really bad person. We have a tendency to judge people in terms of their goodness or badness, but seldom do we refer to others as being "evil." Instead, evil is a label we reserve for those worse than bad. "Badness" we expect to find in many people, but evil relegates individuals to a special classification that suggests some form of satanic affiliation. Interestingly, both bad and evil persons may engage in similar types of undesirable behaviors yet be categorized with different labels. Part of the problem in assigning such labels is determining exactly what constitutes good or evil. Some people believe that gambling is "of the devil," whereas others see it more as a benign form of entertainment or recreation. The same can be said of drinking alcohol, committing fornication, or illegal use of drugs.

But homicide is another matter. Killing for recreation is not only unacceptable, it elicits some of our deepest anxieties about being alone and meeting strangers. We can understand to some degree the typical "domestic" homicide—a husband and wife, or other family members, find themselves in altercations that end in someone being killed. One can even understand why a person with a grudge may finally lash out at his or her tormentor or why an individual dying of an incurable disease is killed by a friend or a family member to halt the suffering. We may not agree in any way with the act of killing—most people believe that killing another human being is wrong. We do, however, understand to some degree the reason for killing and are able to place such homicides in context with everyday life. We consider them to be "crimes of passion" or situational killings that can be explained away as marital problems, family disputes, or acts of mercy. These types of crimes are illegal and wrong in the eyes of society. However, we assume that most of these offenders will not kill again.

Multiple homicide offenders, especially serial murderers, are incomprehensible to society. If someone has murdered children because he enjoys killing, that raises serious questions about the offender's rationality. Surely no one in his or her "right" mind could rape and murder a dozen children simply for recreation. We find it disgusting to imagine such crimes and disturbing to hear words such as "enjoyment" and "recreation" associated with the taking of human life. Evil then becomes the appropriate label for those who apparently enjoy controlling and destroying human life. What greater crime exists than to deny another person his or her free agency, the right of self-determination?

The quest for power and control over the lives of others is exemplified by the case of Josef Mengele (Profile 2-1) a physician and geneticist recruited into the Nazi ranks to direct the processing of concentration camp prisoners at Birkenow and Auschwitz during World War II. While Hitler stepped up his campaign for his "Final Solution," Mengele also promoted his own bizarre agenda for thousands of camp victims. Posner and Ware (1986), in their book, *Mengele*, examine the depths to which one person is willing and able to descend, once given unbridled control over the lives of others.

Mengele was an intelligent, articulate individual who appeared dedicated to his work. Married, with a family, he managed to compartmentalize his life in and out of the camps. Under the guise of science he masqueraded as a researcher, but his rationalizations could not hide the truth. But do all people have such propensities? What, if anything, keeps most of humanity from such diabolical practices? Martin Buber, a noted Jewish theologian,

PROFILE 2-1: JOSEF MENGELE
1911–1979

One of Adolph Hitler's most insidious goals was his Final Solution: genocide, the killing of all Jews in Europe and inevitably throughout the world. Genocide involves people killing large numbers of victims while at the same time remaining emotionally detached from the operation. Special techniques were routinely used to neutralize any guilt associated with wholesale slaughter of humans. Large rations of alcohol were distributed regularly to many of the executioners; they were also provided with better food and housing than their peers. To professionalize the killing, special terminology such as "human material" and "subjects" was used to identify intended victims.

Physicians usually supervised the incoming trains at the death camps such as Auschwitz and Treblinka. Their job was to identify which prisoners would or would not be immediately sent to the gas chambers. For some of the doctors this was a very stressful task that evoked severe anxiety. This was not true of Dr. Josef Mengele, indeed, he regularly volunteered for "selection" duty. At thirty-two, Dr. Mengele was an aspiring geneticist who held a passion for fame and notoriety. Disturbed by the lack of warmth between him and his parents, Mengele was determined to raise himself up in their eyes through a successful career in medicine. He easily accepted the

JOSEF MENGELE, continued

Nazi philosophy that it was possible through selection, refinement, and genetic engineering to create the ultimate "pure" race. At the camps he had an endless supply of human material on which to experiment. Those who were not deemed fit for experimentation were usually gassed and cremated shortly after their arrival, except those prisoners who were forced to labor.

Mengele set himself apart from the other physicians and soon became known as the most feared man in Auschwitz. His "experiments" turned out to be ruthless, diabolical acts of torture that nearly always ended in death. Unlike many who simply followed orders, Mengele undertook his work with a passion. Witnesses reported having seen tables and walls in his laboratory lined with pairs of eyes from his experiments on dozens of victims. His obsession was to conduct comparative research on children, especially twins. He was constantly in search of identical twins. He often performed surgery on the children without anesthetics. In one case he took two children, one of them a hunchback, and surgically sewed them back to back.

Mengele never tired of his work and killed hundreds of children simply to be able to dissect them. In one instance he had a hunchback father and his 15-year-old son, who had a deformed foot, executed, then had all the flesh boiled off their frames. After bleaching their skeletons, Mengele displayed the victims'

bones for his colleagues to see. He also ordered several adult female prisoners to be shot and their breasts and muscles from their thighs extracted to be used as "cultivating material" for future experiments. According to the West German indictment, Mengele was reported to have jumped on pregnant women's stomachs until the fetuses were expelled and even dissected a one-year-old child while it was still alive.

His indifference to suffering was immense. He was charged with having 300 children, most under the age of five years, burned alive. Witnesses recount the night when several dump trucks arrived and parked near a large pit fire that had been started earlier by soldiers. One by one the trucks backed up and emptied their load of screaming children into the roaring fire. Some of the burning children managed to crawl up to the top of the inferno. Under the direct supervision of Mengele, soldiers with sticks pushed the little girls and boys back into the pit.

Mengele went to great lengths to care for children who developed various diseases. Once they were cured he sent them to be gassed. His goal was not to relieve misery but to succeed at his task. One survivor reported how sometimes he would calm frightened children whom he had ordered killed by making their last walk into a game he called "on the way to the chimney."

examined the myths and notions of evil and found that some people are in a process of moving toward evil whereas others have been consumed by it. This may be analogous to a continuum along which we are constantly moving toward increasing degrees of goodness or increasing degrees of badness or, ultimately, evil. Some religions, such as Christianity, refer to the temptations people must endure and overcome in order to achieve a state of goodness; those who succumb become slaves to their own vices and passions. The ultimate notion of evil may be defined by those individuals who appear to have progressed past worldly temptations and have become devils unto themselves, completely without guilt, remorse, or compassion for their victims.

Erich Fromm (1973) refers to human evil as a process that includes the principle of agency or choice.

> Our capacity to choose changes constantly with our practice of life. The longer we continue to make the wrong decisions, the more our heart hardens; the more often we make the right decision, the more our heart softens—or better perhaps, comes alive. . . . Each step in life which increases my self-confidence, my integrity, my courage, my conviction also increases my capacity to choose the desirable alternative, until eventually it becomes more difficult for me to choose the undesirable rather than the desirable action. On the other hand, each act of surrender and cowardice weakens me, opens the path for more acts of surrender, and eventually freedom is lost. Between the extreme when I can no longer do a wrong act and the extreme when I have lost my freedom to right action, there are innumerable degrees of freedom of choice. In the practice of life the degree of freedom to choose is different at any given moment. If the degree of freedom to choose the good is great, it needs less effort to choose the good. If it is small, it takes a great effort, help from others, and favorable circumstances [pp. 173–178].

Dr. M. Scott Peck refers to evil people as the "people of the lie": they are constantly engaged in self-deception and the deception of others. He goes on to say that "the lie is designed not so much to deceive others as to deceive themselves. They cannot or will not tolerate the pain of self-reproach. The decorum with which they lead their lives is maintained as a mirror in which they can see themselves reflected righteously" (1983, pp. 66–75). Peck observed that although it might be difficult to define evil people by the illegality of their actions, we can define them by the "consistency of their sins" (p. 71).

The notion of evil may best be understood if one perceives evil to be both a characteristic of an individual and a behavior. Men and women who commit evil acts are often perceived to possess evil characteristics. Thus serial killers not only *do* evil, but they also possess various developmental characteristics that may contribute to the evil. This differentiation between behavior and characteristics may depend on the type of serial killer. For example, some serial murderers possess highly developed narcissistic qualities. Fromm, discussing the pathology of narcissism, refers to people who exhibit "malignant narcissism." Many of these offenders display an unrelenting will to promote their own wants and needs over everyone else's. As Peck (1983) observes, "they are men and women of obviously strong will, determined to have their own way. There is remarkable power in the manner in which they attempt to control others" (p. 78). The epitome of narcissism may well be the total domination of others.

For example, I researched a case in which the offender is believed to have murdered 12–14 victims during a series of robberies on the West Coast. He usually stalked and attacked dark-haired, attractive women working in stores and other places of business. After robbing his victims he would bind them with tape and force them to engage in sexual acts. This entailed the victim assuming a kneeling position and being forced to perform fellatio on her attacker. During these encounters he held a gun to the victim's head. Sometimes he forced the woman to look him in the eyes until he climaxed, at which point he fired a bullet into her brain. Usually those whom he executed were victims who became hysterical, cried, and begged for mercy. Those who survived had complied with his demands but remained calm, some even joking with their assailant. The killer sought total domination and submission over his victims before pulling the trigger. The victim's death symbolized the attacker's signature on a completed act of total control over another human being.*

When Evil Embraces Good

The notion of evil becomes complicated by the generally accepted belief that those who commit sins can repent and virtually turn their lives around. The Christian Bible is replete with exhortations to repent. Whether or not we accept the Christian principle of repentance, the fact remains that people can and do stop committing sins and crimes. This "change of heart" may precipitate in some a desire to correct the wrong they have done and to become productive rather than destructive members of society. Prisons seem to breed religious conversions, which sometimes do appear to effect a change in attitude and behavior.

Is it possible for convicted and incarcerated serial killers to experience this "change of heart," experience remorse for their crimes and never engage in them again? The scope of this research does not provide concrete answers to this question, but a few brief observations can be made.

Frequently in the processing of offenders a judge is influenced in sentencing by the display of remorse. The general public is incensed when a convicted criminal displays no remorse for his or her crimes. Many people do not or can not fathom homicide beyond the realm of television and expect those who commit such crimes to have some degree of remorse. We tend to equate remorse with the recognition that a terrible wrong has been committed and that the offender, recognizing his or her wrong, feels sorrow.

Recognizing words such as "sorrow" and "remorse" as qualitative terms and difficult to quantify, we are faced with the task of determining sincerity. Many serial murderers, some who have killed dozens of victims and are now in prison, profess a sincere conversion and deep commitment to God and/or Christian principles.

---

*Some of this information was gathered from interviews with the offender and surviving victims in December, 1988.

In one case an offender killed at least 12 victims. Some of those murdered were children whom he tortured and sexually attacked for hours before finally taking their lives. He recalled to me during an interview that on one occasion a young woman he attacked died too quickly. He was outraged that she had not lived longer for him to torture. In his anger he hung her from a ceiling and for several minutes bludgeoned and kicked the corpse. Later that day he found another young woman who died much more slowly. This killer is now a converted Christian who is confident that God has forgiven him for his crimes and that he eventually will be set free.

Another offender killed 11 children over a period of one and one half years in the early 1980s. Seven of the eleven boys and girls were raped or sodomized. Some he bludgeoned to death with a hammer, others he strangled or stabbed to death. Apprehended for only the last missing child, he made a deal with the authorities. In return for money he would be willing to take authorities to the grave sites of other missing children, but without the money there would be no bodies. Parents of missing children in the area naturally wanted to know if it was their son or daughter killed by this mass murderer or whether their child was still alive somewhere. Authorities, without public knowledge, agreed to the exchange, and the killer began locating the dead children. Each time a body was recovered, $10,000 was placed in an account bearing the offender's wife's name. After ten bodies were exchanged the offender terminated the deal. He now resides in an isolation unit in a maximum security facility.

I have corresponded and spoken with the offender on several occasions. He clearly understands what he has done is wrong, but now claims no remorse for his deeds. When asked about his victims he responded, "I have put this whole matter behind me now. They are my brothers and sisters in Christ. All the children are with our Lord Jesus Christ now, and some day I shall be there with them." Claiming to have always been a Christian, the offender is enrolled at the time of this writing at a Divinity College, where he is pursuing coursework in religious studies. He continues to write essays condemning abortion and capital punishment (a reversal of his previous stance) and supporting the power and importance of prayer.

These are only two of many cases of serial killers who ardently embrace God. Whether the embracing of God and/or Christianity will inevitably lead to productive rather than destructive lives remains to be seen.

When Good Embraces Evil

The more perversely and obscenely some murderers tend to behave or are depicted by the media to have acted, the greater the interest by the general public. Most persons are simply fascinated and shocked with the innovative destructiveness of multiple murderers. Most serial killers, especially those males viewed as attractive and charming, quickly draw a following of women, mostly young. These women attend the trial, write letters, and send photographs of themselves hoping to receive some attention from the killer. Some wish to help the offender recover from his aberrant behavior or are simply interested in having contact with someone so dangerous, but from a safe distance. We have yet to adequately explore the impact of media and public attention on serial killers and future offenders. We do know serial murders elicit an immediate response from some people who otherwise would in all probability never have contact with the offender. The relationship between the public and the offender is shaped to some degree by the amount of publicity, the types of victims, and the personality of the offender.

Inevitably some people are drawn to the offender because they have a desire to befriend and understand the killer. In one instance a woman met the offender after he had been convicted and sentenced to prison for killing children. She came to believe that it was God's will that she devote herself to the betterment of this man's life and has every intention of remaining faithful to him. She understands the nature and the extent of his crimes but is convinced that the offender is salvageable. This type of involvement by a convicted killer with morally "straight" members of the community raises several questions. What influence, if any, do such offenders have over members of the community? What factors create attraction between someone who has ritualistically killed children and another person who abhors violence? Is there an attraction between people who strive to do good and those who commit acts of evil? It is easy to ascribe naivete to those who align themselves with the offender, but we fall short in understanding the dynamics of such relationships.

CHAPTER **3**

Biology and Psychology in Serial Murder

The early schools of thought addressing biogenic explanations for homicide included the notion of "inheritance," or the belief that criminality was an inherited trait. For example, the research included the case study of the offspring of Martin Kallikak and Ada Jukes. Among 2,000 descendants researchers identified 450 paupers, 258 criminals, 428 prostitutes, and a variety of other socially unacceptable types (Dugdale, 1910; Estabrook, 1916, pp. 60–61). The inheritance school of thought is discounted by most researchers today because it is impossible to determine if the criminal behavior is a product of inherited or acquired traits. Clearly, the propensity for homicide cannot be explained away by simply knowing the identity of a killer's parents.

Biological and Biochemical Theories of Violent Behavior

The earliest biocriminologists studied the shape of the head and the body, including facial features and bumps on the skull. Cesare Lombroso (1835–1909), often referred to as the "father of criminology," studied physical characteristics of criminals. He believed that people born with traits that lead them to commit crimes have particular atavistic anomalies—that is, physical characteristics typical of distant ancestors. These anomalies, or crimogenic physical traits, were believed to be inherited from degenerate family types and sometimes tempered by environmental factors. However, the work of Lombroso and those supporting such "body-build theories" have been set aside in favor of more scientifically sound research.

Modern research now supports a variety of biochemical factors involved in criminal behavior, such as allergies, environmental conditions, and diet. For example, vitamin deficiency and use of vitamin supplements continue to receive attention as factors in violent, aggressive behavior, but because of limited testing and methodological problems in sampling, little credible evidence of the connection currently exists (Gray, 1986). Hypoglycemia, a state of low blood sugar that affects the functioning of the brain, has been connected to antisocial behavior, including homicide and habitual violence (Hill & Sargent, 1943; Podolsky, 1964; Virkkunen, 1986). Other research has begun to focus on contaminants in our ecosystem—including metals such as copper and lead, food additives such as artificial dyes and colors, and radiation from artificial lighting, television sets and computer screens—that may negatively influence behavior (Ott, 1984).

Considerable attention has also been given to chromosome studies attempting to link an abnormal number of Y chromosomes (XYY) in men to violent behavior, but findings always remain tenuous (Mednick & Volavka, 1980). Other research involving adopted twins has been more concrete, but much more evidence is needed to establish a relationship among heredity, environment, and criminality (Mednick et al., 1983; Rowe, 1986). In reviewing biogenic literature we must proceed with extreme caution to avoid confusing factors that may correlate with violent behavior and those that address causality. The argument that biological factors determine aggressive behavior remains premature, with little substantiating data. When Charles Whitman fired on dozens of students from the Bell Tower at the University of Texas, speculation arose that his violent behavior may have occurred as a result of a brain tumor later discovered during an autopsy.

However, studies continue in the area of hormones and their relationship to violent behavior. Hormone research has ineffectively attempted to link the principal male sex hormone, testosterone, to aggressive and violent behavior (Rada, 1983; Rada et al., 1976; Rubin, 1987). Review of premenstrual syndrome (PMS) research by Horney (1978) found little support in connecting increased amounts of estrogen and progesterone with aggressive behavior in females. Indeed, Johns Hopkins University provides sex offenders estrogen and progesterone therapy to lower their testosterone levels. Some states, such as Texas, Michigan, and California, are recommending the use of hormones to perform chemical castration on convicted rapists. The movement toward biological definitions for explaining violent behavior may be gaining momentum. In Indiana a bill was introduced in the legislature in 1989 to allow sex offenders the opportunity to be surgically castrated in exchange for reduced time in prison. The bill was defeated.

Hans Eysenck (1977), from a biosocial perspective, argued that criminal behavior, including homicide, stems from interactions of environmental conditions and inherited personality traits. In addition he concluded that the combinations of interactions of biological, environmental, and personality factors determine different types of crimes. Unlike those who believe in the "born" criminal, who is genetically programmed for criminal activity, Eysenck attributed criminality to persons born with nervous system characteristics that are distinct from "normal" people. In turn, these characteristics interfere with their ability to conform to the rules, values, and laws of society. He contends that most people are not criminals because as children they were classically conditioned to obey the rules and laws of society—much like the dogs in Pavlov's experiments. According to Eysenck, most people avoid antisocial behavior because they have been trained to recognize the negative consequences.

In addition, Eysenck believes that *extraverts* are more likely than *introverts*, because of the biological differences in their nervous systems, to be involved in antisocial behavior. Serial killers are often viewed as charismatic, thrill-seeking types of individuals (Ted Bundy, Randy Woodfield, Clifford Olson), although cases exist in which serial murderers are found to be quiet, introverted types (Richard Angelo, Donald Harvey). Certainly, this is one perspective that has yet to receive much attention by researchers.

Occasionally there will be serial killers and other violent offenders who, when examined, display abnormalities in their genetic composition. Such findings should stimulate further research rather than hasty conclusions of causality. Certainly, biological research is not without merit, and, in future explanations for homicide, particularly multiple homicide offenders, new findings may well prove to be helpful. However, given the current state of biogenic research, it is unlikely that in the foreseeable future biological factors will be established as the sole link between humans and violent behavior.

Insanity: What Is It?

Most people's immediate response on learning that someone has murdered several persons is that he or she must be crazy. This is especially common when an individual enters a schoolyard, a shopping mall, or a restaurant and begins shooting randomly. Many such killers are found to have a history of mental problems, drug usage, and encounters with the law. For example, in Stockton, California, in January, 1989, an intruder entered the Cleveland Elementary School yard and began firing rounds from a Russian-made AK-47 assault rifle. Five children were killed and at least 30 other children wounded, many seriously, from the 110 expended rounds. The attacker then fired a bullet into his own head, killing himself instantly. Police and psychologists who investigated the case believed that something "snapped" in him and he reacted violently. The man's history indicated a life of drug abuse, arrests, and isolation. In this particular case the attacker appeared unable to cope any longer with an intolerable existence. He could not accept the fact that others around him were becoming successful. The feelings of inadequacy, loss of self-esteem, perceived rejection by others, and failure to achieve can become too much for some individuals to bear. They finally respond by lashing back at society. In this case the killer may have been exacting the greatest possible revenge on society by killing children.

Confronted with such cases, we sometimes employ terms that may blur the distinction between legal and medical definitions of mental disorders. Once an offender is charged with multiple murders, the "not-guilty-by-reason-of-insanity" defense (NGRI) may be used as the defense strategy.

However, as far as the criminal courts are concerned, insanity is a legal term not a psychiatric distinction.

The courts usually determine the state of mind of the accused before a trial commences. During the trial the courts must then determine if the offender was insane at the time of the crime and to what extent he or she is responsible for the crime. Thus the legal system uses the term *insanity* to define the state of mind of an offender *at the time of the offense;* offenders may be deemed insane at the moment of the crime and *only* for that period of time. Insanity pleas have been commonly used by offenders charged with serious crimes such as homicide, especially when the defense team sees little hope of acquitting their client by any other means. Most legal jurisdictions ensure that NGRI offenders are automatically placed in psychiatric facilities, regardless of their present state of mind. In *Jones v. United States* (1983) the Supreme Court ruled that insanity may continue after the criminal act, and therefore the offender could be placed in a psychiatric facility until such time when he or she is determined to have recovered from his or her afflictions. For some offenders confinement in a mental institution is tantamount to a life sentence because they must be clinically evaluated and deemed no longer to be a threat to society before they can be released.

Less than 1% of all criminal cases use the insanity defense, and most of those are unsuccessful. Those who do plead insanity generally are non-violent offenders. Contrary to popular opinion most serial killers never use the insanity plea, although one might expect such a defense. Legal determination of insanity usually stems from specific tests for criminal responsibility. American courts usually apply rules patterned after British law. In the United States, courts generally follow the M'Naughten Rule, the Brawner Rule, or the Durham Rule.

The M'Naughten Rule

The M'Naughten Rule is often used to define insanity because of its simplicity:

> To establish a defense on the ground of insanity, it must be proved that at
> the time of the committing of the act the party accused was laboring
> under such a defect of reason from disease of the mind as not to know
> the nature and quality of the act he was doing; or, if he did know, that he
> did not know he was doing what was wrong [M'Naughten, 1843, p. 718].

The M'Naughten Rule is used in about 16 states to determine if the offender was unable to distinguish between right and wrong as a result of mental disability. Critics of the rule feel it fails to include situations in which offenders can distinguish between right and wrong but are simply unable to control their behavior. Some states used to supplement the M'Naughten Rule with the Irresistible Impulse Test, which allows an insanity defense when it can be determined that the offender understands the difference between right and wrong yet succumbs to uncontrollable impulses (Kadish & Paulsen, 1981). The defense then had to prove only that the offender could not control him- or herself during commission of the crime.

The Brawner Rule

Today the Brawner Rule, or Substantial Capacity Test, is commonly used in the United States to test for insanity because it combines the intents of the M'Naughten Rule and the Irresistible Impulse Test. It states in part:

> A person is not responsible for criminal conduct if at the time of such conduct as a result of mental disease or defect he lacks substantial capacity either to appreciate the criminality (wrongfulness) of his conduct or to conform his conduct to the requirement of the law [*United States* v. *Brawner*, 1972].

Under this test, or rule, the accused need only show a lack of substantial capacity instead of total impairment. This partial incapacity, however, excludes repeated criminal behavior such as acts committed by sociopaths or acts determined to have been committed by people with antisocial personality disorders.

The Durham Rule

Finally, the Durham Rule, known also as the Products Test, held in *Durham* v. *United States* (1954) that "An accused is not criminally responsible if his unlawful act was the product of mental disease or defect." Controversy arose over establishing "mental disease" or "defect" and defining the term "product." Essentially, in such cases the jury has no standards to follow but instead must rely heavily on psychiatrists' decisions about defendants' mental faculties. Consequently nearly all states have discontinued use of the Durham Rule.

Incompetency

Another important issue from a legal perspective is that some defendants are incompetent to stand trial. This has nothing to do with the court's determination of criminal responsibility, because anyone determined to be incompetent does not stand trial and thus has not been found guilty of a crime. The defendant's state of mind at the time of the crime may differ greatly from his or her state of mind later in court. If a person is found incompetent, he or she is usually placed in a mental institution until such time as he or she is considered competent by medical experts, after which the person must stand trial. Few serial murderers are found to be incompetent.

In recent years considerable public pressure has swayed some states to change their use of the insanity defense. For example, Alaska, Delaware, Georgia, Illinois, Indiana, Michigan, and New Mexico have created a guilty but insane defense. Under this plea, offenders are confined to psychiatric facilities until their mental states improve. They are then transferred to prisons to finish out their sentence. Another reason for some states to revise their rules for determining insanity is the federal government's 1984 revision of the criminal code, which abolished the Irresistible Impulse Test.

Public pressure does affect the judicial system. The extremely high visibility of serial murderers, although they are relatively few in number, draws increasing attention to offenders who to some extent have "beaten the system"—for example, by going to a psychiatric institution instead of to prison. The public is becoming frustrated with lengthy appeals, insanity defenses, and competency hearings and is anxious to see the application of swift and certain punishment. However, in our haste for reform we must not remove adequate protection under the law for those who were legally insane when they committed the offense.

Mental Illness and Personality Disorders

We are inclined to believe that persons capable of random homicides must indeed be mentally ill or sick. As a society, we have long harbored feelings of fear and loathing toward those who appear to be mentally unbalanced. Defining the state of the mentally ill according to their behavior, our society has long felt a need to protect itself from them by confining them in a variety of institutions. Part of the problem of defining mental illness stems from the fact that many different labels are used to describe bizarre behavior. "Insane," "mentally ill," "sick," "deranged," "crazy," "mental problems," "psychiatric disorders"—each term describes abnormal behavior.

We have also maintained the use of two classical Freudian labels to describe degrees of mental illness: psychotic and neurotic.

PSYCHOSIS Attaining a clinical consensus on an exact description of psychotic behavior is often difficult. Psychosis has generally been viewed as a severe form of mental illness in which the individual suffers from a severe break with reality and may exhibit dangerous behavior. However, movies such as *Halloween*, depicting escaped mental patients slaughtering unsuspecting victims, create an unwarranted distortion of people suffering from psychosis. Most of the psychotic patients I have encountered generally were not violent. Those who became dangerously violent were usually at a much greater risk of hurting themselves than anyone else. In one instance a young woman who was believed to be in a psychotic state was admitted to a hospital. The day after her arrival she sat quietly by herself staring off into space. Suddenly she jabbed an index finger in behind her right eyeball, partially tearing it from the eye socket. She proceeded to nearly sever two fingers with her teeth before attendants were able to stop her. The woman appeared to have experienced no pain during the self-mutilation and probably would have chewed off all her fingers had there been no intervention. In another case a female patient in moments of psychosis would seek out the edge of a door casing on which to split open her skull. The poor woman would thrust her forehead against the casing until the front of her head began to split open. In such a state she also appeared to have no feeling of pain.

It is exactly these types of images of mental illness that are held and perpetuated by our communities. It becomes easy to believe that "psychotic" people are prone to kill others. However, empirically based research literature discounts notions that psychotics are particularly dangerous people. Henn and colleagues (1976) examined the psychiatric assessments of nearly 2,000 persons arrested for homicide between 1964 and 1973 and noted that only 1% were considered to be psychotic. Similar results were also reported in other studies (Hafner & Boker, 1973; Zitrin et al., 1975).

Until recently persons determined to be psychotic were routinely transferred into institutions for the criminally insane without ever having committed a criminal act—even though, as mentioned earlier, psychotics are more likely to hurt themselves than others. Psychotics are perceived by the public as dangerous to others. By contrast, people who are called "criminally insane" often display few if any overt signs of mental illness. "Criminal insanity" is more of a contradiction in terms, an oxymoron of sorts. Most people who commit crimes are sane, whereas those who truly are insane commit few crimes. The U.S. Supreme Court ruled in *Vitek* v. *Jones* (1980) that administrative hearings are mandatory prior to transferring psychotic individuals to institutions for the criminally insane. Given the deplorable and limited facilities for the truly mentally ill it is unlikely that this ruling will significantly alter the flow of psychotics to such institutions.

NEUROSIS *Neurotic* behavior generally has been defined as a variety of forms of mental disorders of less violent nature than occur in cases of psychotic behavior. As with "psychosis," "neurosis" has remained a vague and nebulous term that has included persons afflicted with high anxieties and compulsive and obsessive behaviors, to name but a few disorders.

Research efforts have failed to substantiate claims that neurotic behavior is common among criminals. Brodsky (1973) in his review of nine studies of prisoner populations found only 1–2% psychotic types and only 4–6% neurotic types among the inmates. Monahan and Steadman (1984) in their exhaustive review on the relationship between mental disorder and crime found little evidence that the mentally ill are more inclined to criminal activity than anyone else. By contrast, many inmates are diagnosed as having personality disorders. A common personality disorder especially among those who commit crimes is the antisocial personality.

THE ANTISOCIAL PERSONALITY　Under the guidance of the American Psychiatric Association, a guidebook entitled the *Diagnostic and Statistical Manual of Mental Disorders (DSM)* was compiled to identify the wide range of mental dysfunctions. Periodically the DSM is revised to reflect current psychiatric thought. Diverging from traditional psychoanalysis and psychodynamic theory, the *DSM III-R* (third edition, revised) was published to focus more on classification and description of mental disorders. The *DSM III-R* reports that personality disorders include a history of antisocial behavior beginning no later than age 15 for males, and for females anytime during the teen years. Antisocial behaviors may include one or more of the following: incorrigibility, theft, fighting during childhood, excessive alcohol/drug use, and aggressive sexual behavior during adolescence. As adults antisocial persons have particular difficulty in developing and sustaining relationships. They tend to demonstrate poor work habits and lack of responsibility, view the world in negative, hostile terms, and frequently show lack of insight into their problems and future plans. The *DSM III-R* suggests there may be a genetic link that perpetuates an intergenerational pattern of antisocial behavior, although such findings remain tenuous.

Serial killers have often been portrayed as antisocial personality types manifesting aggressive, hostile behavior and a tendency to avoid developing close relationships. However, some serial murderers appear to be well-adjusted persons leading rather normal lives; their closest friends and family members have been surprised and shocked by their confessions of multiple homicides. The point is: Offenders do not always come from the same mold. Each killer has evolved through different life events and has responded to those experiences differently. Although it may be argued that serial killers possess "fatal flaws," it remains indefensible to say that such flaws are overtly manifested. In short, some offenders may never reveal enough of themselves in daily life to allow the identification of particular personality disorders. In hindsight we are always able to identify fatal personality flaws once we know what the offender has done. Accurate prediction of homicidal behavior, particularly serial killing, continues to evade researchers and clinicians alike. Understanding the psychopathology of these Jekyll-and-Hyde-like personalities appears increasingly complex as we explore the minds of serial murderers.

Dissociative Disorders

Researchers have recently begun to explore dissociative disorders and their relationships to serial killers. Such disorders include abrupt, temporary changes in consciousness, identity, and motor activity. Gallagher (1987) identifies different forms of dissociation, including multiple personality, the most widely known dissociative disorder. He noted that only a few hundred cases have been reported, and in 1978 approximately 100 cases were being treated in the United States (pp. 117–119).

MULTIPLE PERSONALITY DISORDER (MPD)   Hale (1983) found less than 300 documented cases of multiple personality disorder (MPD), whereas Size-more (1982), herself a case of multiple personality, believes there are no more than 100–200 cases of true multiple personalities. Prince (1908) documented the classical case of Christine Beauchamp, a Radcliffe student who appeared to have three distinct personalities. Thigpen and Cleckley (1957), in their book *Three Faces of Eve*, observed that their patient Eve White experienced at least 22 completely different personalities. Chris Sizemore, who eventually revealed herself publicly as Eve, is not sure of the origins of her personalities but observed that "it was a defense and a unique coping mechanism which created satellite persons to cope with conflicts that were unbearable" (Suinn, 1984, p. 180).

Having more than one personality may be an attempt to suppress or deny severe traumatizations as a child. Gallagher (1987) describes the highly acclaimed multiple personality case of Sybil, who was initially believed to be controlled by three personalities—thirteen others became manifest during treatment. Sybil appeared to have begun developing these personalities at age 3½. An only child born to a mother determined by psychiatrists to be paranoid schizophrenic, Sybil was forced to watch her parents engage in sexual activities and became the target of her own mother's bizarre fantasies. Each morning Sybil was strapped to the kitchen table, and, following a prescribed ritual, objects including knife handles, flashlights, a buttonhook, and bottles were inserted into her vagina. Frequently her mother adminis-tered enemas and forced Sybil to retain the contents while the mother played melodies on the piano. If the child soiled herself she immediately received a vicious beating. There were times when Sybil was burned, had bones broken, was locked in trunks and other confined spaces, and hung upside down.

Sybil's psychoanalyst would later explain that Sybil's personality had split or divided into several selves as a mode of self-preservation from the nightmares to which she was subjected. The "new" personalities denied the existence of Sybil's mother as their mother, thus allowing Sybil to cope with the immeasurable amount of stress and pain placed on her (pp. 118–199). Schreiber (1973) suggested that Sybil was traumatized by her mother's attitude toward being a woman. When Sybil first menstruated, her mother jabbed her in the abdomen and remarked, "It's simply awful. The curse of women. It hurts you here, doesn't it" (p. 118).

Multiple personality as a dissociative disorder may be one way in which some people avoid or escape stressful or painful experiences. Wilbur (1978) in her studies of MPD argues that all personalities diagnosed as dissociative had been battered as children. Stress that fuels anxieties may trigger a dissociative response to adapt to intolerable situations. Without such a defense mechanism the individual may be subject to a psychotic break with reality that inevitably could become self-destructive.

Using multiple personalities disorder to explain serial murder behavior is a rare but usually highly publicized event. In the case of the Hillside Strangler, one of the killers, Kenneth Bianchi, while under hypnosis, suddenly revealed another personality whom he called Steve Walker. Initially, the explanation of MPD was eagerly embraced by many observers. While on the one hand there was Ken, the kind, loving father and responsible individual, on the other hand there was Steve, the other personality, the cold, vicious killer. Psychiatrists postulated that Ken had deeply resented his mother and had repressed these feelings only to have them surface in the form of Steve Walker. Dr. Ralph Allison, an expert on multiple personalities, interviewed "Steve Walker" under hypnosis.

> "I fuckin' killed those broads...those two fuckin' cunts, that blond-
> haired cunt and the brunette cunt. ..."
> "Why?"
> "Cause I hate fuckin' cunts" [Schwarz, 1981].

Bianchi explained to Allison during the hypnosis that he had met Steve while being abused by his mother. Allison recommended to the court that Bianchi was incompetent to stand trial as a result of his dual personality. Dr. Martin Orme of the Department of Psychiatry of the University of Pennsylvania Medical School was brought in to examine Bianchi to see if perhaps he could be faking the multiple personalities. Just before placing Bianchi under hypnosis Orme mentioned to him that it was rare to find a case of MPD with only two personalities. Within moments after being hypnotized "Billy" emerged as a third personality. Several people questioned Bianchi's disorder, including the police and the detectives involved in the case. Further investigation uncovered an academic transcript from Los Angeles Valley College that Bianchi had stolen from another student and then altered. The original owner of the transcript was Thomas Steven Walker. Bianchi, always the manipulator, had successfully deceived several experts. Before his capture he had easily conned a North Hollywood psychologist into allowing him to use some of his office space while he launched his counseling practice. Producing a phony master's degree in psychology from Columbia University, he deftly talked his way into a professional career, albeit short-lived. Bianchi, now under attack for faking MPD, dropped his plea of insanity and admitted guilt for the murders of several young women.

There do not appear to be any well-documented cases of MPD in serial killing. Even in single homicides, MPD is more likely to be used as a decoy defense than to be valid. Coons (1988), in his review of eight one-time murderers who used MPD as an insanity defense, noted that five were found guilty, one not guilty by reason of insanity (NGRI), and two people's guilt was never mentioned. In none of these cases in which MPD was claimed was the defendant ever described properly enough to substantiate an unequivocal diagnosis of MPD.

PSYCHOGENIC AMNESIA   Although MPD has yet to be empirically proved in cases of serial murder, other forms of dissociative disorders that may play a role are only now beginning to receive attention. Psychogenic amnesia, a loss of memory due to psychological reasons rather than organic problems, is considered to be rare and can be triggered by highly stressful events such as war and natural disasters (Frederick, 1981; Hirst, 1982). Frequently, those afflicted display anterograde amnesia, or loss of memory after a traumatic experience (Golden et al., 1983). The *DSM III-R* describes four types of psychogenic amnesia, each stemming from various forms of traumatization. Some traumas, such as viewing a murder or being a rape victim, can trigger nearly complete memory loss regarding one's own personal life.

PSYCHOGENIC FUGUE   Another dissociative disorder, psychogenic fugue, is described by the *DSM III-R* as temporary psychological "flight," or psychological disturbance, precipitated by a traumatic event. Those afflicted may engage in partial or complete identity change triggered by their loss of self-identity. Fugues are still considered rare among dissociative disorders. Kirshner (1973) noted that only 7 out of 1,795 cases of admissions to a medical facility were diagnosed as fugue states.

What we are beginning to learn from studies of multiple personality, psychogenic amnesia, and psychogenic fugue is that memories can be terrifyingly painful for some individuals. Splitting off, blocking out, or not remembering anything may all serve as vehicles to thwart undesirable memories. Indeed, we all to some degree repress certain memories that cause discomfort. Memories of failure, divorce, death(s), rejection, even of always being the last child chosen for a ball team, all can cause that psychological "wincing" that most people prefer not to discuss in detail. Suinn (1984) found that individuals report poor memory of incompleted tasks that imply a sense of failure. He suggested that memory can be very selective when dealing with threatening information, even in the mildest forms (p. 175).

Psychoanalytic Factors

The notion of repression of feelings and thoughts was promoted by Sigmund Freud in linking abnormal behavior to mental problems induced by early childhood trauma. According to Freud, the mind is constantly engaged in balancing the three-part personality structure of id, the ego, and the superego. The id represents the primal component of a person's mental state, the driving force for the necessities to sustain life, including food, water, and sex. The ego develops from birth and serves to guide individuals' behavior to conform to rules, laws, and community standards. It is the pragmatic component of the mental state. The superego is the composite of moral standards and values learned within the family and community, which to some degree have been internalized. The superego sits in judgment of a person's behavior. The id and the superego generally oppose each other: the id seeks pure pleasure and the superego strives for morality and acceptable ethics. The ego, the arbitrator of the personality triad, constantly seeks to mediate between these two forces and generally provides a compromise. To illustrate the psychoanalytic concept, imagine someone being taunted by racial slurs. His immediate feelings (id) might be to strike the offending party in retaliation, but the superego senses that such behavior would not only be an overreaction but inherently dangerous behavior. Torn between the two forces, the ego guides the individual to a compromise. The individual may discount the event as meaningless and choose to ignore the situation or perhaps file harassment charges against the offender.

From the psychoanalytic perspective, violent persons appear to give little attention to morality, ethics, or standards when their id functions have been aroused. For example, Henry Lucas, a confessed serial killer of dozens of victims throughout the southern states, described himself as sometimes quick-tempered. On one occasion the 42-year-old Lucas became involved in a dispute with his 15-year-old lover and confidant. In anger the girl reached over and slapped Lucas who responded by stabbing her repeatedly until she was dead.

Gallagher (1987) in describing the conflict between the id and the superego concluded that abnormal behavior is the product of a conflict between innate human needs and societal norms (p. 47). Such conflicts usually stem from traumatic experiences during childhood that place tremendous stress on an individual. Most often the stress is generated by a conflicted parent-child relationship; the personality of the individual may become fixated or halted as a result of the unresolved conflict.

Such psychological scarring can be devastating to a young person. For instance, Edmund Kemper experienced significant childhood conflict with his mother, which left him with intense feelings of love and hate for her. At age 15 he killed both his grandparents because he was angry and wanted to know what it would be like to kill someone. After a few years of treatment Kemper was released into the care of his mother, which only escalated his feelings of rage toward her. He quietly went on a wild and terrifying homicidal rampage. Picking up female hitchhikers from the University of California at Santa Cruz campus where his mother worked, he sexually attacked and then butchered his victims. During this time Kemper was also fulfilling the terms of his parole and regularly attended sessions with his psychiatrist. During one of his visits the psychiatrist told Kemper how much better he appeared to be functioning and that he was pleased with his progress. During that particular visit, even as they spoke with each other, the head of one of Ed's latest victims lay in the trunk of his car. In this case, as in the cases of many serial killers, appearances were not only deceiving, but costly.

Kemper eventually murdered several young female students before finally killing his mother and decapitating her. Kemper believed that once he had "resolved" the conflict with his mother his rages would subside, and he would not feel compelled to kill more victims. Kemper was arrested again and is now eligible for parole. He feels he no longer is a threat to society.

According to psychoanalytic theory, there are several paths to fixation besides harsh treatment of a child and anxiety-producing infantile experiences. Various forms of sexual assault on a child, including parental abuse, exposure by a child to sexual activities, and acts of incest by older siblings, can also contribute to early childhood traumatizations (Nunberg, 1955). The efficacy of the emphasis on disrupted sexual development of the child is not the focus of this research, but the fact that some serial killers demonstrate symptoms of psychosexual dysfunctioning should be a point for future investigation.

August Aichorn (1934), a psychoanalyst associated with Freudian analysis, studied delinquent youths and concluded that societal stress alone could not explain a life of crime. He noted that a predisposition was also prerequisite for a youth to engage in antisocial behavior. Latent delinquency, a term he coined to describe a state in which a youth constantly seeks immediate gratification while neglecting the feelings or needs of others, centered on a lack of remorse or sense of guilt in satisfying instinctive urges.

Indeed, there now exists considerable literature that lends support to the belief that most seriously violent offenders (excluding serial killers) suffer from various forms of personality disturbances. Lewis et al. (1985) studied a group of nine youths who had been examined prior to their homicidal attacks. They found that all nine had manifested "extreme violence" as children and as adolescents. They also noted that factors that were associated with the violence clustered around neuropsychiatric and family factors. The boys were found to be the offspring of psychotic households filled with violent behavior and physical abuse. Most of the boys were found to have suffered neurological damage as a result of head injuries or seizure disorders.

Smith (1965), based on his studies of eight adolescent murderers, reported that each boy had experienced various forms of deprivation in his life that abrupted his ego development and facilitated violent aggression. Similarly, McCarthy (1978) found a tendency for homicidal behavior among young men who had experienced early deprivation and, in a study of ten killers, noted complex feelings of low self-esteem and deep-seated anger. Sendi and Blomgren (1975) found that sexual abuse of a child by a parent was associated with homicidal behavior. Corder et al. (1976) found psychosis, chronic alcoholism, and criminal behavior among parents of adolescent murderers. Malmquist (1971), commenting on the function of homicide, asserted that it "can serve the illusory function of saving one's self and ego from destruction by displacing onto someone else the focus of aggressive discharge." Pfeffer (1980) concluded that young men who victimize and murder others do so in an effort to neutralize early childhood traumatization.

David Abrahamsen (1973) in *The Murdering Mind* found one common characteristic among people who murder. He observed that all murderers are intensely tormented and are constantly beset by inner conflict:

> The prime marks of the murderer are a sense of helplessness, impotence, and nagging revenge carried over from early childhood. Intertwined with this core of emotions which color and distort his view of life and all his actions are his irrational hatred for others, his suspiciousness, and his hypersensitivity to injustices or rejection. Hand in hand with these go his self-centeredness and his inability to withstand frustration. Overpowered by frequent uncontrollable emotional outbursts, he has a need to retaliate, to destroy, to tear down by killing [p. 13].

Abrahamsen, as well as several others who subscribe to the Freudian perspective of psychoanalytic theory, places a considerable emphasis on psychosexual factors. Indeed, many childhood trauma experiences are sexual in nature. It is these sexual traumatizations that may later surface as aggressive, sometimes homicidal, behavior. Abrahamsen also noted an intimate connection between the offender and the victim as the "intertwining of our murderous and self-murderous impulses. . . . Every homicide is unconsciously a suicide and every suicide is, in a sense, a psychological homicide. Typically, the killer is afraid of killing himself, afraid of dying, and therefore he murders someone else" (p. 38). This effort to assert himself, to show that he is indeed capable and not a weakling, is an attempt to restore his "narcissistic" masculine self-esteem. Violence is an ego defense mechanism against intense inner pain and loss of self-esteem. Asserts Abrahamsen, "Frustration is the wet nurse of violence" (pp. 42–43).

For most, if not all serial killers, frustration appears as a common theme from one homicide to the next. For many, the homicidal act is preceded by sexual torture. In one case, a serial killer in Michigan ritualistically rammed broken branches from trees and bushes into his victim's vagina. Sex as a vehicle to vent the killer's frustration, anger, hate, and fear becomes a powerful destructive tool. By contrast, there are various cases of serial killers who derive sexual gratification from watching their victims suffer and die without sexually assaulting them or overtly using sex in any way to harm or degrade them. One offender reported how he would administer poison to prostitutes and immediately leave, even before the chemical began taking effect. As he walked home he would revel in and fantasize about the agony his victim was now going through.

One might argue, however, that even in the last case the offender may have been vicariously experiencing sexual pleasure. Although some cases of serial murder appear to involve absolutely no sexual motivations, one may argue that latent sexual motivations exist unknown even to the offender. Psychoanalytic literature is replete with examples of defense mechanisms that serve to reduce anxiety states. Freud identified several, including denial, the conscious refusal to admit a factual event; repression, an unconscious exclusion from consciousness of anxiety-producing material or events; suppression, the conscious exclusion of anxiety-producing material; projection, the initial repression of a trait, then attaching it to others; displacement, the venting of unacceptable impulse(s) toward a substitute target; and sublimation, directing unacceptable impulse(s) into socially acceptable channels (Suinn, 1984). Each of these mechanisms appears at one time or another in the personality profiles of various serial killers. A tendency does exist for serial offenders to engage in a process of blocking out past experiences too painful or stressful to accommodate. The magnitude of the role these and other psychoanalytic factors play in the mind of the serial murderer is only now beginning to be explored.

The Psychopath-Sociopath

The term *psychopath* was introduced by J. L. A. Koch in his 1891 monograph *Die Psychopathischen Minderwertigkeiten* in his description of "psychopathic inferiorities." In 1939 Henderson described psychopaths in his book *Psychopathic States* as those afflicted with an illness:

> The term psychopathic state is the name we apply to those individuals who conform to a certain intellectual standard, sometimes high, sometimes approaching the realm of defect but yet not amounting to it, who throughout their lives, or from a comparatively early age, have exhibited disorders of conduct of an antisocial or asocial nature, usually of a recurrent or episodic type, who, in many instances, have proved difficult to influence by methods of social, penal, and medical care and treatment and for whom we have no adequate provision of a preventive or curative nature. The inadequacy or deviation or failure to adjust to ordinary social life is not a mere willfulness or badness which can be threatened or thrashed out of the individual so involved, but constitutes a true illness for which we have no specific explanation [1939, p. 19].

Cleckley (1976) in *The Mask of Sanity* outlined 16 characteristics of psychopaths:

1. intelligent
2. rational
3. calm
4. unreliable
5. insincere
6. without shame or remorse
7. having poor judgment

8. without capacity for love

9. unemotional

10. poor insight

11. indifferent to the trust or kindness of others

12. overreactive to alcohol

13. threatens suicide

14. impersonal sex life

15. without long-term goals

16. inadequately motivated antisocial behavior

Thompson (1953) in *The Psychopathic Delinquent and Criminal* viewed such persons as those who seek momentary gratification, lack discretion, and fail to profit from experience, which leads to repeated failures.

The term *psychopath* operates as a label to describe a potpourri of individuals determined by societal and medical standards to possess antisocial qualities or characteristics. Interchangeably used with the label of *sociopath*, the psychopath often turns out to be exactly what we want him or her to be. Working in a sex-offender unit, I quickly learned these offenders were also regarded by the professional staff as psychopaths. In another section of the hospital were housed the habitual criminals, often also called "psychopaths." Even on the unit designated for persons on civil commitment, "psychopaths" were in abundance (author's files).

Psychopaths are generally viewed as aggressive, insensitive, charismatic, irresponsible, intelligent, dangerous, hedonistic, narcissistic, and antisocial. These are persons who can masterfully explain another person's problems, what must be done to overcome them, but appear to have little or no insight into their own lives or how to correct their own problems. Those psychopaths who can articulate solutions for personal problems usually fail to follow them through. Psychopaths are perceived as exceptional manipulators, capable of feigning emotions in order to carry out their personal agendas. Without remorse for the plight of their victims they are adept at rationalization, projection, and other psychological defense mechanisms. The veneer of stability, friendliness, and normality belies a deeply disturbed personality. Outwardly there appears to be nothing abnormal about their personalities, even their behavior. They are careful to maintain social distance and share intimacy only with those whom they can psychologically control. They are noted for their inability to maintain long-term commitments to people or programs.

Although not all psychopaths can be considered violent, they appear to be more prone to violent behavior than other people. If nothing else, they are viewed as more dangerous than most other people. Hare and Jutai (1959) noted that psychopaths do not "peak" in their careers as do other criminals but instead are able to maintain a consistency in their criminal behavior.

Psychopaths are commonly found in institutions and constitute approximately 20–30% of prison populations.

A common trait of psychopaths is their constant need to be in control of their social and physical environment. Often, when this control is challenged, the psychopath can be moved to violent behavior. One example from the author's experience is David, an intelligent man who was charming, engaging, and who possessed tremendous skills for deceiving others. Transient, he moved from one locale to another seeking out those whom he could use. He had married several times, often before the divorce from his previous spouse was finalized. He carefully and systematically siphoned off, diverted, and used the financial resources of each new wife. He embezzled money from his step-children by forging their names on government bonds. Constantly he borrowed money from others with no plans for repayment. Fastidious in his dress, versed in etiquette, and articulate in speech, he impressed everyone who had never been victimized by him as a responsible, gentle, and kind person. The man also had a passion for organization. He constantly reviewed everything about his life, his daily plans, and his goals. He always knew where he had been and what he did on any given day, any week, month, or year. Indeed, he spent so much time planning and creating checklists he never really accomplished anything. When confronted, he deftly sidestepped the issues, carefully staying out of the focus. He rarely allowed himself to be in situations in which he might not have control. On occasion he would engage in an athletic contest, such as basketball. A personality transformation inevitably occurred if his team was losing or if he did not give a stellar performance. Seething with anger and frustration he would resort to vulgar language, extreme physical aggressiveness, and shouting at other players. Although he had never been in prison, it was only because of his manipulative abilities that he remained free (author's file).

The problem with the label *psychopath* is that researchers and clinicians alike have yet to arrive at a consensus as to the proper definition of the term. Constructing a framework for the sociopathic personality type is still in the early structural stages. The etiology of personality disorders has given rise to a plethora of literature describing various forms of dysfunctional personalities. As mentioned earlier, the publication of the *DSM III-R* is an attempt to provide clarification of such personalities.

For the serial killer, the term *psychopath* seems to "fit." Heretofore, killers could, by societal standards, be labeled through generally accepted standards of stereotyping. Gradually, however, the public was introduced by the media to the "nicest-guy-in-the-world" killers, and it discovered that it had no apparent overt characteristics to enable stereotyping. The catch-all label of *psychopath* serves adequately to describe serial killers mainly because there appears to be a variety of types of serial offenders. This "variety," however, may be more of style than substance. The underlying pathology of serial killers typically is frustration, anger, hostility, feelings of inadequacy, and low self-esteem. These feelings may be manifested in many ways, but the source or underlying pathology appears as a common denominator. The continuum of psychopathic personalities includes representatives of many groups, including adolescents, sexual deviants, intellectual types, hard-core criminals, recluses, and extroverts, to name but a few. Many people may at one time or another play "mind games" with others in order to gain the upper hand in a relationship. Psychopaths become adept at this psychological game playing and ultimately become proficient at controlling their environment.

Psychopaths are easily misidentified because so often their behavior is inconsistent with earlier behavior or statements. Although they may show contempt, anger, and hatred toward certain types or groups of people, they may be particularly accepting of other groups or types of individuals. Feelings are compartmentalized and victims rationalized into objects by the psychopath who seeks outlets for his hostilities. In 1985 in Wisconsin dozens of women received telephone calls from an individual described as an "emotional rapist." His goal was to psychologically gain control over his victims' emotions by persuasively convincing them that they were dying of cancer or a rare blood disease. The only cure, he insisted, was to inflict extreme embarrassment on themselves. Some were ordered to walk down city streets with their breasts exposed, and two others pierced their nipples and walked mutilated among the public. His ability to manipulate his victims amazed everyone, especially those who obediently followed his commands (*Newsweek*, December 16, 1985). The purpose of his ruse was to inflict as much pain, degradation, and humiliation on his victims as possible.

Sex offenders use sex as a vehicle to gain control over their victims by inflicting pain and suffering. Many serial killers are believed to be involved sexually with their victims as a result of childhood experiences. According to Gebhard (1965), "It appears that fewer sexual psychopaths than other offenders were able to make good adjustments with their parents and their peers throughout their childhood" (p. 856). De Young (1982) noted that "the sadist sees the child victim as a representation of everything he hates about himself as well as the dreaded memories of his own childhood" (p. 125). Karpman (1954) noted similar characteristics of masochists: "Aggressive sexual crime symbolizes the inferiority feelings of the masochist and expresses his hostility toward the objects of his lust; these tendencies are integrated in the personality of the sexual psychopath as a result of long-standing emotional conflicts and stresses" (p. 72). The offender, through violent acts, attempts to gain the control he or she has sought since his or her childhood experiences. As Stoller (1975) observed, "Many childhood defeats and frustrations feed into the dynamics of risk, revenge, and triumph" (p. 128).

The sexual psychopath is often referred to in serial murder cases as a "lust killer." The notion of lust suggests one who possesses a particular urge, not only to kill, but to ravage the victim. Even among lust killers, methods of killing vary widely, as do the types of mutilations that may occur before or after the victim has died. In one case an offender described his feelings about killing, focusing on the urge to mutilate and destroy his victims before he could find temporary relief:

UNCENSORED EXOTICS*

Vainly I crouch at the fireside,
For the flames on the hearth cannot warm me.
Vainly I put on coats
Against the cold of the star winds,
Blowing from Outer Gulfs in the darkness beyond Time.
Thick walls and roofs, you are useless
Against the breath of the star winds.
Red logs, why do you crackle,
Since you are mocked by the star winds?
And my bones are chilled within me
And my blood is become as water.
And now from the void behind me
Comes the piping of the piper,
That senseless, complaining piping,
That tuneless, high, thin piping.
Swiftly I turn to assail him
But he keeps ever behind me,
So that I catch but a glimpse of him,
Piping behind the shadows.
Faceless, with malformed hands
Holding a flute of silver,
Blowing his senseless music.
Piping his high, thin piping.
During an age does his playing
Beat to my brain through my eardrums,
Covered by helpless fingers.
Then, with a shout, I surrender,
And leap to do the bidding.
From the wall I snatch my weapons
And rush from the house to the forest.
Where the road winds down the mountain,
Panting I lie in ambush,
Waiting for some poor traveler
Who shall bring me my release.
When he comes with laggard footsteps,
Sudden and fierce is my onslaught.
Like a beast I overcome him
And utterly destroy him.
And I cut out his heart and eat it,
And I guzzle his blood like nectar,
And I cut off his head and scalp him,
And hang his scalp at my belt.
Homeward I walk through the snowdrifts,
And my heart is warm within me,

---

*From J. Paul de River, *The Sexual Criminal*, 1949, pp. 210–211. Courtesy of Charles C Thomas, Publisher, Springfield, Illinois.

And my blood and bones are new again,
And the star winds cease to chill me,
And the piping of the piper
Will be heard no more for a season.

Such an urge to kill is fueled by well-developed fantasies that allow the offender to vicariously gain control of others. Fantasy for the lust killer is much more than an escape, it becomes the focal behavior. Even though the killer is able to maintain contact with reality, the world of fantasy becomes as addictive as an escape into drugs. Ressler and his colleagues (1988) argue that psychological motives for homicide do not find their roots in traumatization or stimulation; rather, offenders murder as a result of their thinking (p. 34). Thought processes, however, are influenced by life experiences that ultimately can affect the types of fantasies developed by individuals. Thus, negative experiences give rise to negative thoughts and fantasies, and positive experiences lay the foundation for positive thoughts and constructive fantasies. It is unlikely to find individuals who fantasize about helping others and then go out and kill other human beings. People who feel good about themselves do not kill others. The better a person's self-concept, the less need he or she has to control and dominate others. One may wonder why so many people subscribe to magazines or prefer entertainment established and operated on the premise of violence. Perhaps those who have carefully controlled lives allow others to stand proxy for them in acting out their fantasies of hostility and aggression. The boxer smashing his opponent's face, splattering blood; the matador who is gored by the horns of an enraged bull; the hockey player who slashes his opponent with his stick—each brings the fans to their feet, eager for more.

But most people do not kill, they just enjoy watching others do it on television and at the movies, or reading about it in books. Murderers take their fantasies farther. Perhaps some of us have fantasies that resemble those of the murderer, but yet we maintain control. Edmund Kemper spoke of the rage inside him that would not subside. He also discussed his fantasy of performing his next murder. By the time Kemper shoved a gun in the face of his first college co-ed, he had already mentally rehearsed the scenario "hundreds of times." Once he pulled out the gun he knew there was no turning back (Home Box Office, 1980). How often and how close do the fantasies of nonoffenders take them to the brink of killing?

Ressler and his colleagues (1988), in their study of 36 murderers, noted fantasy more as a process than merely an experience. Fantasies may begin at a very early age and appear to escalate over time. They reported several cases in which offenders were involved in early construction of aggressive fantasies including "sexualized rituals" or the repetition of sexual acts. They challenge the notion that murderers involved sexually with their victims make the decision to kill as adults: "The power of life and death and the realization that one decides whether to control, injure, or kill is a very early experience for these men" (p. 38). Given the fact that many serial killers report histories of traumatization, including sexual abuse, we may be well served by identifying exactly when they remember wanting to kill. Knowing the type of offenders to be questioned, one must always recognize the degree to which the subject can "color" his or her responses. Such a precautionary note would also suggest a need for more subjects able to provide reliable information.

Another manner of exploration of multiple homicides focuses on sociological explanations. Chapter 4 explores the various structural and social-process theories that may also be useful in understanding the dynamics of serial killing.

CHAPTER 4

 Social Construction of Serial Murder

Those involved in criminological research often find themselves drawing on various sociological theories. Two theories that are often quoted are social structure theory and social process theory.

Social Structure Theory

Social structure theories focus on individuals' socioeconomic standing, suggesting that poor people commit more crimes because they are stifled in their quest for financial or social success. Specifically, offenders, as a result of their racial, ethnic, or subcultural standing, are blocked in various ways from achieving the "American dream" through legitimate means. Consequently, they seek success through deviant methods. Structural theories offer cogent explanations for many types of crimes except for serial murder. Generally, serial killers do not belong to a racial or ethnic minority and do not appear to be particularly motivated by social or financial gain. Certainly, serial offenders exist who rob their victims, but even then the financial reward is peripheral to the attraction of killing another human being. The few exceptions to this often are found among female serial killers, who constitute a small portion of the total number of serial murderers (see Chapter 6). Occasionally, as in the case of Belle Gunness of Indiana, who advertised in newspapers for suitors, then promptly killed them once she gained access to their money, women will kill their husbands, fiances, or lovers in order to improve or maintain their lifestyle. Over a 14-year period one offender is believed to have murdered seven of her eight children for insurance purposes. Each time she needed money another child would suddenly pass away. Even in these cases, however, we cannot be sure that money was actually the primary motive.

One structural theory that may at some point provide greater insight into serial murder is the perspective of urbanism. Murder rates tend to be highest in densely populated cities such as Detroit, Miami, Birmingham, New York City, and Washington, D.C. Urban homicide rates tend to be associated with social disorder, alienation, drugs, fear, disassociation, poverty, and broken homes (Messner & Tardiff, 1986). High-density populations increase the probability of victimization because of impersonalization and frequent encounters with strangers (Sampson, 1987).

Serial killers have been located in and around most major U.S. cities, although they also appear in some of the most isolated areas in America. Where the offenders are, of course, will depend on what type of serial killers they are and what kinds of victims they are after. High-density populations are attractive for those wishing to "melt" into their environment. Several of the most "effective" serial killers have operated in some of the more populated areas of the country. Whether serial murderers are attracted to such locales or they already live in the area is not exactly clear. It is clear, however, that California, the most populous state in the United States, reports more incidents of serial killing than any other state in the nation. According to the study discussed in this book, incidents of serial killing in California appear to be more than double those in other populous states with relatively high reportings of serial murder. For the serial offender who is specifically looking for women or children, the larger cities obviously offer an ample supply of unsuspecting victims. Ted Bundy was particularly at ease when working the crowds of people in shopping malls. Christopher Wilder specifically went to shopping malls to lure his victims by posing as a photographer. Yet, for some of these offenders, it is not the crowds they seek but the potential victims who walk, work, or play alone. Although areas with dense populations would seem likely places for serial offenders to find victims, further research is warranted on the connection between population density and occurrence of serial murders.

Social Process Theory

Social process theories contend that criminal behavior is a function of a socialization process. This includes a host of sociopsychological interactions by the offender with institutions and social organizations. Offenders may turn to crime as a result of peer group pressure, family problems, poor school performance, legal entanglements, and other situations that gradually steer them to criminal behavior. Process theories recognize that anyone, regardless of race or socioeconomic status, has the potential for criminal behavior. Central to the social process theory, as to some aspects of psychoanalytic theory, is the effect of the family on youths who engage in delinquent or violent behavior. Considering the dramatic rise in divorce rates from 35 per 1,000 married in 1960 to 131 per 1,000 married today and the growing number of single parents, extensive research continues in the area of family dynamics (*Boston Globe*, 1988).

Theories of aggression vary extensively, but for understanding the etiology of serial murder, Albert Bandura's book *Aggression* (1973) provides valuable insights. According to social learning theory, a component of social process theory, one might explain the aggressive behavior of the serial murderer by examining the offender's past (see Chapter 3). Special attention by researchers should be given to childhood experiences for evidence of victimization or the witnessing of violent behavior. In earlier studies, Bandura and Walters (1963) noted that particularly aggressive boys were also hostile and antagonistic and that they experienced feelings of rejection from their fathers.

Brown (1984), in an application of social learning theory, found that emotional neglect and abuse were correlated with all forms of reported delinquency. But, he also noted a lack of correlation between physical abuse and any form of delinquency. This may suggest to those who study the psychodynamics of the serial killer that evidence of the social learning of aggression may be subtle. Children who witness family violence are (according to ratings by their mothers) likely to demonstrate diminished social competence and behavioral problems (Wolfe et al., 1985). This "exposure to violence may have an indirect, yet significant, effect on children " (p. 663). The social learning of violence, therefore, need not be the result of one's having been a victim but simply a result of viewing violence. Wolfe and his colleagues add: "It is suspected by some researchers and clinicians that girls from violent families may not express signs of maladjustment in childhood, yet they may suffer higher rates of mental health and family problems in adulthood than many girls from nonviolent homes" (p. 663). Again, this suggests that the evidence of learned social aggression may not manifest itself in some cases for several years. The direct and indirect influence of family violence on future adjustment difficulties of boys was examined by Jaffe and his colleagues (1986), who found similar patterns of adjustment problems for those who had been abused by parents and those who had witnessed violence between their parents. Both of these groups differed from a control group in that they exhibited more aggressive behaviors toward others.

Ruth Inglis, in her book *Sins of Fathers* (1978), noted a strong relationship between abused children and subsequent violent behavior. In comparing abusive and nonabusive families, Webster-Stratton (1985) found that, in addition to low family income, "family history of parent abuse as a child was highly correlated with more negative and controlling interactions with children, which was correlated with the abusive family. This finding seems to support the social learning model that parents learn abusive parenting techniques from their own parents and then carry them out with their children, thus continuing the 'coercive cycle' across generations" (p. 67).

In another study done by Dean et al. (1986), maltreated and nonmaltreated children were asked to tell stories about kind or unkind behavior initiated by a child toward a child, by an adult toward a child, or by a child toward an adult and then asked to explain what the recipient would do next. In contrast to their nonmaltreated counterparts, maltreated children between the ages of six and eight years told more stories in which children reciprocated the kind acts of adults and fewer stories in which adults or peers reciprocated the kind acts of children. A second finding was that maltreated children of all ages justified their parents' unkind acts on the basis of their own bad behavior (pp. 617–626). This finding is echoed in many of the statements and accounts of serial killers.

Alice Miller in *For Your Own Good* (1984), an examination of child rearing and the roots of violence, provides a subjective qualitative study of child abuse in which she explores the private hells of children who later become offenders. She discusses "soul murder" or the extraordinary beatings and sexual abuses perpetrated upon young children by parents and relatives. She argues that "the earlier this soul murder took place, the more difficult it will be for the affected person to grasp and the less it can be validated by memories and words. If he wants to communicate, his only recourse is acting out" (p. 231). Other theoretical frameworks also warrant examination.

Neutralization Theory

Sykes and Matza (1957) and Matza (1964) viewed the process of delinquent youths becoming criminals as a matter of neutralizing their personal values and attitudes as they drift between conventional behavior and illegitimate behavior. Matza points out that people are not criminals all the time. Often criminals participate in the normal functions of everyday life. Occasionally they drift toward illegal behavior just as they sometimes drift toward conventional behavior. In order for them to rationalize their drift toward illegal behavior they must use learned techniques of neutralization. These techniques include denial of responsibility, denial of injury, denial of victim, condemnation of the condemners, and the appeal to higher loyalties—in other words "it was not my fault," "no harm was done," "they had it coming," "society is to blame," and "I did it for them not me."

Denying the victim is a technique commonly used to shift blame and accompanying guilt. It also serves to lessen the value of the life destroyed. Bandura (1974) described methods by which offenders can make inhuman behavior legitimate:

> Attribution of blame to the victim is still another exonerative expedient. Victims are faulted for bringing maltreatment on themselves, or extraordinary circumstances are invoked as justification for questionable conduct. One need not engage in self-reproof for committing acts prescribed by circumstances. A further means of weakening self-punishment is to dehumanize the victim. Inflicting harm upon people who are regarded as subhuman or debased is less likely to arouse self-reproof than if they are looked upon as human beings with sensitivities [pp. 861–862].

Current research into the behavior of serial killers suggests they frequently dehumanize their victims before taking their lives. It appears to expedite the murder when, psychologically, instead of attacking another human being, they attack something without name, feelings, or identity.

Henry Lucas, who confessed and recanted confessions to dozens of murders, once stated that when he had found a victim he would never ask her name and if she gave it he would forget it immediately because he did not want to know his victim's names or anything about them. Charny (1980), in explaining the process of dehumanization of others, noted that the process is actually much more subtle and commonplace than we would expect:

> Dehumanization is a process of ridding the other of the benefit of his humanity. The process extends along a continuum, leading to the ultimate step of removing the other person's opportunity to live. The "little" everyday dehumanizations we practice on one another are stations on a way toward the ultimate act whereby one person takes away another's very life. Thus, it is not simply the insult that we inflict upon another that is at stake in everyday dehumanizations. The fact is that we are learning to practice a devastating process, rehearsing it, achieving gratification from it, and perhaps preparing ourselves to participate one day in the removal of other people's actual lives [p. 100].

One might argue that serial murderers drift between conventional and nonconventional behavior. Several serial killers have been known to be gainfully employed, married with families, active in civic organizations, and educated, and they were considered part of mainstream society.

Complete denial of injury to victims by offenders is a common ploy used by many serial killers. Others not only deny any involvement but readily name another person as the guilty party. One serial killer was found guilty in 1983 of murdering several women and presently awaits execution on San Quentin's death row. His female accomplice received two lengthy prison sentences. In December 1988 the male offender, in a letter to me, reaffirmed his complete innocence with regard to any of the killings.

> The sum total would prove beyond doubt to you that [she] was following a script for murder, and that she was and at times is... wife of Theodore Robert Bundy. ... It is utterly easy to show that [she] selected her own internalized victim/motivation and externalized into the script of a book about a man she idolized.

> She lived one of the most bizarre lives from that point forward of any serial killer to date. She became a practicing lesbian. She engaged in degradation-sex, and S/M. She lept the gender line with such frequency in her life, even marrying a flagrant homosexual, that her roles in sex and S/M became so blurred she would often be involved in utterly contradictory encounters with gender-blended persons, groups or persons, and in such a role-blended way with her sado-masochism she wanted to torture her deceased victims as she wished she dared be so tortured.

> You won't find a cesspool as vile as this case. But god damn it, I can prove I am a mere "substitute" for her partner... whom she murdered. She could not testify against a dead man, so the next best deal shown to her was to testify and accuse against some living person. I was a man who stayed in her apartments, renting a room and bathroom, and on

three occasions, dumb enough to let her talk me into sex with her. She had a man, proximate to vehicles, weapons, and herself. It was all the police wanted. In the aftermath of the terror of the Hillside Strangler case in Los Angeles, the authority-attitude was, solve this damned case fast.

Within the first 18 days, August 11, 1980, to August 29th, 1980, they committed themselves trustingly to her stories.

That sealed it.

The Ted Bundy legacy is still going on. If you don't have the sense and energy to see that everything I've said, and tons more, proves truly that [she] is the strangest of them all, then live on in the mediocrity of assuming those who are on death row MUST be guilty... [author's files, November 30, 1988].

John Wayne Gacy, killer of 33 young males in Chicago, has denied any involvement in the murders and suggested that someone else must have placed those 27 bodies in the crawlspace of his home while he was at work.

Other serial killers have admitted murdering women, especially prostitutes, but insist there have been no real victims because they were, in the offenders' eyes, scum of the earth. Thomas N. Cream argued that he had aided society and ended the suffering of scores of prostitutes. Another offender, Robert Carr, explained that those who died by his hands "grew" a great deal during their brief stay with the killer. Others killed because they believed it was God's will or because of allegiance to their partners or to assist the survival of society.

The problem with neutralization theory as an explanation for serial murder is its verifiability. One would have to be able to demonstrate that an offender first neutralized his moral beliefs before drifting into violent behavior. As it appears now, serial murderers who rationalize their behavior are believed to construct explanations ex post facto, or after the homicides occurred. Given the current understanding of serial murder behavior, empirical evidence of neutralization will not likely appear in the foreseeable future.

Social Control Theory

Classical control theorists would argue that people do not commit crimes such as murder because of their fear of punishment. Punishment then, they believe, can serve as a deterrent to committing crimes. For homicides in general, capital punishment or long prison terms usually do not deter people, because many homicides are "crimes of passion" in which the offender kills his or her victim as a result of an altercation. Briar and Piliavin (1965) pointed out that fear of punishment alone is not sufficient for everyone to refrain from criminal behavior. They believe that a sense of commitment to society, family, and education will serve as a deterrent to crime. Reckless (1967) argued that youth can become isolated or insulated from criminal influences through what he termed "containments" including a

positive self-image, ego strength, high frustration tolerance, goal orientation, a sense of belongingness, consistent moral front, reinforcement of
norms, goals, and values, effective supervision, discipline, and meaningful
social role.

• Hirschi (1969) expanded social control theory and introduced four elements of the social bond, which apply to all social classes. These four
elements—attachment, commitment, involvement, and belief—are bonds
that individuals strengthen or weaken in relationship to the society in which
they live. He noted that attachment to peers, schools, various social institutions, and especially family is critical if the individual is to develop a sense of
conscious concern for others and a general acceptance of the social norms.
Hirschi also believed that having a commitment to personal property, conventional goals, reputation, education, and so on will make people less
likely to commit crimes and risk losing what they have worked to establish.
Similarly, involvement in conventional endeavors allows little time for criminal behavior. Finally, if one shares a set of common beliefs with others, there
exists a greater likelihood of conformity to societal expectations.

Hirschi found that youths who appeared to be closely attached to their
parents were less likely to commit crimes. In comparison, most serial killers
do not appear to have close relationships with their families. The majority
appear to have experienced gradual or traumatic breaks with one or both
parents while in their youth. The lack of commitment to conventional values
is noted in the histories of other serial murderers who became heavily
involved in drugs, alcohol, and other "marginal" behaviors. In addition,
serial killers usually do not have meaningful, close relationships with peers
but remain distant and isolated.

The application of Hirschi's social control theory may eventually provide
additional insight into serial killers. These offenders do not appear to have
the requisite ties to family, peers, and community that Hirschi found among
those who tended not to engage in criminal behavior. The theory, however,
was developed for measuring delinquent youths, not adults. Although serial
offenders report weakened social ties we have yet to examine youths who
later become serial offenders in order to determine whether they had experienced weakened social bonds before their acts of homicide. Certainly there
are case histories of offenders that reveal weakened social bonds, but such
reports are usually developed after the homicides. In short, we find what we
want to find: instead of a weak social bond causing one to become violent,
becoming violent to the point of killing may cause the offender to weaken his
or her social bonds.

Labeling Theory

Erving Goffman (1961) in his classical treatise on institutions noted the
stigma attached to persons who have spent time in an institution such as a
prison or a psychiatric facility. This stigma is the result of having attracted the

attention of society through abnormal or unacceptable behavior. Labeling theorists Lemert (1951) and Schur (1972) viewed negative labels such as "former mental patient," "ex-convict," "delinquent," "stupid," and "slut" as inflicting psychological damage on those to whom the labels are attached.

Labeling theory views abnormal behavior as a process by which a person graduates from primary deviance to secondary deviance (Lemert, 1951). According to labeling theorists the original deviant act, of which the origins vary significantly, is called *primary deviance*. In turn, by being labeled a deviant the offender is carried along in a societal process of negative social sanctions that inevitably engender hostility and resentment in the offender. Then the offender reacts negatively to the label by acting against society and so concludes the process by affirming the negative label or deviant status.

The labeling process takes a certain amount of time for the offender to absorb the labels and for those labels, in turn, to affect the offender's self-concept. The negative feelings created by the labeling multiply into feelings of inadequacy, low self-esteem and anger. Clifford Olson, killer of eleven children in British Columbia, Canada, during the early 1980s, explained to me that society played a major role in his homicidal behavior. The courts had kept him in prison for nearly 30 years and then allowed him to go free. He was already an habitual criminal and a perceived threat to society. As Olson ruefully noted, "They never should have let me go." He claimed that the effects of prison made him much more dangerous. Combined with alcohol, he said, they triggered his murder rampages (author's files).

The types of labels, their visibility, and the manner in which they are applied, including their intensity, duration, and frequency—as well as the individual's ability to cope with the process of labeling—may all help to determine an offender's commitment to a criminal career. The more an individual succumbs to the labels of failure and imperfection, as well as to remarks critical of his or her behavior, the more he or she discounts positive feedback.

The labeling process is expedited by the selective application of those labels. For example, Becker (1963) described people who create rules as moral entrepreneurs: "Social groups create deviance by making rules whose infractions constitute deviance and by applying those rules to particular people and labeling them as outsiders. From this point of view, deviance is not a quality of the act a person commits, but rather a consequence of the application by others of rules and sanctions to an 'offender'. The deviant is one to whom the label has successfully been applied; deviant behavior is behavior that people so label" (p. 9).

Labels, by the nature of their construction, are inconsistently applied. The poor, racial minorities, and the socially disadvantaged are more likely to be labeled. The facts that most serial killers are white and many appear to maintain at least middle-class socieconomic standing does not disprove labeling theory. It is plausible that some serial offenders have been affected by negative labels created to differentiate between the rich and the poor, white and nonwhite, the powerful and the powerless. In essence, labeling can create psychological disparities between individuals regardless of their race or socioeconomic standing. Wayne Williams, who is believed to have been involved in the murders of 22–28 young black men and boys in the Atlanta, Georgia, area was described as one who hated his own race and preferred white people and who killed blacks because they reminded him of his own standing.

It is unlikely, however, that all serial killers destroy human life because of their socioeconomic status or race or because the law is applied to favor the powerful people in society. Individuals who have experienced a traumatic event or process of events involving extreme criticism, or those who are forced to feel the pain of failure when their egos allow only perfection, may eventually respond negatively. Inevitably their feelings of low self-esteem and worthlessness become their internalized "master status," constantly reminding them of their weaknesses. Psychologically, the effects of labeling are stress and anxiety, which in turn feed into a need to right the wrongs and restore balance. Labeling theory then is not concerned with the origins of serial killers' behavior but with the formation of the killers' status as the result of experiencing traumatic events during their formative years.

Etiology of Serial Killing

So far we have briefly examined a number of psychological and social theories of deviant behavior. But how can we then explain the phenomenon of serial murder in a manner that will include all varieties of serial murderers and satisfy the psychologist, the psychiatrist, the criminologist, the geneticist, the sociologist, the biologist, the phenomenologist, and other scientists and researchers who investigate homicidal behavior? Because research into serial murder is in its infancy, the haste to draw quick conclusions about its etiology is not only speculative but dangerous.

Some data and literature, however, allow researchers some leeway in formulating tentative models to explain the construction of serial murder. We do know that alcohol and drugs are often cited as contributing factors to serial murder; some offenders even suggest it as a primary causal factor. Ted Bundy's declaration that pornography led him to his career in killing caused considerable debate regarding the degree of influence such material has on people who become murderers. Many people believe that pornography and/or alcohol cause people to kill. Yet millions of people in the United States frequently consume alcohol and indulge in pornography and never physically harm anyone.

The current belief in pornography and alcohol as causal factors in serial murder belies a much more complex set of variables. If our society were to ban pornography should one expect the incidence of serial murder to decrease? If we restrict or ban the use of alcohol would that affect serial murderers' behavior? Such a Band-Aid approach to a cure for serial killing ignores a host of more obtuse factors. Also, by joining the bandwagon of "porno makes murderers" we continue to avoid issues that may in some way attribute some of the responsibility to nonoffending citizens.

As long as we continue to seek quick answers without first constructing a framework for the discussion of serial murderers' behavior, we will continue to treat the symptoms of the illness rather than the illness itself. For example, we continue saying that anyone who kills, especially serial killers, must be insane. No one would argue that what these offenders *do* is insane by society's standards, but the vast majority of serial killers are not only judged sane by legal standards but are indistinguishable from nonoffenders as they move within our communities. However, there exists a degree of security for us in believing that such crimes occur as a result of insanity or violent pornography. Such cause-and-effect thinking creates a dichotomy of "them" and "us." "Normal" people are not considered to be high risks for insanity nor do they generally indulge in violent pornography. Therefore, criminal behavior is completely out of our control, and in no way must we bear any responsibility for such actions.

As mentioned previously, common belief that pornography, drugs, alcohol, or insanity directly causes serial homicides negates the more difficult and complex explanations. Such thinking is not only simplistic, but fallacious. It is my belief that such factors *can* contribute to serial murder, but only as appendages to an etiological process.

Trauma-Control Model of the Serial Killer

We are beginning to learn that serial offenders are influenced by a multitude of factors that inevitably lead them to kill. It is unlikely that any one factor is directly responsible for homicidal behavior. People are no more likely to be born to kill than offenders are to acquire homicidal inclination from watching violence on television. However, this does not preclude the existence of a predisposition for violent behavior or the fact that we may be influenced by what we see.

In addition, no one factor has been useful thus far in predicting who may be prone to serial murder. Social scientists have long engaged in creating models for predicting criminal behavior. Unfortunately, in serial murder research, everyone wants to be the first to predict causation. Whether the explanation is excessive television viewing, head traumas, biogenics, childhood victimization, or a host of other "causes," it has been offered too quickly, without having a basis of sufficient and valid data.

Among serial killers there may exist one or more predispositional factors that may influence their behavior. As mentioned in Chapter 3, some violent offenders have been known to possess an extra Y chromosome, but some men who possess an extra chromosome never become violent offenders. Similarly, there are many who drink heavily and indulge in pornography— even violent pornography—and never become serial killers. Thus even for those influenced by predispositional factors, whether they be biological, sociological, psychological or a combination thereof, an event or series of events, or traumas, seem to be required that gradually influence a person to kill. Figure 4-1 shows a proposed trauma-control model for understanding the process by which individuals may become involved in serial murder.

In discussing the trauma-control model, the destabilizing event(s) that occur in the lives of serial offenders will be referred to as *traumatizations*. These include unstable home life, death of parents, divorce, corporal punishments, sexual abuse, and other negative events that occur during the formative years of the offender's life. There are literally millions of U.S. citizens who experience one or more of these traumatizations in their lives and never become offenders of any sort. Also, it is possible that individuals who have some predilection for criminal behavior and who experience some form of traumatization do not become violent offenders.

In the case of serial murderers, the triggering mechanism within the trauma may well be the individual's inability to cope with the stress of the events. For serial murderers the most common childhood traumatization reported was rejection, including rejection by relatives and parent(s). It must be emphasized that an unstable home was reported as one of the major forms of rejection. The child or teen feels a deep sense of anxiety, mistrust, and confusion when psychologically or physically abused by an adult. Eth and Pynoos (1985) noted some of the effects of traumatization when children witnessed murder, rape, or suicidal behavior. These effects included images of violence involving mutilations, destabilization of impulse control, and

FIGURE 4-1 Trauma-Control Model for Serial Murder. (Predispositional factors and facilitators may or may not influence the serial killing process.)

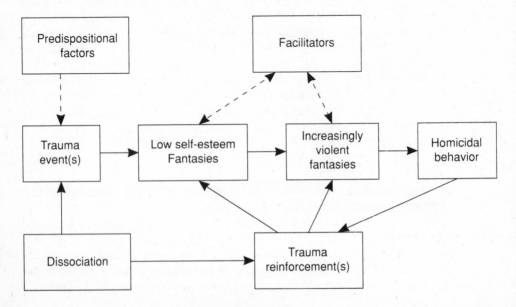

revenge fantasies. However, instability in the home environment may not be sufficient to trigger homicidal behavior. Other factors may be involved that in combination create a synergistic response, or enhanced reaction.

The combined effect of various traumatizations is greater than any single trauma. In other words, the combined effects should be viewed exponentially rather than arithmetically. As Nettler (1982) observed, "In synergistic situations, a particular effect may be 'more than caused.' It is not merely a metaphor to speak of 'causal overkill'" (p. 77). Other possible contributing forms of rejection include failure, ostracism in school, and exclusion from a group. Most individuals appear to constructively cope with rejection or at least to deal with the stress of rejection from a "self-centered" perspective. In other words, the individual deals with his or her feelings without the involvement of others. This may include physical exercise, hobbies, travel, and so on. Others may become self-destructive through, for example, excessive eating, anorexia nervosa, bulimia, and other types of eating disorders. In more severe cases, rejection may prompt individuals to take their own lives rather than live with such uncomfortable feelings. Rejection as a stressor may contribute to a number of psychosomatic illnesses. For some people, confronting rejection may necessitate seeking out others who are able to provide emotional support to again restore their psychological equilibrium.

Some individuals deal with rejection within a more destructive framework—perhaps by beating the family dog, breaking objects, or assaulting a spouse, a friend, or a relative. Each person deals with rejection differently depending on its perceived degree, frequency, and intensity. Similarly, children cope with various childhood traumatizations in numerous ways. In the case of children who later become serial killers, many have experienced some form of childhood trauma that was not or could not be effectively countered by therapeutic strategies. In some cases there appeared to be series of traumatizations that psychologically affected these offenders. At this juncture in our research we can only speculate as to the number or strength of predispositions or predilections offenders may have had toward violent behavior. However, we do know that most of them have a history of childhood traumatizations. Hazelwood and Warren (1989) reported in their study of 41 serial rapists that 76% had been sexually abused as children. Considering that some serial killers in this study were rapists before they graduated to murder, we must not ignore the implication that sexual victimization during childhood may readily manifest itself in a negative manner during adulthood.

Traumatization experienced by the offender as a child may nurture within him or her feelings of low self-esteem. A common characteristic of most, if not all, serial offenders is feelings of inadequacy, self-doubt, and worthlessness. They do not cope constructively with the early trauma(s) and subsequently perceive themselves and their surroundings in a distorted perspective. It is during this time of childhood development that a process of dissociation occurs. In an effort to regain the psychological equilibrium taken from them by people in authority, serial offenders appear to construct masks, facades, or a veneer of self-confidence and self-control. The label of *psychopath*, given to most serial killers, may actually describe a process of maintaining control of oneself, of others, and of one's surroundings.

The offender may suppress the traumatic event(s) to the point where he or she cannot consciously recall the experience(s). This can be referred to as splitting off, or blocking out, the experience. Tanay (1976), in describing this state of dissociation, noted that the murderer appears to carry out the act in an altered state of consciousness. Such an ego-dystonic homicide, whereby the individual is faced with a psychologically unresolvable conflict, results in part of the psychic structure splitting off from the rest of the personality. Danto (1982) noted that dissociative reactions are types of anxiety states in which the mind is "overwhelmed or flooded by anxiety" (p. 6). For some children, certain traumatizations can generate extremely high anxieties. To defend oneself against a psychologically painful experience a person may block the experience from recall or, instead, not consciously suppress the fact the trauma occurred but suppress the hurt, fear, anger, and other feelings caused by the event(s). However, the pain of a traumatic event will eventually surface in some way. For the offender, a cycle of trauma and quest for regaining control can be generated at a very early age.

Facilitators

At some point in the trauma-control process the offender may begin to immerse him- or herself in facilitators. Facilitators may include alcohol and other drugs, pornography, and books on the occult. Alcohol appears to decrease inhibitions and inhibit moral conscience and propriety, whereas pornography fuels growing fantasies of violence. During the Reagan Administration, the Meese Commission found that violent pornography was linked to violent sexual behavior. However, the connection made between pornography and violence can be misleading, because saying the two are "linked" can be interpreted in several ways. In any case, the serial murderers who insisted that pornography was a major factor in their killing young women and children should not be ignored. In February, 1989, Richard Daniel Starrett was arrested and charged in the murder of a 15-year-old girl in South Carolina. He was also believed to have participated in the abduction and sexual assault and murders of several other young women and girls. Starrett observed that the proliferation of pornography influenced his violent behavior. As police searched a rented miniwarehouse, they seized 935 books and magazines belonging to Starrett that depicted nudity and sexual violence. Also found were 116 posters depicting bondage, violence, or sex, 18 calendars depicting sex or violence, and books on sex crimes, as well as dozens of hardcore videos.

Murray Strauss and Larry Baron (1984) found that states with the highest readership of pornographic magazines, such as *Playboy* and *Hustler*, also had the highest rape rates. Dr. Victor Cline (1990), of the University of Utah, outlined a four-factor syndrome that appears similar to the process experienced by serial killers who are reported to have used pornography extensively. The offender first experiences "addiction" similar to the physiological/psychological addiction to drugs, which then generates stress in his or her everyday activities. The person then enters a stage of "escalation," in which the appetite for more deviant, bizarre, and explicit sexual material is fostered. Third, the person gradually becomes "desensitized" to that which was once revolting and taboo-breaking. Finally the person begins to "act out" the things that he or she has seen.

We must remember, however, that some serial murderers do not use pornography to any extent. Given the current state of limited research in serial homicide, it is dangerously premature to suggest facilitators as *causal* factors. What we can say is that a tendency to use pornography, alcohol, and texts on the occult has been noted frequently in serial offenders. But, we must recognize that pornography is produced in many different forms, both qualitatively and quantitatively. There exists not only difficulty in defining the parameters of pornography but also in discerning the effects it may or may not have on any particular person. In a recent study conducted by the Federal Bureau of Investigation, it was found that 36% of serial rapists collected pornography (Hazelwood & Warren, 1989). Does this mean they all read *Playboy*, *Penthouse*, and *Hustler* or perhaps the many publications that include hardcore acts of sadomasochism, bestiality, and other forms of sexual degradation? Can we give the same weight to all forms of pornography, including acts of violent sexual conduct?

Also, can we exclude the possibility that pornography, like alcohol, may affect those people who harbor a predisposition for such stimulation more than others? In addition, pornography may actually serve as a retardant to serial offenders. If we are to believe, regardless of the presence or absence of pornography, that serial killers will commit acts of murder, then it is possible that some people may find sufficient gratification in and catharsis through various forms of pornography to avoid violence. As a release valve, the pornography lessens the demand for victims. We might argue that some serial offenders might have been motivated to kill earlier if pornography had not been available through which they could exercise their fantasies of control.

Proper scientific verification of these and other implications of pornography are needed in the construction of serial murder etiology. We must be cautious in suggesting there exists anything more than a tendency for pornography to affect those offenders involved in serial killing, regardless of how any of us may feel about pornography. If an argument is to be made that pornography (hardcore) is a primary causal agent for serial murder, then how are we to explain the behavior of serial killers who lived before the media explosion of the twentieth century? Serial murderers have existed for several hundreds of years, if not longer. Before technology permitted society to produce violent and sexually graphic material, serial killers were at work in America.

However, one could also argue that the emergence of large numbers of serial killers beginning in the 1960s was a direct result of the media explosion of recent years. Alcohol and pornography are not mandatory elements in the construction of a serial killer, but they tend to provide vehicles the offender uses to express the growing rages from within. In most instances these facilitators tend to be present to some degree in the profile of a serial killer. It is my contention, however, that without alcohol or pornography the offender in all likelihood would kill anyway. The circumstances of the acts may be altered, but the murders would inevitably occur. The offender still must gain control of inner feelings, anxieties, anger, rage, and pain. Using alcohol, pornography or other such types of graphic literature may be useful in expediting the offender's urge to kill.

FANTASY   The most critical factor common to serial killers is violent fantasy. Prentky and colleagues (1986), who studied repetitive sexual homicides, found that daydreams of causing bodily harm through sadism and other methods of sexual violence were common among offenders. The researchers concluded that the offender attempts to replicate his fantasies. Since the offender can actually never be in total control of his or her victim's responses, the outcome of the fantasy will never measure up to his or her expectations. In any case, each new murder provides new fantasies that can fuel future homicides. Ressler and his colleagues (1988) concluded that "sexual murder is based on fantasy" (p. 33). Fantasy becomes a critical component in the psychological development of a serial killer. Although fantasies are generally associated with sexual homicides, they are likely to be found in the minds of most, if not all, serial killers.

The following case illustrates how consuming and powerful fantasies can become: Carl had been arrested for attempted rape and murder. Visiting a young woman in whom he was interested, Carl suddenly attacked and tried to rape her. During the course of the attack the girl's mother returned home. Enraged, Carl killed the mother and fled the home. Carl was adjudicated to be insane at the time of the attack and was confined to a mental institution until he could be considered safe to return to the community. After seven years and extensive therapy in a sex offender program, Carl was permitted to begin a community reintegration program. Working as an electrician's helper, Carl worked during the day and stayed at the hospital at night. He was also allowed certain weekend privileges provided he followed the specific rules of his therapy program. One of Carl's problems had been his propensity for fantasy. When he was younger, he loved to set fires so he could view the flashing lights of the police and fire trucks. Over time he had graduated into some extremely violent fantasies that were believed by psychiatrists to have contributed to his homicidal behavior. During his years in the sex offender program Carl appeared to learn how to control his fantasies. On weekends he attended dances, movies, and other recreational activities.

He was not permitted, however, to attend movies that contained any explicit sexual violence for fear he could still become caught up in his own fantasies of violence. One evening he violated his weekend pass by attending the movie *Dressed To Kill* featuring Angie Dickinson. Later, he would report how he had attempted to "pick up a girl" during the movie but was rejected. Even before the violence in the movie had ended, Carl was also ready to kill. Going to his car engulfed in raging fantasies of violence, Carl located his electrician's knife and waited in the shadows while four unsuspecting female college students exited from the theater. His fantasy was to enter their car and cut each girl's throat. Walking quickly to the rear door of the vehicle, Carl reached for the handle. Just as he was about to open the door, the driver, unaware of his presence, stepped on the accelerator and drove off.

Frustrated and in the grips of his violence fantasies, Carl later explained how he had then gone to the local park, hunting for a lone female jogger. He had decided to cut her into pieces. Waiting in some bushes for several minutes, Carl saw a woman jogging toward him. It was 11:30 P.M., and the park was deserted. Fortunately for his intended victim, a male jogger emerged from another direction at about the same time. Thwarted in his bid to kill and in fear of detection, Carl returned to his car. After driving around for a while and unable to locate any more suitable victims, Carl calmed down and returned to the hospital where he explained to hospital staff his evening's experiences. It was decided that Carl was still in need of closer supervision, and his passes were revoked (author's files).

Most people's fantasies generally are perceived as harmless and often therapeutic. Fantasies can involve a continuum of benign to aggressive thoughts that usually generate little or no action on the part of the fantasizer. For serial offenders, however, fantasies appear to involve violence, often sexual in nature, whereby the victim is controlled totally by the offender. The purpose of the fantasy is not the immediate destruction of another human being but the total control over that person. The element of control is so intense in the serial killer that in some cases the actual death of the victim is anticlimactic to the fantasized total control over the victim. In a case mentioned in an earlier chapter, an offender who is believed to have killed 14 young women used to place his revolver on the forehead of his victim and order her to perform fellatio. Those victims who cried and begged for mercy would invariably receive a bullet in their heads during the sexual assault. Those victims who cooperated with the killer but remained calm and did not show fear were spared. During an interview with one of the victims who survived the assault I was told how she, a store owner, was ordered to kneel on the floor. In this instance the offender had placed tape over his victim's mouth. After he had taped her mouth the killer proceeded to rub his penis against her face and insisted she look him in the eyes while he performed his sexual assault. The victim later recalled how she managed to remain calm and did exactly as he ordered her to do even though her attacker held a gun to her head. After a few moments the killer realized his victim was not responding the way he expected (and according to his fantasies), and so he abruptly fled the store (author's files).

The control fantasy becomes the highlight of the attack. The sexual assault is one vehicle by which the offender can attempt to gain the total control of a victim. Sexual torture becomes a tool to degrade, humiliate, and subjugate the victim. It is a method to take away all that is perceived to be personal, private, or sacred from the victim. The offender physically and mentally dominates his or her victims to a point where he or she has fantasized the ultimate control over another human being. Once that sense of control has been reached, the victim loses his or her purpose to the offender and is then killed. One serial killer noted in a personal interview that he developed a ritual for torturing his victims and that he seldom varied from those methods.

It is during the sexual assault, torture, and degradation that fantasies of the original childhood trauma may manifest themselves in acts of violence. In some cases, ten or twenty years may have lapsed since the traumatic event(s) occurred; in others, only a short period of time may have passed. During the time elapsed between the traumatic events(s) and the homicides, the offender may have completely split off from the traumatic experience and have protected him- or herself further by assuming a life of control and confidence. Psychologically the offender has been drawing farther and farther away from self-control but desperately seeks to retain control of his inner self. Often the victims selected by the killers stand as proxies for the traumatic event(s) experienced by the offenders. In one instance an offender had received electroshock treatments as corrective therapy for his involvement in a gang rape while he was a teenager. In 1984, 22 years after his electroshocks, the offender tortured some of his victims by wiring their toes to electrical outlets and then turning the power on and off. In yet another case, an offender had been sexually abused, beaten, bound with heavy cords, and left in terrifyingly dark closets. Several years later he began torturing boys by beating them, tying them with heavy cords, and holding them captive in dark places. His attempts to replicate his childhood traumas were nearly successful except he lacked the elusive sense of control. Each victim experienced more extensive tortures and depravities than the previous victim until he died, at which time the killer butchered the corpse. His last victim was slowly dismembered and disemboweled while still alive (author's files).

Fantasies may be fueled by pornography and facilitated by alcohol. The anger that has continued to grow over the years is allowed to be expressed in images of violence and death. Once the total domination and destruction of the victim has occurred, the killer momentarily regains the sense of equilibrium lost years before. One offender described this as the "restoration stage," which allows the killer to "feel good" again. He explained that for many serial killers, the frequency of victimization is a direct function of the degree of completion of the restoration. In other words, if the offender is stymied or frustrated in some way as he ritualistically kills the victim, he or she may be prompted to quickly seek out another victim. Once the killer is able to complete the ritual of killing and feeling that sense of control restored, he or she may not need to kill again for some time.

But fantasies can never be completely fulfilled or the anger removed or the lack of self-esteem reversed. For some, the experience of killing may generate new fantasies of violence. Exactly what does occur in the killer's mind between murders? It is possible for some offenders to become so consumed by their attempts at fantasy fulfillment that killing becomes a frequent experience. Yet, there are many serial killers who wait long periods of time, months or even years, before they seek out their next victim. According to one offender, he felt good about himself and more in control of his life directly following a murder. Eventually he would experience another failure in his life, such as criticism of job performance or rejection by a girlfriend. He believed that such events should not have bothered him, but they seemed to act as catalysts for depression and low self-esteem. The sense of failure or rejection never failed to put him into a spiral of self-pity, anger, loss of confidence, and increased fantasies. Sometimes it would be months, but inevitably he would go hunting for young women to torture and kill (author's files).

The trauma-control model of violent behavior then becomes a cyclical experience for serial offenders. Fantasies, possibly fueled by pornography or alcohol, reinforced by "routine" traumatizations of day-to-day living, keep the serial killer caught up in a self-perpetuating cycle of violence. Contrary to some claims, serial killers do not all wish to be caught, although some do and even allow themselves to be apprehended. Ed Kemper, after murdering several women in California, drove to Colorado, called the police and told them he was the killer they were searching for. Kemper was accommodating enough to wait by the pay phone until police arrived and arrested him. Some serial killers can go on for many years and never allow their fantasies to become so consuming that they lose control of their surroundings and their abilities to remain obscure. For the killer, the cycle becomes a never-ending pursuit of control over one's own life through the total domination and destruction of others' lives.

CHAPTER 5

Victims

Criminologists have recognized for some time the need to understand the victim and his or her involvement with the offender. Hewitt (1988) reviewed the body of literature of victim-offender relationships in homicides based on data from a large heterogeneous population. He then examined demographic characteristics of victims and offenders in the often publicized community of "Middletown, U.S.A." (Muncie, Indiana) and found the victim-offender relationships to be similar to those in larger cities. Studies in victimization assist in clarifying the victim side of the offender-victim relationship, measure in part the degree of vulnerability and culpability of certain victims, and often reveal the social dynamics of criminal acts. Case study analysis in serial murder has begun to provide researchers with insightful information, however tenuous. Elliot Leyton (1986), for example, in his book *Hunting Humans*, provides an in-depth investigation into the lives and minds of a few contemporary serial killers and their relationships with their victims. The purpose of this chapter is to contribute to this body of knowledge by focusing on the victims of serial murderers and demographic factors associated with their victimization. Such demographic data can assist in determining variations, if any, between victims of homicides in general and victims of multiple murderers. Also, from a historical perspective, we are able to challenge current notions pertaining to serial murderers and their victims by drawing on this database of serial murder victims.

One of the most perplexing questions researchers are unable to answer is "How many serial murderers have killed or are presently killing in the United States?" Agents from the Federal Bureau of Investigation conservatively estimate the number of offenders currently active in the United States at 35, but it may be as high as 100 or more. This does not mean there are 35–100 *new* offenders each year but rather that 35–100 serial killers may be

Portions of this chapter are based on material from "Etiology of Victimization in Serial Murder," by E. W. Hickey. In S. A. Egger (Ed.), *Serial Murder: An Elusive Phenomenon* (Praeger Publishers, New York, 1989). Copyright 1989 by Steven A. Egger. Used with permission. Material also used from "Responding to Missing and Murdered Children in America," by E. W. Hickey, in *Helping Crime Victims*, Albert R. Roberts (Ed.), pp. 158–185, copyright 1990 by Sage Publications, Inc. Reprinted by permission.

active in a given year. From the 203 offenders in my study, 67% committed their murders over a period of at least one or more years. For this group the median number of years for an offender's homicide spree was 4.3 years. Controlling for gender, female offenders reported 74% of their group spanning one or more years, with a median of 8.4 years. Males reported 65% of their group spanning one or more years, with 4.2 years as the median. Possible explanations for females operating over roughly twice the amount of time as their male counterparts may in part have to do with their methods of killing and the types of victims selected.

Between 1795 and 1988 the number of identified serial killers surged during the last 25 years (Figure 5.1). The number of offenders between 1980 and 1989 is slightly lower than those in the previous decade. We should expect to see a continued increase in the numbers of cases of serial murder beyond the year 2000 but not at the same dramatic rate of increase experienced during the 1970s. Certainly media attention has been instrumental in creating public awareness of the serial murderer. It is unlikely, however, that media attention alone is responsible for the recent "emergence" of serial killing.

According to the time frame of this study, over half of the 159 cases (203 offenders) appeared since 1970. Although we recognize that the "dark figure," or the unknown killer, will always exist, the study's data may be viewed as indicating trends in serial murder. One of the trends indicates a nearly ten-fold increase in the number of cases during the past 20 years in comparison to the previous 174 years. Although the debate continues over causal explanations for this dramatic rise in serial murder, we must not forget the victims. The dynamics of victimization will in all likelihood enable researchers to better understand the etiology of serial murder.

Demographics of Victimization in Serial Murder

As indicated in Table 5.1 the number of known victims of serial murder has risen markedly since 1950. For those who fall prey to these offenders their plight is a deplorable one indeed, but the odds of becoming a victim are minuscule when one considers the size of the population as a whole. Of all types of crimes, homicide in general has one of the lowest victimization rates. If we were to take all of the victims in this study on serial killers between the years 1975–1988 and assumed for a moment these deaths occurred in one year instead of 14 years, the serial murder rate would still only be approximately .2 per 100,000 population. Inversely proportional to the nominal risk of falling prey to serial murderers is the amount of fear and public awareness of this phenomenon. We run a greater risk of being a victim of domestic homicide and an even greater risk of being a victim of other violent crimes than we do of dying at the hands of a serial killer.

Having minimized the risk the general population experiences we must recognize that rates will vary considerably when we control for specific segments of the population. In short, some of us are at much greater risk than others. As noted in Table 5.1, the number of victims per case has steadily declined over the years. (This may in part be explained by greater

FIGURE 5.1 Number of Serial Killers in the United States by Decade, 1795–1988*

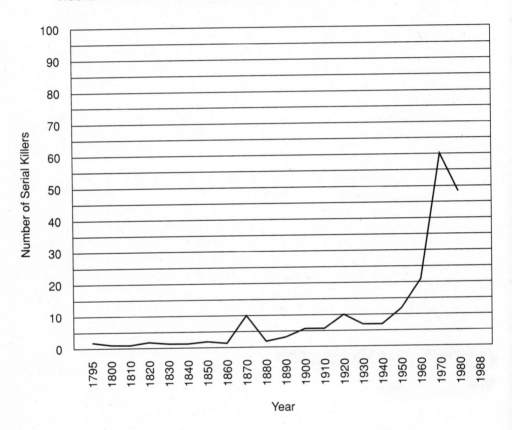

Number of Serial Murder Cases and Offenders in the United States, 1795–1988

YEARS	TOTAL NO. OF CASES	NO. OF CASES PER YEAR	NO. OF OFFENDERS	PERCENTAGE OF OFFENDERS	NO. OF OFFENDERS PER YEAR
1795–1988	159	.82	203	100	1.0 (194 yrs)
1795–1969	76	.45	95	47	.55 (174 yrs)
1970–1988	83	4.2	108	53	5.4 (20 yrs)

*Note: There were 60 offenders identified during the ten-year period 1970–1979. In the nine-year period between 1980 and 1988, 48 offenders were identified, which is indicated by the sudden decrease in the graph above. Given the comparative rates between these two time periods, however, little difference exists between the actual numbers of offenders. In brief, since the 1980s there appears to be a plateau in offenders.

TABLE 5.1 Victims/Serial Murderer Comparisons in the United States, 1795–1988 (N = 159 Cases/203 Offenders)

YEARS	TOTAL NO. OF CASES	NO. OF CASES PER YEAR	NO. OF VICTIMS	NO. OF VICTIMS PER CASE	NO. OF VICTIMS PER YEAR	
1795–1988	159	.82	1,483–2,161	9–14	8–11	(194 yrs)
1795–1824	5	.16	44–47	9	1–2	(30 yrs)
1825–1849	2	.08	58	29	2	(25 yrs)
1850–1874	8	.32	64–150	8–19	3–6	(25 yrs)
1875–1899	7	.28	97–214	14–31	4–9	(25 yrs)
1900–1924	14	.56	184–251	13–18	7–10	(25 yrs)
1925–1949	13	.52	133–174	10–13	5–7	(25 yrs)
1950–1974	51	2.04	492–675	10–13	20–27	(25 yrs)
1975–1988	59	4.21	411–592	7–10	29–42	(14 yrs)

accuracy in police investigations and efficiency in apprehension of offenders.)

The three states in my study reporting zero cases of serial murder all have small populations (Table 5.2). Generally, states with larger populations and large metropolitan areas are more likely to report cases of serial murder. Except for California, the most populous state, there does not appear to be regionality in serial killing. Instead, serial murder appears to be correlated with population density more than regional variations. Inevitably, we expect to find cases in every state. California reported more than double the cases found in any other state between 1795–1988, and that trend appears to continue in recent years (Table 5.2; Figure 5.2).

Four states, two northern and two southern, reported between 16 and 25 serial homicide cases. In group three we again see representation both from the north and south. In each succeeding group of states we see an equitable distribution from each region of the United States. In contrast, homicide rates in general can vary dramatically from one geographic region to another in the United States.

Gastil (1971) and, later, Doerner (1975), explaining the consistently higher murder rates in the southern states, concluded that a regional sub-culture of violence exists in this area. Blau and Blau (1982), controlling for income inequality, found, however, that poverty and southern location were not related to homicide rates, and the number of blacks in the community was a poor prediction of violence. This lack of consensus regarding a regional subculture of violence is pervasive among current researchers. Unlike homicide cases in general, in which, according to police records, blacks are responsible for over 50% of the deaths, black serial murderers constitute only 10% of the offenders in my study. Since 1975, however, 21% of all reported offenders in this study were black.

TABLE 5.2 Distribution of Serial Murderers by State, 1795–1988 (N = 203 Offenders)

STATE		NO. OF CASES IN WHICH ONE OR MORE VICTIMS WERE KILLED
California		50 +
Texas Florida New York Illinois		16–25
Georgia Ohio		11–15
Washington Oregon Utah Colorado Kansas Oklahoma Louisiana Alabama Tennessee	Kentucky Indiana Michigan Pennsylvania Massachusetts Connecticut New Jersey Virginia	6–10
Idaho Montana North Dakota Nevada Arizona New Mexico Alaska Wyoming Nebraska Minnesota Wisconsin Missosuri	Arkansas Maryland Mississippi North Carolina South Carolina West Virginia Delaware Vermont Rhode Island New Hampshire New Hampshire South Dakota	1–5
Iowa Hawaii Maine		None recorded in this study

Serial murderers are often portrayed by the media as killers who travel wantonly across the United States in search of victims. As noted earlier, Hickey (1985, 1986) created a mobility classification typology for serial murderers and identified three distinct killer types (Table 5.3). First are place-specific offenders, or those who murder within their own homes, places of employment, institutions, or other specific sites. For example, John Wayne Gacy, Jr., murdered 33 young males in his home, spanning nearly a seven-year period. Second are the local serial killers who remain within a certain state or urbanized area to seek out victims. In 1986 Michael D. Terry confessed to killing six male street prostitutes whom he encountered all within a 14-square mile area of downtown Atlanta, Georgia. Third are the traveling serial murderers, distinguished by their acts of homicide while traveling

FIGURE 5.2 Frequency of Serial Murderers by State 1795–1988 (Based on Activity of 203 Male and Female Serial Killers)

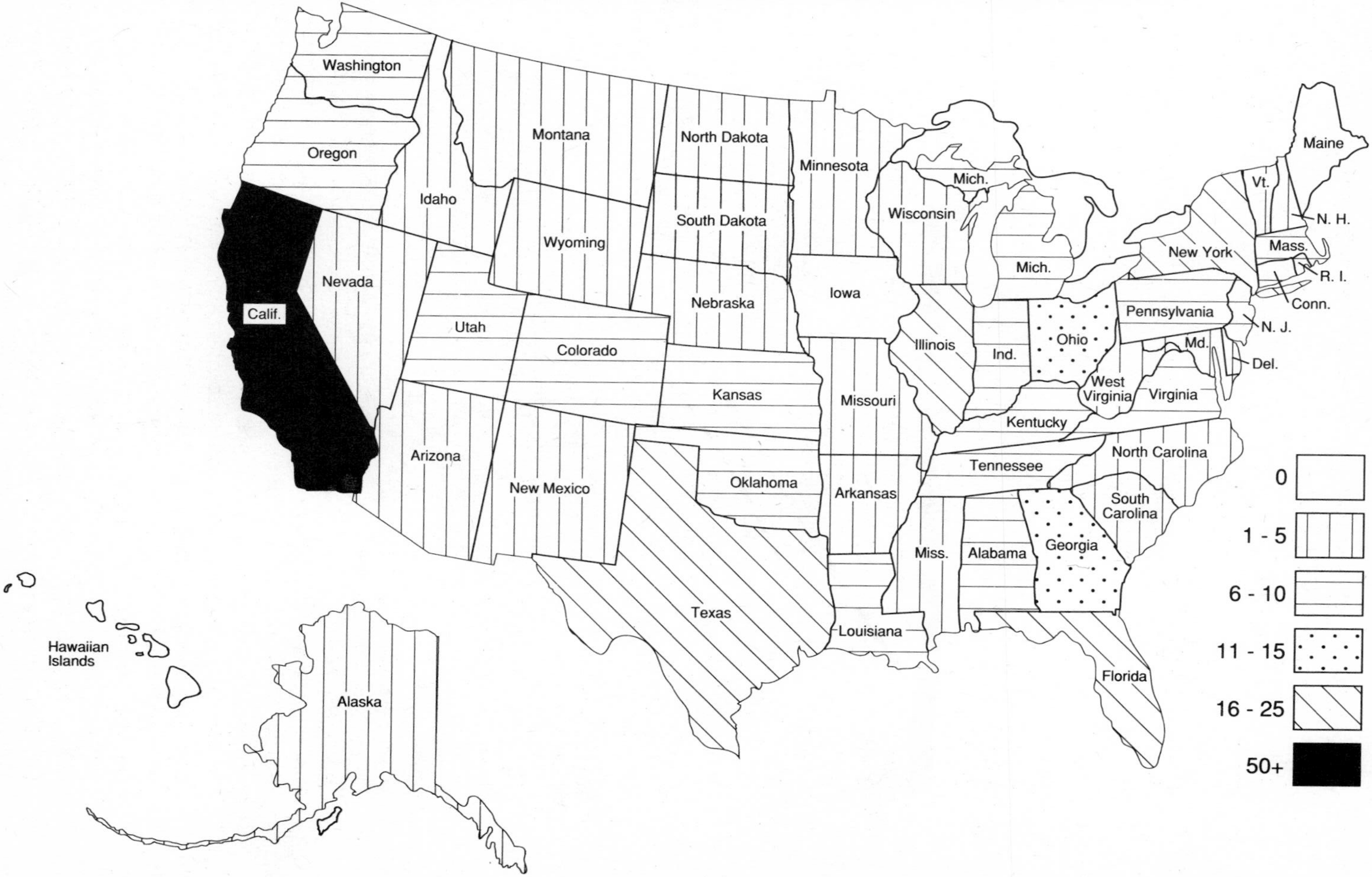

TABLE 5.3 Victims of Serial Murder in the United States, 1795–1988, by Mobility Classification

MOBILITY CLASSIFICATION OF KILLERS	PERCENTAGE OF VICTIMS (N=1483–2161)	NUMBER OF CASES	PERCENTAGE OF OFFENDERS (N=203)	AVERAGE NUMBER OF VICTIMS PER OFFENDER	AVERAGE NUMBER OF VICTIMS PER CASE
Total	100	159	100	7–11	9–14
Traveling	32–35	46	28	10–16	10–16
Local	29–32	70	45	5–7	7–9
Place-specific	36	43	27	10–14	12–18

through or relocating to other areas in the United States. Randall B. Woodfield, also known by the moniker the "I-5 Killer," is believed to have murdered as many as 13 victims while he traveled the 800-mile stretch of freeway through Washington, Oregon, and California.

By using these typologies to analyze our victim data I found that overall, 36% were killed in specific places, whereas 29–32% were murdered by offenders identified as local killers. The traveling killers accounted for 32–35% of the victims. From these data I noted that the majority of serial killers (71%) operated in a specific place or general urbanized area but did not travel into other states. By grouping these two mobility typologies I found that 65%–68% of all the victims were killed by men and women who generally stayed close to home. My data indicate a shifting in mobility since 1975, with those who travel out of state declining to 23% and place-specific offenders also declining to 19%. Conversely, those offenders classified as local killers increased dramatically to 58%. One explanation for these changes may be related to the increase in urbanization. With nearly three fourths of the U.S. population distributed among large urban areas such as Los Angeles, New York, and Chicago, offenders are able to maintain anonymity and also have access to a large pool of victims.

Also, the number of place-specific offenders has decreased largely in part because of methods of killing. Poisons such as arsenic and cyanide, once commonly used by women killers to murder their families and friends, are now more easily detected. Consequently, between 1975 and 1988 the number of victims killed by place-specific offenders in this study declined from 36% overall to 16-19%. The percentage of victims killed by local offenders between 1975 and 1988 rose sharply from 29–32% to 49–51%. The change in the percentage of victims killed by traveling offenders during this time was negligible. In short, since 1975 I found that approximately the same percentage (65–70%) of all victims were killed by offenders who carry out their murders in one state but the majority of these homicides were done by the local killer.

Two major homicide studies by Wolfgang (1958) and Pokorny (1965) found that the number of victims of homicides was divided almost equally between those killed in the home and those killed in areas outside the home. By comparison, serial murder victims were more likely to be killed away from their homes, suggesting that they may be vulnerable in areas of the community where their assailants have easy access.

According to the numbers for the three mobility groups in Table 5.3, place-specific cases were the least common but were responsible for the greatest percentage of homicides and the greatest average number of victims per case. These findings contradict the general belief that serial killers are primarily offenders who travel across the United States, murdering as they go. According to these data, perhaps a greater area of concern should be focused on serial killing in hospitals, nursing homes, and private residences.

A commonly held notion about serial murder is that offenders have a tendency to operate in pairs or groups, making the abduction and/or killing of a victim an easier task. Of the 203 offenders surveyed, 37% appeared to have at least one partner in committing their homicides. Of all offenders who started killing since 1975, 35% were found to have at least one partner. Similarly, the percentage of all victims killed by these "team" offenders between 1975 and 1988 totaled 25–31%. Although the number of team offenders in this study appears to have increased, the majority of offenders apprehended tended to commit their murders alone.

Another important issue concerns the types of victims serial killers single out. One of the most common beliefs concerning serial killing is that the offender often develops a pattern in his or her modus operandi. However, to a great extent the offender's behavior is directly related to the type of victim selected. For homicides in general, victimologists agree that sometimes the offender and the victim are "partners in crime" — or at least that the victim precipitates his or her own demise. Many domestic disputes that lead to fatalities are initiated by the victim. Karmen (1990) refers to this notion of shared responsibility as victim blaming. Homicides in general often include this element especially because of the prior relationship of the victim to the offender. In Wolfgang's (1958) study and Pokorny's (1965) Cleveland study, a replication of Wolfgang's work, the findings showed a similar pattern. In both studies, those directly involved in the homicide were usually family relatives or close friends. A common assumption, however, is that victims of serial murder are killed primarily by strangers. Using the three categories of family, acquaintances, and strangers as potential victims, Figure 5.3 indicates that stranger-to-stranger serial homicides increased markedly between 1950 and 1974. According to these data, the number of offenders killing at least one stranger can be projected to increase steadily to the year 2000, in comparison to the 1950–1975 data.

As stranger-to-stranger homicides appeared to continue a steady rise, acquaintance and family serial killings declined in my study group. I may speculate a slight increase of reports of offenders' killing one or more acquaintances or one or more family members by the year 2000 because of

FIGURE 5.3 Number of Serial Offenders Reporting Killing at Least One Family Member, Acquaintance, or Stranger in the United States, 1795–1988

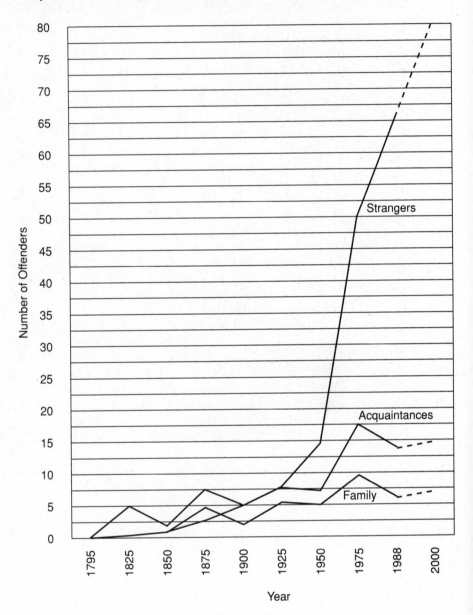

increased media attention. This increase is expected to be relatively small, however, in comparison to stranger-to-stranger homicides.

To further illustrate this apparent rise in stranger-to-stranger serial murder, offenders were surveyed regarding preferences toward strangers, acquaintances, or family members as victims (Table 5.4). Historically, 7% of offenders were found to murder family members only, with female offenders most likely to do so. Only 4% of all offenders targeted acquaintances only, and these offenders were all males. In contrast, 62% killed strangers only, male offenders again most likely to do so.

Combined, at least 44% of all offenders in this study killed one or more acquaintances or one or more family members, although the trend continues to lean toward increased stranger-to-stranger homicides. Since 1975 only 3% of offenders were found to have killed family members only, and only 8% killed at least one family member. No offenders were believed to have killed acquaintances only, and of those murdering at least one acquaintance, only 18% had done so between 1975 and 1988. By contrast, those offenders murdering strangers only increased sharply to 75%, and, overall, 96% had killed at least one stranger.

Various reasons can be offered for such a dramatic trend. Killing strangers is probably perceived by most offenders as providing safety from detection. Also, the anonymity and thrill derived by seeking out unsuspecting strangers certainly must attract many (Leyton, 1986). Perhaps even more important, offenders can much more easily view strangers as objects and thereby dehumanize their victims. On his capture, one offender confessed that he did not want to know his victims' names or anything about them, and if they did give a name he would quickly forget it.

Another factor influencing victim selection is the degree of power and control the offender is able to exert. Serial killers rarely seek out those who are as physically or intellectually capable as themselves. Instead, by either randomly or carefully targeting victims, serial killers mentally and/or physically stalk their prey. Because strangers seem to be the primary target, offenders were also surveyed as to the specific type of stranger-victim they most commonly murdered (Table 5.5).

Although many of the categories under the heading of "strangers" in

TABLE 5.4 Preferences of Offenders toward Murdering Family, Acquaintances, or Strangers as Victims in the United States, 1795–1988

	PERCENTAGE OF MALE OFFENDERS (N=169)	PERCENTAGE OF FEMALE OFFENDERS (N=34)	PERCENTAGE OF TOTAL (N=203)
Family only	3	26	7
At least one family member	10	50	17
Acquaintances only	5	0	4
At least one acquaintance	25	38	27
Strangers only	68	29	62
At least one stranger	89	56	84

TABLE 5.5 Rank Order of Types of Victims Sought Out by Serial Murderers

A. Strangers
1. Young women alone, including female college students and prostitutes
2. Children (boys and girls)
3. Travelers, including hitchhikers
4. People at home, including entire families
5. Hospital patients, including the handicapped
6. Business people, including storeowners and landlords
7. People walking on streets/in stores
8. Older women alone
9. Police officers
10. Employees
11. Derelicts/transients
12. People responding to newspaper ads
13. Racial killings

B. Acquaintances
1. Friends and neighbors
2. Children (girls and boys)
3. Women alone, including waitresses, prostitutes
4. Adult males
5. People in authority, including landlords, employers, guards
6. Members of one's own group—i.e., gangs and inmates
7. Patients

C. Family
1. Own children
2. Husbands
3. Wives
4. In-laws
5. Other relatives—i.e., nephews, nieces, uncles
6. Mother of the offender
7. Siblings
8. Grandparents

Table 5.5 are not mutually exclusive, they do represent the actual types of strangers reported in our study. Thus, "young women alone" in category one may also fit into the category of "hitchhikers" or "people walking on streets." "Young women alone, including female college students and prostitutes," was the most commonly noted stranger-victim category. The second category of "children (boys and girls)" was also frequently noted as desirable victims. Combined, these two categories accounted for most of the stranger-victim serial murders.

When offenders murdered acquaintances, friends and neighbors appeared to be the most common victims, although they were followed closely by "children (girls and boys)." With the addition of "women alone, including waitresses and prostitutes," these first three categories represent the majority of the acquaintance-victims. In the family grouping, offenders were most likely to kill their own children, husbands, or wives, although several other relatives were represented. The most salient factor among the groupings of strangers, acquaintances, and family members was that most of the victims were women and children. Whatever the specific motives of the killers were, they chose to act out their aggressions on those perceived to be weak, helpless, and without power or control. Males certainly were not exempt from victimization, but they were in the minority. These figures differ from those for homicides in general; in 1986 about 75% of approximately 20,000 murder victims were males. In addition, the typical murder victim in general

TABLE 5.7 Percentage of Offenders Murdering in Specific Victim-Gender Categories

GENDER OF VICTIMS	PERCENTAGE OF OFFENDERS
Only:[1]	
Females	31
Males	21
Both	48
At least one:[2]	
Female adult	69
Male adult	59
Both	40
At least one:[3]	
Female teen	24
Male teen	16
Both	4
At least one:[4]	
Female child	21
Male child	21
Both	10

[1] $N=199$ [2] $N=199$ [3] $N=200$ [4] $N=198$

behavior of males. The Philadelphia study also revealed that most murders were intraracial: blacks killing blacks and whites killing whites.

As discussed earlier, the victims of serial murder appear to be increasingly falling prey to strangers. Unlike homicides in general, where the victim often knows the offender and provocation plays an important role in the killing, involvement of victims of serial murder in their own victimization may be best determined by the degree of facilitation created by the victim, or the degree to which the victim had placed him- or herself in a vulnerable situation (Table 5.8). For example, picking up hitchhikers can place the driver or the passenger of a vehicle in a highly facilitative position for killing. Low facilitation was defined as sharing little or no responsibility for the victimization. For example, a child is abducted by a stranger while playing in his yard, a patient is poisoned to death during a hospital stay, or a woman is abducted from a shopping mall during daytime business hours. Usually these types of victims are completely unsuspecting of any imminent danger.

Data on offenders were examined regarding the methods used to obtain victims, and, in turn, data on victims were examined as to their lifestyles, Cor...ne of employment, and their location at the time of abduction and/or Tee...ng. The overall trend indicated that 16% of victims in this research were Adults a... facilitative in their own deaths. Some were hitchhiking, others All age grou...s prostitutes, and still others placed themselves in one way or ...mercy of strangers. Three fourths of all victims were generally

*$N=202$, except for elde...
† Calculated on the number ...

TABLE 5.8 Degree of Victim Facilitation in Serial Murder Cases in the United States, 1795–1988*

FACILITATION	NUMBER OF VICTIMS	PERCENTAGE OF VICTIMS	PERCENTAGE OF CASES	NUMBER OF VICTIMS PER CASE
High	233–327	16	17	9–13
Low	1023–1561	72–75	78	9–13
Combination	161–193	9–12	5	20–24
Total	1417–2081	100	100	—

*Based on 150 cases, 194 offenders.

in the right place at the wrong time and became a homicide statistic. In some cases, offenders selected victims from both categories of high and low facilitation. Since 1975, a slight decrease was noted in these categories of facilitation, with a 6% increase in combinations of high and low. Whether this reflects a trend in offender versatility, a statistical aberration, or simply problems in consistently defining and measuring facilitation over time will require further exploration.

Although some people argue that much of the preceding research substantiates the contention of those claiming our society has experienced a dramatic emergence of serial killing, others may argue that such claims are the product of vague definitions, variations in reporting, the omnipresence of high-tech media, or a statistical artifact. However, of greater concern than the extent of serial murder is its reality. The pervasiveness of serial murder will unlikely ever challenge that of domestic homicides. What does seem to be increasingly apparent is that we are confronted with a phenomenon for which we have little explanation and which we have little ability to deter. The risk of victimization in our general population appears to be extremely small, yet there are those who are at greater risk as a result of their age, gender, place of residence, or lifestyle. The fact that relatively few individuals are victims of serial murderers should in no way alter our concern for the victims or the dynamics of victimization.

The etiology of victimization should be of concern to researchers who wish to expand their explanations of criminal behavior. Victim profiling can be an effective tool in understanding causation as well as providing direction for deterrence. Victims in this study, except for California, exhibited little regionality. Increasingly they were targets of offenders who operated locally in areas with higher populations. Unlike homicides in general, where the victim often knows his or her attacker, serial murder usually involves stranger-to-stranger situations. Young women and children were at greatest risk of victimization, especially those who were alone or could be isolated. Considering age groups, offenders appeared to kill young adults in greater proportion, yet in recent years the elderly were frequently selected as victims. Most victims did not facilitate their deaths as a result of their lifestyles, although in recent years an increasing number of victims appeared to place themselves at risk.

Missing and Murdered Children

In 1979 six-year-old Etan Patz walked along a busy New York street to await his school bus. He had walked that one block to the bus before, but today was the first time his mother felt he was capable of going alone. Etan never arrived at the bus stop and has not been seen or heard of since his disappearance ten years ago. In 1981 six-year-old Adam Walsh was abducted from a shopping mall when he was momentarily left unattended. Part of his corpse was eventually recovered by investigators.

These two cases attracted extensive media coverage and motivated the creation of the Adam Walsh Child Resource Center in Ft. Lauderdale, Florida. However, in many other instances the offender, not the victim(s), receives the national media attention. In 1981–1982 eleven children disappeared in the area of Vancouver, British Columbia, Canada. Eventually, Clifford Robert Olson was arrested in the murder of the eleventh missing child. Although Olson was a suspect in the other disappearances no one was sure what had become of the children and teenagers, ages 12–17. Olson, a man with an extensive history of criminal behavior, offered to take investigators to the graves of several victims in return for money. Without the money there would be no names or bodies returned, and parents might never know if their child had been one of his victims or had disappeared for some other reason. If Olson did kill their children, the families wanted to know and desperately wanted the bodies returned for a proper burial. After some deliberations the Canadian government agreed to pay Olson $10,000 for each body returned to them. The killer responded by leading them to ten gravesites. Olson's wife was given the $100,000 and has since divorced him and relocated with her son. Olson now resides in a prison in Kingston, Ontario, where he must serve a minimum of 25 years before he will be eligible for a parole hearing (author's files and interview with offender).

These type of abductions, murders, and serial killings of children generally precipitate alarm and fear in any community. The true extent of the problem of missing and murdered children is often subject more to speculation than fact. In 1983 the U.S. Department of Health and Human Services stated that 1.5 million children are reported missing every year. The executive director of the National Center for Missing and Exploited Children, a nonprofit clearing house set up by the government in 1984, indicated that strangers were responsible for the abductions of 4,000 to 20,000 children each year. In addition the Center reported that 25,000 to 500,000 are victims of parental kidnapping (*Newsweek*, October 7, 1985). Other organizations such as the Federal Bureau of Investigation strongly disagree with such figures and report much smaller numbers of victims.

Part of the problem of disagreement over current data can be traced to (1) methodological issues in data collection and (2) operationalizing definitions of categories of missing children. Only in recent years has national attention been focused on the plight of missing children. Much more is needed in the area of national surveys that can be compared to regional and statewide data. A need is also apparent for consistency in defining the types of missing children. Most missing children can be classified as runaways, many leaving home several times in one year. Each time they run away, however, they can be counted again as missing children. Most runaways eventually return home, whereas others can be classified as parental kidnappings (Abraham, 1984).

The following categories suggest ways to expand definitions of missing and murdered children:

1. *Runaways*—children who voluntarily leave home without parental/ guardian permission.

2. *Parental abductions*—children abducted by the noncustodial parent or the parent who does not have legal guardianship.

3. *Relative abductions*—children abducted by a relative, such as an uncle, aunt, or in-law who takes a child from the parent or legal guardian.

4. *Discarded children*—children who are forced to leave their homes by rejecting parents or guardians.

5. *Disposable children*—children who are murdered by their parent(s) or legal guardians.

6. *Stranger abductions*—children who are taken by persons who are strangers to the victim and the victim's family.

7. *Abbreviated abductions*—children who are abducted for a short period of time (minutes or hours) and then released. These may never be recorded in police records.

8. *Aborted abductions*—children who manage to escape the attempted kidnapping.

The National Center for Missing and Exploited Children recently released the number of children reported to them as missing between June, 1984, and January, 1988 (Table 5.9). As expected, runaways represented the greatest percentage of children found alive, whereas stranger abductions accounted for the greatest percentage of those children found dead.

Abraham (1984) found that only three out of every ten children kidnapped by a parent will ever see the other parent again and that physical and sexual abuse of the abducted child is common. Table 5.9 indicates that nearly one fourth of the children that were abducted by a parent or a relative and

TABLE 5.9 Missing and Murdered Children Reported to the National Center for Missing and Exploited Children between June 13, 1984 and January 7, 1988

	PERCENTAGE FOUND ALIVE (N=8,562)	PERCENTAGE FOUND DEAD (N=117)	PERCENTAGE STILL MISSING (N=7,832)	PERCENTAGE OF TOTAL (N=16,511)
Runaways	65	13	28	50
Parental abductions	28	3	54	38
Relative abductions	5	20	15	9
Stranger abductions	2	64	3	3
Total	100	100	100	100

U.S. Department of Justice, 1988.

later found had been murdered. These findings also challenge the generally accepted notion that 95% of missing children are runaways. According to the National Center, parental and relative abductions accounted for nearly half of all missing children reported to their agency. In contrast to their earlier findings of several thousands of children being abducted by strangers each year, their data indicated approximately 150 stranger abductions per year during the three-and-one-half-year study (Federal Bureau of Investigation, 1988).

In 1987 the FBI reported that 2,398 children had been murdered (Table 5.10). These deaths included those reported to the National Center for Missing and Exploited Children as well as children who were killed by their parents or legal guardians and those categorized as discarded children. Death tolls could be much higher if we were able to account for all the children still missing.

TABLE 5.10 Number of Murdered Children in the United States in 1987 Reported to the U.S. Federal Bureau of Investigation, by Gender

AGE	PERCENTAGE OF MALES (N=1,662)	PERCENTAGE OF FEMALES (N=735)	PERCENTAGE UNKNOWN (N=1)	PERCENTAGE OF TOTAL (N=2,398)
Less than 1 year	8	13	—	10
1–4	9	21	—	13
5–9	4	8	100	5
10–14	7	12	—	8
15–19	72	46	—	64
Total	100	100	100	100

Federal Bureau of Investigation, 1988.

According to the FBI approximately one fourth of all male children murdered in 1987 were 14 years of age or younger. By comparison over half of all female children murdered that year were 14 years of age or younger. When controlling for all age categories, male children were more than twice as likely to be murdered. When the 15–19 age group is excluded, the ratio nearly evens out between males and females. In other words, the percentages of male children being murdered in all age categories with the exception of the 15–19 group are similar to those of female children in respective age groupings. The dramatic difference between murders of males and females aged 15–19 may be explained in part as a result of drug- and gang-related violence. Yet these data also reveal that nearly one fourth of all children reported murdered in 1987 were four years of age or younger (Federal Bureau of Investigation, 1988). This figure, of course, includes children killed by their mothers or fathers, as well as abducted and murdered child victims.

Although in 1987 blacks constituted less than 13% of the U.S. population, they represented half of all the murdered children reported to the FBI (Table 5.11). Although males were more likely than females to be murdered between the ages of 15 and 19, blacks were more likely than whites to be murdered in the same age group (Federal Bureau of Investigation, 1988). Again this can be explained in part by the socioeconomic conditions under which the majority of blacks are forced to live. When we exclude the 15–19 age group, black children represented 41% of all children murdered (aged 14 and younger). It appears that even young black children are at significantly higher risk of being murdered than their white counterparts.

In January 1989, the Office of Juvenile Justice and Delinquency Prevention published a bulletin of the preliminary estimates of stranger abduction homicides of children. The data were gathered from the FBI's Supplemental Homicide File and represent the first findings from the National Studies of

TABLE 5.11 Number of Murdered Children in the United States in 1987 Reported to the U.S. Federal Bureau of Investigation, by Race

AGE	PERCENTAGE WHITE ($N=1,140$)	PERCENTAGE BLACK ($N=1,193$)	PERCENTAGE OTHER ($N=47$)	PERCENTAGE UNKNOWN ($N=18$)	PERCENTAGE OF TOTAL ($N=2,398$)
Less than 1 year	12	7	17	22	10
1–4	15	10	15	5	13
5–9	6	4	13	17	5
10–14	10	8	4	17	8
15–19	57	71	51	39	64
Total	100	100	100	100	100

Federal Bureau of Investigation, 1988.

the Incidence of Missing Children. They estimated between 1–2 stranger abductions per 1 million general population per year with teenagers between the ages of 14 and 17 with the highest rates. Such figures indicate that the risk of a child being abducted and murdered by a stranger is much lower than previous estimates (U.S. Department of Justice, 1989). They noted that child murders by strangers that may have involved abduction ranged from a low of 110 in 1980 to a high of 212 in 1982. They found no evidence to suggest that these types of homicides are on the rise. Where strangers are concerned, the preliminary data suggest that girls are at greater risk than boys; in addition, the rates for black children were three times higher than for white children. This report, along with five other major studies cited, dispels the myths that thousands of children are being abducted and murdered each year and that cases are on the rise (U.S. Department of Justice, 1989). As the report also observed, most of these data originate from police statistics, and the conclusions, therefore, are tentative. Nonetheless, the preliminary report is encouraging. Studies presently being conducted will continue to shed light on the problem of missing and murdered children. The fact remains, however, that some children do fall prey to strangers, some of whom are serial offenders. The following section explores factors involving children in my study who were victims of serial killers.

Children as Victims of Serial Murderers

If we are to protect children from adults who would kill them we must be willing to look beyond the traditional notions of victim-offender relationships. Although researchers are still attempting to measure the extent of the serial murder phenomenon, the evidence is clear that young women and children are the prime targets of such attacks. According to the case files of 203 known serial killers in the United States, 62 (31%) had killed at least one child. The child-killer group comprised males (73%) and females (27%); only 7% of the offenders were black (author's files).

Although a consensus has not yet been reached to explain the low numbers of black offenders, there has been an increase in the number of black serial murderers in the past ten years. It is possible that blacks have been overlooked during the emergence of the serial murder phenomenon. Most serial offenders are white and lower middle-class or middle-class, and their homicides tend to be intraracial. The fact that some major urban centers are now predominantly black and are politically controlled by black citizens may in part explain why increasing attention is being focused on the plight of missing and murdered black children. In 1981 Wayne Williams, who is black, was arrested in the killings of 25–30 black youths in Atlanta, Georgia. The murders and their investigation attracted national media and government attention. In recent years a few blacks have also been involved in interracial serial killings and have received considerable publicity for their crimes. In 1985 Alton Coleman and his companion Debra Brown, both black, went on a killing spree in the Midwest, murdering several victims including young children both black and white.

My study of 203 known serial killers in the United States also showed that 73% of serial offenders who killed one or more children had murdered at least one female child, whereas 68% had targeted at least one male child. A few of the 62 offenders (19%) targeted children only. Nearly half (45%) of the child killers were parents of one or more children. Eighty-one percent of the female offenders were mothers of one or more children, whereas only 29% of the male offenders were fathers.

As expected, female killers of children from this group were more likely to murder victims from their own families or other relatives, whereas males were more likely to be total strangers to their victims (Table 5.12). In addition, female offenders were much more prone to use poisons to kill their victims; males who killed children frequently mutilated, strangled, shot, or bludgeoned their victims.

By using the mobility classifications to analyze the child homicide data, most of the offenders were found to have stayed within one state or killed their victims in a specific area (Table 5.13). Only 26% of child killers in this study were categorized as the "traveling" type. As expected, most female offenders were typed as place-specific, with the murders occurring in their own homes or places of work, such as hospitals. By contrast, the largest group of male offenders operated in a local area, whereas nearly one third traveled, and one fourth stayed in a specific area. One implication derived from these data is that children, when targeted by a serial killer, can be at risk both in and out of the home. Although the likelihood of a child being murdered by a serial offender is remote compared with the much higher risk of being the victim of domestic homicide, the fact that any risk exists underscores the need for increased education regarding the etiology of serial murder.

TABLE 5.12 Relationship of Serial Murderers to Their Child Victims in the United States

RELATIONSHIP	PERCENTAGE OF MALE OFFENDERS ($N=45$)	PERCENTAGE OF FEMALE OFFENDERS ($N=17$)	PERCENTAGE OF TOTAL ($N=62$)
Strangers	49	18	40
Strangers/acquaintances	29	18	26
Family	7	29	13
Family/acquaintances	—	35	10
Family/stranger	9	—	6
Acquaintances	4	—	3
All	2	—	2
Total	100	100	100

TABLE 5.13 Mobility Classification of Serial Murderers in the United States Who Have Killed One or More Children

MOBILITY	PERCENTAGE OF MALE OFFENDERS (N=45)	PERCENTAGE OF FEMALE OFFENDERS (N=17)	PERCENTAGE OF TOTAL (N=62)
Place-specific	24	71	37
Local	44	18	37
Traveling	32	11	26
Total	100	100	100

For male offenders the primary motive reported for the killing of children was sexual gratification (Table 5.14). In one recent case spanning several months the offender lured several young boys into his control and then sexually molested them. He later confessed to killing the boys for fear that they would tell someone about the molestation.

The female offenders were much more likely (50%) to kill children for financial reasons. In several cases female offenders have insured their own children, other relatives, or even neighbors in order to collect the insurance. In addition, both male and female offenders often reported deriving enjoyment (43%) from the killing of children. Overall, males were much more inclined to report a combination of motives for killing (61%) compared with their female counterparts (38%).

TABLE 5.14 Reported Motives of Serial Murderers in the United States Who Have Killed One or More Children

MOTIVES	PERCENTAGE OF MALE OFFENDERS (N=44)	PERCENTAGE OF FEMALE OFFENDERS (N=16)	PERCENTAGE OF TOTAL (N=60)
Sexual gratification	64	13	50
Enjoyment	43	44	43
Monetary gain	30	50	35
Personal reasons[1]	30	25	28
Perverted acts[2]	25	6	20
Revenge	18	6	15
Mental illness	5	—	3
Combination of motives	61	38	55

[1] Males generally reported "an urge to kill," whereas female offenders reported they "were not good mothers," "children were a burden," or they were trying to hide other crimes.
[2] Perverted acts for males included necrophilia and saving body parts as trophies or souvenirs. Only one female offender engaged in necrophilia.

Another important key to understanding the serial killer of children is to dispel notions of lunacy, mental illness, or psychosis. As mentioned in Chapter 3, very few offenders—whether they kill children or adults—are ever found to be insane by legal definitions. Instead, as I have described earlier, I prefer to refer to such killers as psychopaths (Chapter 3). This label is intended to include persons with particular personality defects that often are not discernible to those around them. Such individuals often possess several or all of the following characteristics: charismatic; above average intelligence; little or no conscience or sense of guilt or responsibility; highly manipulative; compulsive lying; void of feelings for others, especially victims; and outwardly friendly (author's files).

For some offenders, killing children may represent an act of revenge on an unjust society or perhaps a desire to prevent others from experiencing the joy and happiness in life they themselves felt denied. Such reasons for murder make children prime targets for offenders. They are viewed as being more trusting, naive, and powerless than adults and are more easily abducted.

Certainly not all psychopaths are violent offenders, and possessing psychopathic characteristics does not always lead individuals to criminal behavior. However, the majority of offenders in this study do possess many psychopathic personality defects. The ability and need for these offenders to control others is tremendous. Children become prime targets because they can be easily controlled and manipulated. Given a conducive environment for these child-killers, abductors, and molesters, children have little resistance to their persuasive powers. Parents need to be just as concerned about where their children *go* in their unsupervised time as they are about teaching them not to "take candy from strangers."

On January 24, 1989, Robert Theodore Bundy was executed in the state of Florida for the murder of 12-year-old Kimberly Leach, whom he kidnapped from the grounds of her junior high school in 1978. Bundy also lured a 15-year-old girl into his car while she was attending a youth conference at Brigham Young University, Provo, Utah, in June, 1975. Because of his charisma and ability to persuade his victims to ignore precautions with total strangers, he was able to abduct, sexually torture, and murder several dozen young women. His usually fail-safe plan involved approaching potential victims in the daytime and in places where the victims felt no danger. He often feigned an arm or leg injury and simply asked an intended victim to help him carry something to his car. He was also known to have posed as a police officer and would talk victims into entering his vehicle. By the time the victims may have sensed danger they were already under the killer's total control.

Luring Children

We have all heard horror stories about abducted children. Unfortunately, child abductors can be particularly creative in their methods of finding suitable victims. One 16-year-old offender being evaluated for a sex-offender program in a psychiatric facility in the western United States noted how simple it was for him to find child victims to molest. His favorite "hunting grounds" were shopping malls because he always found parents who were willing to leave their children, sometimes even young children, alone for a few minutes around the toy counters. The children whom he approached, escorted to the washroom, and molested inevitably seemed to trust him. Some of his victims were so young he was sure they would not understand what had occurred once he allowed them to leave. On a "good" night he claimed he could lure three to four children to the washrooms.

In another case a 15-year-old offender who had been arrested in Hawaii for sexual molestation of children was never prosecuted because his family relocated. A few months later the offender abducted a two-year-old child while she played inside her fenced front yard. After raping and strangling the infant, he left the body in a vacant building.

In 1977 Operation Police Lure was organized in Oakland County, Michigan, by a law enforcement task force in response to a series of seven unsolved child homicides. At the time some people believed that a serial killer was responsible for several of the abductions. In the area where the children were probably lured and abducted, a survey was administered to students in 54 elementary and junior high schools in grades four through nine in an effort to gather more data on child molestation and abduction. The children reported 782 incidents of attempted or actual cases of molestation that had never been reported to authorities. Police investigators also found that children aged 10–12 were the most likely targets and that males and females were victimized at about the same rates. Although victims were approached at different times of day, 3:00–6:00 P.M. was the time most frequently reported. Children profiled the offenders as white males, usually in their twenties or thirties, who often attempted to lure them by asking for help, such as looking for a lost puppy. When vehicles were used, the abductors and molesters also seemed to prefer two-door blue models (Wooden, 1984).

Child abductors, of course, do not come in only one mold and generally do not fit the stereotype of the peculiar looking "dirty old man." Some very benign looking individuals are arrested for child abductions/molestations. Creating a new stereotype of such offenders becomes problematic because it excludes many variations of the traditional stereotype. There are, however, some important concepts that should be noted about the nature of child abductions. Although coercion, bribery, and other such methods to lure victims are frequently employed, asking for help from a child is not only effective from an offender's perspective but also creates difficulty for parents in protecting their children. The thought of helping find a lost animal, such as a puppy or a kitten, can easily distract the child from paying attention to the person seeking the assistance. Similarly, the offenders may use a badge or a blue vehicle to appear as an authority figure to the intended victim. Most children are taught or have learned by experience a degree of respect for authority figures and will automatically respond to their commands.

Wooden (1984) outlines a variety of child lures used by offenders, including the appeal to a child's ego by telling him or her that he or she is to be in a beauty contest or a television commercial. Some offenders tell the child an emergency has occurred, and they have come to escort the child home immediately. Wayne Williams (involved in the Atlanta child murders) was known to have posted employment advertisements for young men throughout the area in which he resided. In the case of Ted Bundy and others like him similar themes are used but in a more sophisticated manner. Wearing a cast to evoke sympathy or displaying fictitious business cards initially alleviates fears of dealing with a stranger. Offenders who have become adept at manipulating can exert complete control over others, especially children. The following tragic story illustrates how devastating the control that some offenders have over their victims can be.

A CHILD KILLER'S STORY*

I remember it was late fall and I was living in T_____, Arizona, on the run from the law in Montana. At 26 I had already committed several violent crimes and was basically out of control. Deep into depression and frustrated I found myself walking across a field about 4:00 P.M. one cold, dreary day. I thought I was alone when I noticed two girls also walking across the field. Immediately I knew I was going to kill them. Moving in their direction I began to speak to them in a friendly voice. They said they were on their way to play badminton. Both were 11 years of age but one looked physically more mature than the other. It was really very easy, and I was so persuasive, the girls did not even hesitate when I suggested we go to a secluded area. They were such trusting children.

I pulled out my knife and told them to do as I said or I would hurt them. I could see the surprise and fear in their eyes as I ordered the smaller of the two to remain where she was while I moved the second child to another area. They were prevented from seeing one another. Each child was staked out on the ground "spread eagle" and their clothes torn off. They didn't dare scream for each time they tried I beat them. I systematically tortured them, going back and forth but spent more time with the smaller child. I had other plans for the prettier girl. The more they responded to the torture the more I tried to hurt them. I burned them with cigarettes, I beat them repeatedly and hurt them sexually. After about two hours the first child was not responding very well, she was very cold, her eyes appeared glazed, and she appeared to be in shock. I took the handle of her racquet and strangled her to death.

I untied the other girl and told her to get dressed and that if she did as I said we would come back for her friend. I told her not to worry that I would not hurt her anymore but she must obey me. I gave her my coat as her blouse had been cut away in the attack. As we left I noticed it was

*This story was edited from a taped interview I conducted with a multiple homicide offender December 5/6, 1988. By request of the offender his identity will remain anonymous.

after 6:00 P.M. I decided to take her to my home and kill her there. We walked quickly across the field, the child trying her best to keep up with me. As we started along the sidewalk a police car came around the corner and pulled up beside us. They had their public address system on and were looking for the two missing girls. Apparently the mother of the child walking with me had gone out looking for her daughter when she realized she had left for the courts without her coat. When neither of the girls could be located, the concerned parents had contacted the police.

Now I was walking less than five feet from the patrol car. The girl was behind me several feet and in a moment I expected the child to run to their car and give me away. I quickly walked down the street anticipating the command to halt. After about 30 yards I suddenly heard the little girl yelling at me "Mister, Mister, please slow down you're walking too fast!" I glanced over my shoulder and was amazed to see her still walking behind me. The police had seen us but there was nothing about our behavior that was suspicious and she was hurrying after me. I took her hand and we walked on. In a few moments we approached another street corner when suddenly she saw her father drive by in a car. "There goes my Daddy! He's looking for me," I remember her saying. She did not call out and her father drove on oblivious to how close he had come to finding his missing child.

She walked with me to my place without any struggle or protest. I again went through my ritual of removing her clothes and staking her out. She was all mine from about 7:00 P.M. till 3:00 the next morning. She never screamed because she knew I would not take her back to her friend if she failed to obey my every command. When I finished, I suffocated her to death. Later that day I borrowed a car and carried her body into the mountains. Searchers found the first child about an hour after we left the secluded area and the second child about a day after I dumped her body. They never would have caught me had I not left the sack in which I had wrapped the second child. It was an odd weave and had the child's blood on it. Police showed the sack on television and someone recognized it as mine. I was captured in another state a few days later.

The offender's initial charisma and his subsequent intimidating and brutal methods were used in succession to gain total control over the children. Even the offender admitted surprise in finding his second victim following him past the police car. In frustration we want to understand why a victim would not run from her attacker. This is reminiscent of the Stockholm Syndrome, in which the victim begins to identify with his or her captor. The child, concerned for her friend and mentally numbed from her ordeal, was incapable of fleeing her assailant.

Protection and Prevention

Many people today feel a sense of impending doom because they believe that they will inevitably fall prey to criminal victimization. A great deal of this fear is created by constant media reports that focus on the most heinous crimes committed in our society. However, we must never forget that there are many factors that play a role in the dynamics of victimization. Age, race, gender, socioeconomic status, place of residence, employment, education, lifestyles—all of which can affect the types of crimes committed in particular areas—must be considered when considering the risk factors. Even then crimes do occur that appear to have little or no correlation to most risk factors. It becomes disconcerting for people to feel they may be at risk and yet powerless to effectively respond to such concerns. Regardless of their utility, most strategies embraced by adults to protect themselves—such as enrolling in self-defense courses, carrying a weapon, or increasing home security—are not viable for children. More important, we may delude ourselves into believing that law enforcement can provide sufficient protection for children and that school officials can always provide adequate supervision.

The perception of increasing randomness of child victimization outside the home has initiated awareness and action on the part of concerned parents and community activists. The experience of victimization often serves as a catalyst for involvement in victims' rights and victim advocacy groups. Some of these organizations function primarily as support groups, whereas others focus attention on introducing legislation aimed at addressing the rights of victims, including the handling of criminals in our judicial system. The murder of a child has effects that extend far beyond the loss of life, as is evidenced by the experiences of parents of child victims. Although some may seek vengeance on offenders, others become involved with groups that actively work to prevent future victimizations, assist other victims being processed through the criminal justice system, and provide counseling, because after the media headlines subside, the agony may just be beginning for many of those related to a murder victim. The following statement provided by Ruth Kuzmaak and her husband, Dr. John Kuzmaak, of Portland, Oregon, describes the effect of their daughter's homicide on the Kuzmaak family and the frustrations they continue to face ten years later.

THE KUZMAAK STORY

I write the following not to enlist the reader's sympathy. I do not want sympathy. I write instead hoping that others will have a better understanding for those persons who have endured criminal victimizations.

I keep searching for the right descriptive words to convey the emotional impact our daughter's murder made on us. "Devastating" just doesn't make it—"ravaged" is closer, engulfed, overwhelmed, drowning in sadness, numb, oblivious to EVERYTHING else, totally immersed in the horror, the why, the who, what she had to go through in her closing minutes of her short life, how terrified she must have been, did she scream for help and no one came, did she fight, the pain, how it felt to be strangled, what her dying thoughts were, how she must have held out hope until the last that she would be rescued, her shock and disbelief that this was happening, and as the information unfolded itself to us in bits and pieces that first day, the anguish of hearing how badly she was beaten, then a couple of hours later crying out when I heard that she had been repeatedly stabbed. Then, the ultimate horror to learn that the cause of death was strangulation. To be deprived of breath—lungs bursting—"Oh, God, oh God," I would wail, tears streaming, hands clenched and imploring.

That is how I remember the day, March 21, 1979. A decade has passed, but the emotions go on, the anger, the sorrow, and the loss.

I wanted to go to the funeral home to see her, but everyone told me that I should remember her the way she was in life, not in death, so I didn't. I have regretted it over and over—that I didn't have the courage to look at her after she had suffered through so much. It was something I should have done.

A big, black Cadillac picked us up in the morning she was to be buried. We drove slowly to the funeral home, parking in the rear. Shortly, the back door opened and men in dark suits started carrying out her casket to the hearse.

"There she is," said our son. She had been so vibrant, so much fun to be with, so bright, and so loving, and here she was being carried out in a coffin. Gone from life. Gone from us.

I counted 75 cars winding up the hill behind us at the cemetery. Many more had mistakenly gone to the funeral home. Plainclothes police photographed the cars and the people. I asked that the poem, "Thana-topsis" be read. The minister asked if she had been baptized, and I said she had.

Within six weeks I had lost 22 pounds, going from 141 to 119. My husband and I kept working at his dental office, which helped considerably during the day, but the nights were a horror. I would wake up two and three times an hour, and each time I had to face, once more, the reality. I had always been an avid reader, and so I would grab a book and start reading until I once more fell asleep. Books became my narcotic.

Relatives, friends, and our dental patients were extremely kind to us during this time. They say that sorrow needs a good support system and we had one. But, within a few months all but Ken, Janet, Aunt Lois, and Donna's girlfriend, Chris, had dropped away and out of our lives. When I did have occasion to talk to people they avoided the subject. It was as though Donna had never existed. One night we went out with a couple we had known for years. I was describing a court hearing we had gone to. We had heard that the defendant might be a suspect in Donna's murder, and he was being tried on another charge. Our friend, a dentist, interrupted with, "Ruth, could we talk about something else? This is so depressing."

Increasingly, we became more isolated.

We could get so little information from the police that we would think up ruses in order to try to get them to say more. "Was she raped? Sodom-ized? No?" Then, we would wrack our brains trying to figure out why they called it a "sex crime." Ken and I had long conversations, filled with theories and speculations.

An enormous boulder had been dropped in our river of life and we all struggled to stay afloat. Within 18 months I had breast cancer. Grandma Kuzmaak developed a giant stomach ulcer from which she never recovered. I was glad that my mother had died for she just couldn't have stood it. Janet had lost her best friend, for she and Donna had been very close in both ages and affection. The 12-year-old neighbor girl of Donna's had to have psychiatric help.

Nightmares were constant for me. They were filled with vicious, evil, predatory men, and in some of them I was trying to shelter Donna from them. But, I had good dreams, too. In them, Donna was again a small, little girls in pigtails. She had always been such a gentle child.

About 1982, Janet talked me into going on a local television talk show. The audience was to be made up of parents of murdered children. During the program, I complained about the inaccessibility of information from the police about what had happened to her. Afterward, Dr. Larry Lewman came over to me and said that he had done Donna's autopsy and that this information was open to us. No one had told us this.

We went down to his office two days later and he went over the autopsy with us. I learned that her nose had been shattered, that she had received a violent blow on the back of her head, that she had been stabbed nine times in the chest and also in the vagina, and strangled with her pantyhose. The vaginal sexual mutilation was why the police considered it a sex crime. Now, we knew.

I started reading everything I could get my hands on about the mentality of these sexually sadistic killers. It was an ugly education. I added new words to my vocabulary such as necrophilia. Although Donna's autopsy showed no semen, I learned that these killers frequently masturbated on or near the body.

We met with other victims and formed a group called "Crime Victims United." This, then, became the focus of my life. I could channel my energies, my rage, and Donna's murder into something really worthwhile.

It took us two attempts to pass a statewide victims' rights measure. No longer would surviving family members be forced to sit in the hall during the trial. We got equal peremptory challenges (before, the defendant had twice as many as the state), victims could make victim impact statements in court, prior convictions could be raised to the jury, and many other important changes.

My husband, Jack, showed gritty determination in these efforts, getting thousands of signers in order to get it on the ballot in each of the elections. Having accomplished this goal, however, I believe he feels now that "enough is enough." But, I go on. We have had several arguments about it recently.

Our children have been quite supportive of our efforts, though one day Janet said to me, "Mom, we're here, too." And. . . that really hurt!

Recently (11/25/88), I watched Dr. Martha Gluckman of Patuxent Institute being interviewed on "Nightline." She was being questioned about the paroles given to convicted murderers and rapists at Patuxent and also the unsupervised weekend passes.

One inmate had been convicted of murdering his girlfriend and her parents. He had been sentenced to three life sentences to be served consecutively starting in the early 1980s. Already he had been given 12 weekend unsupervised passes.

Another inmate, Charles Wantland, murdered a 12-year-old boy three weeks after being paroled. He had served only six years of a 30-year sentence for murder.

Yet another sex offender convicted in 1972 was serving a life sentence for rape, perverted practices, assault, and kidnapping. He was paroled in 1980 and within a year convicted of three more rapes.

Dr. Gluckman vigorously defended the passes and furloughs, saying, "George Bush said he wants a kinder and gentler nation, and I think it should start with Corrections." The remark left me totally outraged.

On Memorial Day and Donna's birthday we go to the cemetery. I can't keep the tears from flowing each time I stoop to arrange the flowers.

I can talk about Donna's murder with the kind of detachment I use when discussing the weather. But, I still can't really THINK about it. This statement has made me think about it, and it has been difficult. But, I truly hope that it will be of benefit in helping people understand.

Our daughter's murder is unsolved [Hickey, 1990(b)].

The Kuzmaak story represents the experiences of many families affected by the murder of a loved one. In this case the homicide is believed to be the work of a serial killer.

Agencies for Missing, Murdered, and Exploited Children

At the national level a multitude of agencies are now beginning to organize themselves to specifically address the issues of missing, exploited, and murdered children. Established in 1984 by the U.S. Department of Justice, the National Center for Missing and Exploited Children operates as a national clearinghouse for information about missing and murdered children and sexual exploitation, including child pornography and prostitution.

National Center for Missing and Exploited Children
1835 K Street, N.W., Suite 700
Washington, D.C. 20006
(202) 634-9821

A hotline (1-800-843-5678) is available to anyone with information about missing children. The Telecommunications Device for the Deaf (TDD) hotline is 1-800-826-7653. The U.S. Department of Justice offers a variety of brochures addressing parental kidnapping, child protection, runaways, and sexually abused or exploited children and covering whom to contact if your child is missing and a host of other topics regarding children. Anyone or any group interested in the safety and welfare of children would be well served to contact this agency.

The parent agency that directly coordinates the many federal agencies pertaining to children is the U.S. Department of Justice, Office of Juvenile Justice and Delinquency Prevention, Washington, D.C. 20531. The U.S. Department of Justice's Coordinating Council on Juvenile Justice and Delinquency Prevention includes representatives from the Department of Health and Human Services and the Department of Education. This council, working in conjunction with the Attorney General's Advisory Board on Missing Children, coordinates communications with the Federal Bureau of Investigation and the National Obscenity Enforcement Unit (both agencies of the Department of Justice), the U.S. Department of State, the U.S. Postal Service, the U.S. Customs Service, the Interstate "I SEARCH" Advisory Council on Missing and Exploited Children, and the National Center for Missing and Exploited Children. The U.S. Department of Justice is very active in collecting and disseminating information about missing and exploited children and has recently published a report summarizing the progress made in the 1980s. This report, *Missing and Exploited Children: Progress in the 80's*, is available to the public and is an excellent resource for better understanding the extent to which the federal government has begun to address the issue of exploited children.

Another agency that now has national recognition in addressing the issues of missing, abused, and neglected children is the following:

Adam Walsh Child Resource Center, Executive Office
3111 South Dixie Highway
Suite 244
West Palm Beach, Florida 33405
(407) 833-9080

Several states have created clearinghouses for missing and exploited children; these agencies usually can be contacted through the state police and are coordinated with the National Center for Missing and Exploited Children. In the state of Indiana, for example, extensive information packets are available upon request.

Missing Children Clearinghouse
Indiana State Police
State Office Building
100 N. Senate
Indianapolis, Indiana 46204
1-800-831-8953 (Indiana only)
(317) 232-8248 (out of state)

A sample of privately sponsored crime victim groups and organizations can be obtained from:

Citizens for Justice and Crime Victims United
P.O. Box 19480
Portland, Oregon 97219
(503) 246-5368

This politically active crime victims' support group, which meets regularly to discuss current legislative issues pertaining to victims' rights and listen to various speakers dealing with the laws, courts, stress management, counseling, and so on, publishes a regular monthly newsletter.

The following nonprofit all-volunteer organization formed in response to problems within the criminal justice system.

The Stephanie Roper Committee and Foundation, Inc.
14804 Pratt Street #1
Upper Marlboro, Maryland 20772
(301) 952-0063

The committee addresses administrative and legislative reform in the sentencing and parole of violent offenders and the establishment of victims' rights. The foundation provides direct services to victims and their families by offering comfort, support, and assistance throughout the period of dealing with the criminal justice system. It also maintains an active court-watch program to monitor the application of victims' rights under law.

CHAPTER 6

The Female Serial Murderer

The orientation of criminological research focuses primarily on male criminality, especially in the area of violent crimes such as homicide. However, during the 1970s, when the United States experienced a growth in the women's liberation movement, some scholars hastily observed "a tremendous increase of serious crimes by women" (Deming, 1977). In her book, *Sisters in Crime*, Freda Adler predicted "a new breed of women criminals," who would be significantly involved in violent crimes (Adler, 1975, p. 7). Yet other research discounts such notions (Chapman, 1980; Schur, 1984; Steffensmeier & Cobb, 1981). Weisheit (1984), in his review of women and crime perspectives, noted that "the factors leading to the current interest in female criminality—the perception that female crime was on the rise, the link between liberation and crime and the sexist nature of previous research on female criminality—have been challenged" (p. 197). In any case, the number of women who kill is still relatively low in comparison with the number of men who kill.

Because of the constant focus on male criminality, women are seldom viewed by the public as killers. Certainly, our crime statistics support this view. Since those women who kill do so primarily in domestic conflicts, there is even less reason to suspect women to be multiple killers. Consequently, those few females who are serial murderers may be even less likely to come under suspicion than their male counterparts or females who commit other types of murder. Of those women who commit multiple murders, rarely does one go on any kind of rampage like that of Richard Speck, who killed eight nurses in Chicago in 1966, or of James Huberty, who in 1984 during a ten-minute shooting spree killed 21 victims and wounded 19 others in a McDonald's Restaurant in San Ysidro, California. Female serial killers, especially when they act alone, are almost invisible to public view. These are the quiet killers. They are every bit as lethal as male serial murderers, but we are seldom aware one is in our midst because of the low visibility of their killing.

This chapter focuses on the cases of 34 females, some acting alone, others with partners, who murdered hundreds of victims. Many of these killers tended to fall into one of two categories: "black widows" and nurses. Black widows were women who killed their husbands, children, or other relatives. Frequently they remarried several times in order to kill again and again. Those who made up the nurse group victimized people over whom they had control. Elderly men and women, and especially babies, became their targets. Of course, some female offenders fit neither group.

We can only speculate on the annual victim count produced by this group of females. They appear to be atypical of female criminality. They tend to be viewed as anomalies, aberrations in female homicide patterns. They are ignored because there has not been an appropriate "pigeon hole" in which to place them and because of the belief that they represent a statistically small number of offenders. The public displays more amusement than concern about cases like that of Linda Sue Jones of Torrance, California. In September, 1988, Mrs. Jones admitted trying to kill two previous husbands in order to collect insurance. The day after she was sentenced to 20 years in prison, Jones married again in a ceremony performed by the same judge who sentenced her. It is less troublesome simply to label such people "insane" and somehow less important, at least statistically, than other female offenders. The Ted Bundys, the John Gacys, and the Edmund Kempers are also atypical of males who commit homicide, but yet they have attracted a host of researchers. However, important comparisons can be made between women who are serial killers and and other women who commit homicide.

Emergence of Female Serial Murderers

Thirty-four female serial killers were identified, which constituted 17% of all serial murderers in this study. Eighteen percent started their killing between 1800 and 1899, whereas the remaining 82% appeared since 1900. Fifteen of the females, or 44% of all female killers, had accomplices when they murdered and therefore are included in Chapter 8, which deals with team killers. This analysis focuses on the behavior, and when possible, the personal lives of these women, who ranged in age from 14 to 54 at the time they first began to kill. They are responsible for the deaths of 261–471 men, women, and children or 18–22% of all victims killed by offenders in this study. Figure 6.1 indicates the progressive increase in the number of female offenders since the year 1800 and the particularly sharp increase since 1970.

Approximately one third of these females began their careers in killing since 1970. Like the statistics for male serial offenders, this number may be explained in part by improved police investigation techniques, population growth, and increased media attention. However, although relatively few in number, female serial killers seem to be increasing in number and thus merit attention. Consider the number of victims believed to have been killed by these few offenders. The average number of victims per female offender ranged from 8 to 14 (Table 6.1) (the numbers are 8 to 11 victims for their male counterparts). Since the number of actual cases of female serial killing (31) was less than the number of offenders (34), the average number of victims per case was slightly higher (8–15) than the 8–14 victims per offender. As

FIGURE 6.1 Frequency Distribution of Female Serial Murderers in the United States by Year, 1800–1988

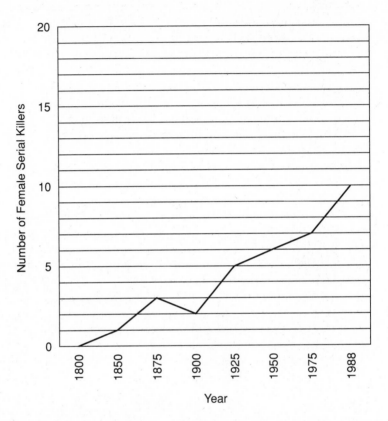

Number of Cases of Serial Murder Committed by Females in the United States, 1821–1988

YEARS	TOTAL NUMBER OF CASES	NUMBER OF CASES PER YEAR	NUMBER OF OFFENDERS	PERCENTAGE OF OFFENDERS	NUMBER OF OFFENDERS PER YEAR
1821–1988	31	.18	34	100	.20 (168 yrs)
1821–1969	20	.13	23	68	.15 (149 yrs)
1970–1988	11	.55	11	32	.55 (19 yrs)

with male offenders, the number of victims per case has continually decreased since 1900. Inversely, as the number of victims per case decreased there was a noticeable rise in the total number of victims since 1975.

The average age of the female offender was 32, slightly higher than that of their male counterparts. Most of these females went on killing for several years before they were finally apprehended. The average killing period for

TABLE 6.1 Victim/Female Serial Murderer Comparisons in the United States, 1821–1988

YEAR	NUMBER OF CASES	NUMBER OF CASES PER YEAR	NUMBER OF VICTIMS	NUMBER OF VICTIMS PER CASE	NUMBER OF VICTIMS PER YEAR	
Total	31	.19	261–471	8–15	2–3	(167 yrs)
1821–1849	1	.03	2–5	2–5	.07–.17	(29 yrs)
1850–1874	2	.08	26–56	13–28	1–2	(25 yrs)
1875–1899	2	.08	39–108	20–54	2–4	(25 yrs)
1900–1924	5	.20	61–65	12–13	2–3	(25 yrs)
1925–1949	6	.24	58–88	10–15	2–4	(25 yrs)
1950–1974	5	.20	30–58	6–12	1–2	(25 yrs)
1975–1988	10	.71	45–91	5–9	3–7	(14 yrs)

this group of females was 9.2 years, with a span of a few months to 34 years. Thirty-two percent of the women were categorized as homemakers, or not employed outside the home, whereas 18% were nurses. Table 6.2 shows that only 15% of these women were noted as having a criminal history, or a criminal "career." Others hired out as housekeepers, worked as waitresses, or operated small businesses. About 20% reported no particular employment status. Most of these offenders were transient or living with relatives.

Overall, about 67% of these female serial offenders were reported as having no legitimate employment outside the home. Weisheit (1984), in his research on incarcerated female homicide offenders, found that between 1981 and 1984 77% of offenders had been unemployed at the time of their offense. He reported that the median age during this time frame was 27 years, 65% of the female offenders were black, and 76% had children (p. 478). Although the percentage of female serial offenders having children

TABLE 6.2 Reported Occupation of Female Offenders*

OCCUPATION	PERCENTAGE
Homemaker	32
Nurse	18
Criminal career	15
Hired housekeeper	6
Other: Farmer, waitress, storeowner	9
None	20
	100

*N=34

is the same as female homicide offenders in general, some interesting differences exist between the two groups. For example, the female serial offenders were older, (median age of 33 since 1975), and 97% were white. The contrasts diminish, however, when we examine the reasons for women committing homicide.

With regard to murders in general, Wolfgang (1967) noted a preponderance of killings among the lower socio-economic classes, where interpersonal violence was more "acceptable."

> When homicide is committed by members of the middle and upper social classes, there appears to be a high likelihood of major psychopathology or of planned, more "rational" (or rationalized) behavior. The fact that they commit an act of willful murder, which is in diametric opposition to the set of values embraced by the dominant social class establishment of which they are part, often means that these persons are suffering severely from an emotional crisis of profound proportions. Or they have been able. . .to meditate and mediate with their own internalized value system until they can conceive of the murder act without the consequence of an overburdening guilt and thereby justify their performing the deed. This self-justificatory behavior undoubtedly requires the actor considerable time and much introspective wrestling in order to remain within, yet contradict his supportive value system. . . . Our thesis contains principally the notion that the man from a culture value system that denounces the use of interpersonal violence will be restrained from using violence because of his positive perspective that conforms to his value system, not because of a negation of it.

> The absence of that kind of value system is hardly likely to be a vacuous neutrality regarding violence. Instead, it is replaced by a value system that views violence as tolerable, expected, or required. As we approach that part of the cultural continuum where violence is a requisite response, we also enter a subculture where physically aggressive action quickly and readily can bleed into aggressive crime. The man from this culture area is more likely to use violence, similarly because of a positive perspective that requires conforming to his value system. Restraint from using violence may be a frustrating, ego-deflating, even guilt-ridden experience. Questions of the risks of being apprehended and the distant, abstract notion of the threat of punishment are almost irrelevant to he who acts with quick, yet socially ingrained aggressivity, neither reasoning nor time for it are at his disposal [pp. 6–7].

This notion of subcultural violence, Wolfgang noted, was based on a differentiation in value systems. He separated out middle- and upper-class people and explained homicide in those classes as a result of "major" psychopathology, of planned, rational behavior. This explanation may well fit the two thirds of female serial offenders (author's data) who were classified within the various tiers of middle- and upper-class social hierarchies. Regardless of the social class, however, all but one of the offending women were white.

Weisheit (1984) found that between 1981 and 1983, 42% of the female homicide offenders in his study killed for money, up from 18% between 1940 and 1966 (p. 486). Overall, 53% of female serial killers were motivated at least partially by money, and 41% murdered only for money. Weisheit also reported that women were less likely now to kill in response to abuse than in the past. By contrast, since 1975 female serial murderers have been much more likely to kill in response to abuse of various forms, although this motive may have been less apparent than the desire for money. Several of the cases in my study, especially those of recent years, report various forms of physiological and psychological abuse at the hands of husbands, lovers, friends, and other family members. In addition, women, regardless of social class, may be motivated to kill in response to a list of unfulfilled needs. Sometimes the needs are economic, and other times they are emotional. For some, the needs for economic and psychological well-being are virtually the same.

In earlier decades of American history, spouse abuse was not considered a justification or an explanation for female homicide. Today, however, emphasis is placed on understanding the nature of domestic violence and its relationship to murder. Women may be more likely now (than they were before the emergence of the women's movement) to explain homicidal behavior as a result of physical and/or mental abuse. The fact that women who commit homicides in general are increasingly reporting their motives as economic does not negate the possible link between societal discrimination against women and domestic violence. In short, women who kill more than once may manifest their behavior differently according to social class, but the stimulation for their behavior may stem from parallel class-related motivations. Whether the stimulation be psychopathology or a tolerance for violence, both may be the product of abuse the offenders have endured. Further discussion of motivations for killing will be discussed later in this chapter.

Victim Selection

Regardless of gender, homicide usually involves an offender and a victim who are acquainted or related to each other. Weisheit (1984) observed in studying victim-offender relationships in which the offender was female that "once again, the data fail to support the notion of a new breed of murderess" (p. 485). While this fact is true of homicides in general, such is not the case when females are involved in serial homicides. Instead, nearly one third of female serial killers reported having killed strangers only and over half had killed at least one stranger (Table 6.3). Overall, one fourth of female offenders killed only family members, whereas half of all these offenders murdered at least one member of their family. Although female serial offenders killed family and strangers in almost equal numbers, since 1975 there has been an increase in killing strangers. Table 6.4 indicates the percentage of victims targeted by female offenders. Overall, since 1975

TABLE 6.3 Percentage of Female Offenders Killing Family Members, Acquaintances, and/or Strangers*

RELATIONSHIP	PERCENTAGE
Family only	26
At least one family member	50
Acquaintances only	0
At least one acquaintance	38
Strangers only	29
At least one stranger	56

*N=34

victims were more likely to be strangers to their killers than an acquaintance or a family member.

Among the groupings of strangers, acquaintances, and family members, female offenders appeared to have preferences in the types of victims selected. Table 6.5 shows the rank order of victims; when the victims were classified as strangers, both young boys and girls were the most likely targets. However, in the case of female serial killers who acted alone, patients in hospitals and nursing homes were the preferred victims. Either way, where strangers were concerned, offenders went after the weak and the helpless. When family members were victims, husbands overwhelmingly became the primary target. Indeed, some female serial killers have given new meaning to the term *serial monogamy*. (For example, consider the case of Nannie Hazel Doss [1925–1954] described in Profile 6-1.)

In the case of child victims, some offenders took years to systematically kill each child. Acquaintances were least likely to be killed by offenders, but of those who were singled out, friends seemed to receive the most attention. Unsuspecting men wishing to marry the offenders did not fare much better.

Female offenders generally did not have a specific age group of victims

TABLE 6.4 Distribution of Victims by Their Relationship to Female Offenders*

TYPE OF VICTIM	NUMBER OF VICTIMS	PERCENTAGE OF ALL VICTIMS OF FEMALE OFFENDERS
Family	47–85	18
Strangers	109–186	39–42
Family and acquaintances	52–57	12–20
Strangers and acquaintances	22–112	8–24
Family and strangers	31	7–12

*N=261–471

NANNIE – THE "GIGGLING GRANDMA" continued

laced with arsenic. She was arrested in Tulsa, Oklahoma, October 6, 1954, where she was working as a baby-sitter and a housekeeper.

Nannie Doss was convicted and sentenced to life in prison, where she continued her obsessive reading of romance novels and wrote her memoirs for *Life* magazine. In 1965 she died in prison of leukemia at the age of 60.

male child. There was little difference between males and females when the victims were teenagers. Not surprisingly, female offenders were more likely to select at least one male adult victim. Conclusions based on these data must be considered tenuous at best, considering the small numbers of victims. However, we do know that males are much more likely to be victimized than females when the female serial offender concentrates on killing adult members of only one gender. In the case of children, it is unlikely that any real gender preferences exist considering the small difference between the numbers of male and female child victims.

Table 6.7 shows the mobility classification of female offenders. Traveling serial killers are almost exclusively males who move from city to city and across state lines, killing victims at random or seeking out a specific type of victim. Due to a lack of crime data correlation, this type of offender has been recognized only in the past few years. Six traveling offenders (18%) were identified as females. Among serial killers who have at least one partner and travel from state to state, again only a small proportion involved female offenders. Seven offenders, or 20% of female killers, were classified as local killers, or serial offenders who sought out their victims within the boundaries of one state or city. The third type, the place-specific killer, repeatedly murdered her victims in the same location. Some of the common locations were nursing homes, hospitals, and private homes. Nearly two thirds of all female serial murderers were identified as place-specific.

Each mobility category was examined for the number of victims killed. Those females identified as place-specific were responsible for nearly three

TABLE 6.7 Victims of Female Serial Murderers in the United States, 1821–1988, by Mobility Classification

	NUMBER OF VICTIMS	PERCENTAGE OF VICTIMS	NUMBER OF CASES	NUMBER OF OFFENDERS	PERCENTAGE OF OFFENDERS	AVERAGE NUMBER OF VICTIMS PER OFFENDER	AVERAGE NUMBER OF VICTIMS PER CASE
Total	261–471	100	31	34	100	8–14	8–15
Traveling	42–59	13–16	6	6	18	7–10	7–10
Local	34–63	13	5	7	20	5–9	7–13
Place-specific	185–349	71–74	20	21	62	9–17	9–17

quarters of the homicides. Although those offenders classified as traveling or local killed similar numbers of victims per case, place-specific offenders murdered more victims per case and per offender. Sixty-two percent of all female offenders were categorized as place-specific whereas only 20% of all male offenders followed this same pattern. Since 1975 half of the female offenders were classified as place-specific. One reason they killed more victims was because they went undetected for longer periods of time; because the murders occurred in one place, there was less likelihood of detection. In addition, one typically does not imagine a serial murderer as a mother, a grandmother or the nice lady next door. The rarity of such murders compared with other types of homicides may have influenced the length of time required to apprehend female serial offenders. Profile 6-2, which describes the case of nurse Terri Rachals, illustrates this point.

Homicides in general often have victims who place themselves in precarious positions, such as domestic disputes, or who provoke the attack by striking the first blow. As mentioned earlier, many victims play a prominent role in their own demise by facilitating the encounter with the offender (see Chapter 5). Generally, victims of serial murder played little or no part in their own deaths. Female offenders (91%) almost exclusively killed victims (96%) who were categorized as low facilitation homicides (the victims played a small role, if any, in their own deaths).

Methods and Motives

Female offenders, as indicated in Table 6.8, were most likely to use poisons at least some of the time to kill their victims. Some of the poisons administered to induce death quickly or gradually were large doses of potassium chloride, which attacks the heart, and strychnine or arsenic. Arsenic was popular for hundreds of years as a method of murder. In the 1800s arsenic could be purchased at any chemist's shop and was commonly used in small quantities by women to improve their facial complexions. Male customers often purchased arsenic to use in their gardens to kill rats and mice. As Gerald Sparrow noted in his book *Women Who Murder* (1970), "the poison eaters" regularly ingested arsenic to improve their attractiveness. The *Chambers Journal* and *Black Woods Magazine*, published during the 1850s, carried a series of articles on the poison eaters.

It is not generally known that eating poison is actually practiced in more countries than one. In some districts of Lower Austria and in Styria, as far as the borders of Hungary, the strange habit of eating arsenic is quite common. The peasantry in particular are given to it. They obtain it under the name of Hedri from the traveling hucksters and gatherers of herbs, who get it from the glass blowers, or purchase it from cow-doctors, quacks or mountebanks. The poison eaters have a two-fold aim in their dangerous enjoyment: one of which is to obtain a fresh healthy

TABLE 6.8 Methods and Motives of Female Serial Murderers in the United States, 1821–1988

METHOD		MOTIVE	
Some poison	52%	Money sometimes	53%
Poison only	45%	Money only	41%
Some shooting	30%	Enjoyment sometimes	38%
Some bludgeoning	27%	Revenge sometimes	9%
Some stabbing	12%	Sex sometimes	9%
Shooting only	9%	Revenge only	6%
Bludgeoning only	9%	Enjoyment only	3%
Some suffocation	9%	Sex only	3%
Some torture	9%	Perverted acts sometimes	3%
Suffocation only	6%	Combinations of the preceding motives	35%
Neglect only	3%	Other motives including: (1) drug addiction, (2) cults, (3) cover up other crimes, (4) children become a burden, feelings of being an inadequate parent, and so on	24%
Some drowning	3%		
Some torture	3%		
Combinations of the preceding methods	24%		

$N=34$

appearance, and also to acquire a degree of sexual desire. On this account gay village lads and lasses employ the dangerous agent, that they become more attractive to each other; and it is really astonishing with what favorable results their endeavors are attended, for it is just the youthful poison eaters that are, generally speaking, distinguished by a blooming complexion and an appearance of exuberant health [Sparrow, 1970, p. 88].

Sparrow goes on to describe the "miraculous cosmetic properties" found in arsenic. Thus, we see that arsenic was readily available without suspicion to anyone wanting to use it to commit murder. Although arsenic does not mix well with cold water, it is nearly undetectable in hot food and drinks, especially coffee or cocoa. The length of time required to kill a person with arsenic varies depending on such factors as the amount of poison administered and the general health of the intended victim. A large dose brings on death usually in a few hours, but death may be prolonged by using small amounts. In such cases the victim may live for several weeks or even months. Arsenic poisoning is a particularly gruesome manner of death because it causes severe and frequent vomiting coupled with intense pain. Naturally, fever, vomiting, and pain may be indicative of several maladies, so arsenic poisoning was seldom raised as a diagnosis. Once a killer was discovered and the victims exhumed, arsenic could be easily detected because it acted as

PROFILE 6-2: TERRI RACHALS
1985–1986

In March, 1986, registered nurse Terri Rachals was indicted on six counts of murder and 20 counts of aggravated assault stemming from alleged poisonings of patients at Phoebe Putney Hospital in Albany, Georgia. The grand jury accused 24-year-old Ms. Rachals of injecting 11 patients in the hospital's surgical intensive care unit with potassium chloride, causing the deaths of six of them. (Potassium chloride is a colorless chemical used in small, diluted amounts in the treatment of nearly all surgery patients. It is used in large doses by states that perform executions by injections.) Her alleged victims ranged in age from 3 to 89 years, including both males and females. All died between October 17, 1985, and February 11, 1986. The 20 incidents of aggravated assault involved nine patients (many of them received more than one injection). Most of the patients injected by Ms. Rachals did not die because they were able to receive immediate attention.

Nine patients died of cardiac arrest in November, 1985; the usual number was three to four deaths per month. The potassium levels in the bodies of several of the victims were found to be abnormally high. An investigation concluded that the only way the high potassium content in the IV line could be accounted for was through human intervention.

Nurse Rachals had worked at the hospital since 1981 and was described as an excellent, reliable surgical intensive-care nurse. There had never been any serious problems with Nurse Rachals at the hospital nor did she have any police record. Very active in her church, she sang in the choir and regularly attended Sunday School with her husband, Roger, who suffered from cerebral palsy, and was a printer at an Albany supply company. The couple resided with their two-year-old son, Chad, in a middle-class suburban Albany neighborhood. Neighbors refused to believe she could be capable of such atrocious acts.

"If you believe your mother could do it, then you'd believe that she could do it. She's not a murderer. That's the craziest thing I've ever heard," stated one neighbor. Another friend said that "Mrs. Rachals would be the last person one would suspect of harming anyone. They were just so nice, so average."

One month after the last victim died, Nurse Rachals confessed to the Georgia Bureau of Investigation that she injected five of the patients, three of whom died. Later she recanted her confession stating that she was confused at the time of her statement. Before her trial Nurse Rachals spent several months undergoing intensive psychiatric evaluation but was found competent to stand trial. The defense worked very hard to build their case around a woman who was molested as a child by her adoptive father and subsequently experienced blackouts. The father denied the molestation charges. At age 16, after five years of his alleged sexual advances, Terri moved out. The defense stressed that there were periods when she could not account for her actions because she suffered from a mental illness that caused her to do unusual things she could not remember. She reacted to stressful events by entering fugue states in which she experienced personality changes and could not recall where she had been or what she had done, said Dr. Kuglar, the superintendent of the Georgia Regional Hospital in Augusta.

Dr. Omer L. Wagoner, a licensed psychologist appointed by the court to examine Mrs. Rachals, agreed she suffered personality disorders but not a "dissociative order" and said he believed

TERRI RACHALS continued

she "thoroughly knew the difference between right and wrong." Mrs. Rachals, he stated, "believed she was relieving them (the patients) of their pain and misery" by causing their hearts to stop with potassium injections.

Because of the weight of circumstantial evidence and testimony that questioned Mrs. Rachals' state of mind at the time of the killings, she was convicted of giving an 89-year-old patient a heart-stopping chemical. She was given 17 years for her conviction, but under the State of Georgia Board of Pardons and Parole guidelines, Mrs. Rachals was eligible for parole after serving 24 months. Although she was found to be guilty and mentally ill, state psychiatrists decided she could be adequately served on an outpatient basis and was confined at the Women's Correctional Institution near Milledgeville, Georgia.

a strong preserving agent after death. Today, pure arsenic is no longer readily available, but it is often found in pesticides. We are now more likely to hear of killers, especially nurses, using potassium chloride, which is difficult to detect once the body has been prepared for burial. Succinylcholine, another relatively undetectable drug, is used as an anesthetic to relax muscles during surgery. An excessive dose inhibits the chest muscles from functioning, and the victim simply stops breathing (Helpern & Knight, 1977, p. 26). This drug was used by Nurse Genene Jones (Profile 6-3).

Poisoning was so common a method for killing that nearly half of the female offenders in this study used poison only to commit their murders.

PROFILE 6-3: GENENE JONES
1978–1982

In February, 1984, Nurse Genene Jones was sentenced to a maximum term of 99 years for the murder of 15-month-old Chelsea McClellan. Testimony showed the little girl died after injections of succinylcholine, a hard-to-detect drug that paralyzes. An expert witness stated at her trial that the drug has long been a favorite for killing because it is difficult to trace. Under Texas law, a 99-year term is equivalent to a life sentence; therefore, Ms. Jones will be eligible for parole in 20 years.

Jones was also charged with using the drug to harm six other children at a physician's office where she worked for three weeks. It is believed her motive was a need to prove there were enough sick children to justify construction of a pediatric intensive care unit in Kerrville, Texas. However, the scope of her criminal behavior also extended to a hospital in San Antonio, Texas, where she was charged with injuring at least one child. Investigators believe that as many as 46 babies and children were murdered at San Antonio hospital during the time Nurse Jones worked there. It is believed that the children were given injections that stopped their hearts. A team of experts from the Centers for Disease Control, Atlanta, Georgia, found that seven were killed by a deliberate overdose of the heart drug digoxin. Digoxin was not ruled out in at least 21 other deaths. Ms. Jones was never tried for these homicides.

Almost all these women were offenders who acted alone to kill their victims. Other female offenders resorted to more violent methods, such as shooting, bludgeoning, or stabbing. Not surprisingly, all female offenders who had an accomplice(s) used violent means to kill the majority of their victims (see Chapter 8). About one fourth of the female offenders used a combination of methods in their killings.

Female serial killers differed noticeably from their male counterparts in methods and motives. Males were much more mobile and attracted more attention than the women. Although both groups selected the powerless as victims or at least those who were easily rendered powerless, their methods of killing usually differed. Males often selected more violent means of killing, including sexually attacking and frequently mutilating the corpse. Women in this study, with a few exceptions, generally were not sexually involved with their victims nor did they kill them by particularly violent methods. These comparisons lead us toward the inevitable question of why do these women commit multiple murders?

We must begin our discussion of motives with the premise that the reality of female crime is largely unknown. Historically, female crime has been explained in terms of a biological framework. The likelihood of a woman committing a crime was believed (and many still subscribe to such interpretation) to be linked to hormonal changes, menstruation, maternity, and other physiological explanations. Only recently have theorists begun to consider social structural influences on women and crime. Of these influences, money was found to be the most common motivator to murder. This seems to contradict motives stated for homicides in general, at least at the North Carolina Correctional Center for Women in Raleigh, where John T. Kirpatrick and John A. Humphrey conducted a study of 76 women who had killed. They noted that "in order for women to kill, it had to be perceived by them as a life-threatening situation affecting their physical or emotional well-being" (*New York Times*, 1987). (But are women who kill under these circumstances really any different from women who are classified as serial killers? Although the list in Table 6.8 does show a ranking of motives, more involved explanations may exist that reflect social and cultural influences generally ignored in the epidemiology of homicide.)

At the turn of the nineteenth century, researchers involved in the study of criminal behavior leaned heavily toward a biological explanation for crime. Lombroso and Ferrero (1916) insisted that biological factors were the keys in understanding criminal behavior in women:

> We have seen that the normal woman is naturally less sensitive to pain than a man. . . . We also saw that women have many traits in common with children; that their moral sense is deficient; that they are revengeful, jealous, inclined to vengeances of a refined cruelty.

> In ordinary cases these defects are neutralized by piety, maternity, want of passion, sexual coldness, by weakness and an underdeveloped intelligence. But when a morbid activity of the physical centers intensifies the

bad qualities of women, and induces them to seek relief in evil deeds...it
is clear that the innocuous semi-criminal present in the normal woman
must be transformed into a born criminal more terrible than any man. . . .
The criminal woman is consequently a monster [pp. 150–152].

Sigmund Freud's influence was felt as psychobiological explanations for
female crime began to emerge. Pollak (1950) argued that women appeared
less often in criminal statistics because of their innate ability to deceive
others. This, according to Freud, was due to the fact that they are born sans
penis. Consequently:

> Man must achieve an erection in order to perform the sex act and will not
> be able to hide his failure...and pretense of sexual response is impos-
> sible for him, if it is lacking. Woman's body, however, permits such
> pretense to a certain degree and lack of orgasm does not prevent her
> ability to participate in the sex act. It cannot be denied that this basic
> physiological difference may well have a great influence on the degree
> of confidence which the two sexes have in the possible success of
> concealment and thus on their character pattern in this respect [1961,
> p. 10].

Gradually, other studies involving professional researchers began to
make tentative connections between female criminality and alcohol,
women's liberation, menstruation cycles, and hormonal imbalances. The
latter connections appear to have found more credence among professional
researchers.

Dr. Eva Ebin, professor of psychiatry at State University of New York,
noted that some women experience a postpartum syndrome that can cause
them to become psychotic. She observed a shift in a woman's personality
that causes her to "break" under stress. Caring for a newborn may create
stresses that the mother is not emotionally prepared to handle. In Pennsylvania in 1985 a woman killed her month-old son by tossing him into a
mountain stream, and in 1986 a West Virginia mother wrapped her newborn
child in a plastic bag and dropped her into the Shenandoah River. In both of
these instances the mothers fabricated stories of their children being kidnapped. Dr. Ebin explains these concocted stories as "a trick of the mind. It's
a dissociative reaction. It's wishful thinking that they hadn't done it. They
need to believe it in order to go on" (*Washington Post*, 1988).

Resnick (1970) reported that two thirds of the mothers who commit
felicide (the killing of a child over 24 hours old) suffer from various forms of
psychosis, such as severe depression, and that they make frequent suicide
attempts. Resnick also found that mothers who committed felicide were
motivated by altruistic reasoning—that the children were better off dead. In
addition, Rosenblatt and Greenland (1974) reported that before killing their
children, over 40% of the mothers intimated their fear or intent of killing to
friends, physicians, or social service agency personnel.

We have only recently begun to connect female crime to stress-related factors and to understand how stress affects behavior. It is believed by some experts that stress is the generic cause of many diseases, both physiological and psychological. The Kirpatrick/Humphrey study found that societal factors, such as the fact that women do not earn as much as men, could be facilitating variables in homicide. But these factors should not be considered the primary cause. More likely the cause is linked to the women's life histories and to the kinds of and the severity of the stress they encountered. Nearly all of the women in the study came from very violent upbringings and experienced high levels of domestic violence—seeing their mothers and fathers fighting, often with weapons (*New York Times*, 1987).

In addition to witnessing conflict, several offenders in the Kirpatrick/Humphrey study were beaten or sexually abused as children. Half of the women had lost a loved one either in childhood or adulthood. "Loss is an important source of stress because not only is it stressful in itself but it also precipitates other stress, as when they have to move in with grandparents or drop out of school due to the death of a parent. . . . These are women who feel at once overpowering aloneness and simmering resentment of others" (*Ibid.*, 1987). (Christine Falling, described in Profile 6-4, appeared to have experienced many of these stressors.)

The available biographical data on female serial murderers also indicate several instances of broken homes, displaced children, and other emotionally traumatic experiences. However, we must again proceed with caution in suggesting that stress explains all such criminal behavior. Our society includes many victims of child abuse of all varieties, as well as children who are displaced or who experience other traumas or stresses, who do not become murderers or criminals of any type. Although there are exceptions, according to the available data female multiple murderers generally do not appear to have experienced more traumas as children than other criminals or perhaps even noncriminals. A critical factor may be their inability as children or as adults to constructively deal with their own sense of victimization. This inability may be fostered by significant others, strangers, and the various societal institutions that affect everyone to varying degrees. Simply because we ascertain that children who later become mass murderesses have been exposed to the same traumatizations that other children experience does not mean they are able to cope with those experiences in similar fashions.

If we are to accept the taxonomy of motives in Table 6-8, then women's motives for serial murder appear to center on financial security, revenge, enjoyment, and sexual stimulation. Those who murdered children seemed to display little or no psychosis. Although data are limited regarding biographical information, several cases in my study revealed histories of child abuse—including sexual molestation, prostitution, and neglect—extreme poverty, and unstable marital relationships.

PROFILE 6-4: CHRISTINE FALLING
1980–1982

Nineteen-year-old Christine was a high school dropout with the vocabulary of a sixth grader. Obese, epileptic, and intellectually stifled, Christine lived in Perry, a town in southern Florida where poverty is a way of life. She had been born into an unstable family; her mother, Ann, was only 16 and already had two children, and her father, Tom, age 65, worked in the woods. Frequently her mother would leave for periods of time and Tom would have to care for the children. Eventually Christine and her sister were adopted by a couple named Falling. Conflict quickly generated between the couple and the two girls, resulting in frequent family fights. Finally at age nine, Christine and her sister were placed in a children's refuge near Orlando.

Christine's personality profile by age nine indicated some potentially serious problems. She had been known on more than one occasion to torture animals, such as cats, by throwing them high into the air or wringing their necks. She later explained this behavior by saying she was trying to find out if cats really had nine lives. Staff members at the refuge described her as a compulsive liar and thief, a child who would break rules to gain attention. She frequently was the brunt of her peers' jokes because of her obesity and dull-wittedness. After continuing problems with the Falling family, Christine, now 12, left in search of her mother near Blountstown, Florida. She found her mother and then married a man in his mid-20s. After six weeks of fighting, the marriage ended. A year later she began making frequent visits to the hospital claiming an array of problems and ills. During this two-year period, the hospital recorded at least 50 visits from Christine.

Christine began baby-sitting and gained a reputation as one who loved children, especially babies, and was very good at caring for them. Unfortunately, no one knew what methods Christine used to quiet the infants. Two-year-old Cassidy "Muffin" Johnson became her first victim on February 25, 1980. One year later four-year-old Jeffrey M. Davis succumbed to Christine's loving care. Three days later, while the funeral was being held for the boy, Christine was caring for two-year-old Joseph, a cousin to the victim. He also died while sleeping, his parents still at the funeral. In one year, three children died strange and unexpected deaths while in the care of the young baby-sitter. Always distraught at the tragic deaths, Christine appeared as baffled as everyone else about the causes of death. Physicians explored a variety of medical explanations but no one was ever quite sure what had happened.

Christine decided to stay away from children for a while and became a housekeeper for 77-year-old William Swindle. The day she began caring for him, Mr. Swindle was found dead on his kitchen floor. No autopsy was performed, and it was assumed he died of natural causes. Christine next baby-sat eight-month-old Jennifer Y. Daniels, the daughter of her stepsister. Mrs. Daniels had left Jennifer momentarily with Christine while she went into a store. On her return Christine announced the child had just stopped breathing. Cause of death was listed as sudden infant death syndrome.

In 1982, after moving back to Blountstown, Christine was asked to baby-sit ten-week-old Travis D. Coleman. He too, died in his sleep. Five deaths and several near-death situations all with small children, all in two and one half years, all in the care of the same person, finally caused people to start questioning Christine. To avoid the death penalty, she eventually con-

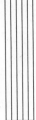

CHRISTINE FALLING continued

fessed in a plea bargain to killing Muffin, Jennifer, and Travis. Christine described her method of killing as "smotheration" and stated in her confession: "I love young'uns. I don't know why I done what I done. . . . The way I done it, I saw it done on TV shows. I had my own way, though. Simple and easy. No one would hear them scream."

Christine was given a life sentence and will not be eligible for parole until the year 2007. She is presently incarcerated in Florida's Broward Correctional Institution.

Psychopathology of Female Offenders

Female serial murderers appear to exhibit traits similar to those of male serial murderers in terms of psychopathology. For example, the women tended to be insincere, amoral, impulsive, prone to exercise manipulative charisma and superficial charm, without conscience, and with little insight, since they failed to learn from their mistakes. Guze (1976) concluded from a 15-year longitudinal study of female felons in prison that psychopathology was the most frequent personality diagnosis for these offenders. Cleckley (1976), in his text *The Mask of Sanity*, describes psychopaths as irresponsible, unpredictable, pathological liars who display a flagrant disregard for truth. He concluded that psychopaths are of above-average intelligence but are self-destructive in that they frequently involve themselves in high-risk ventures, generally blame others for their failures, and have no long-range goals. They are able to mimic the behavior of others but carry no actual burden of remorse for their crimes. It is unlikely that every psychopath possesses all of these characteristics or that he or she constantly exhibits any of these traits. Instead, psychopathic behavior may be cyclical, like the Dr. Jekyll/Mr. Hyde syndrome. Although fewer in numbers, female serial killers must be considered to be as lethal as their male counterparts. Jane Toppan, from the witness stand at her trial for murder, stated: "This is my ambition—to have killed more people—more helpless people—than any man or woman has ever killed." These predominately stay-at-home killers operate carefully and inconspicuously and may avoid detection for several years. One hopes that future research will focus more attention on exploring the psychopathology of female offenders. We have only begun to explore their motivational dynamics.

Sentencing Female Offenders

To some extent our society has become increasingly desensitized to death. The media often provide a distortion of reality that is pervasive throughout much of our movie industry. The "splatter movies" with their endless sequels perpetuate bizarre images of those who kill. Some of these movies surpass our own worst nightmares. However, although male offenders have received media profiling that incites fear and paranoia in our communities, women fail to receive similar caricaturization. Even those few female killers who have received national attention do not instill the fear that male killers do. Certainly, this is not unexpected, because males do most of the killing and are usually responsible for most of the sadistic and perverted acts committed against victims. Our underestimation of the ability of women to commit murders as heinous as those that males commit may be a factor in the perceived differential treatment of women in the criminal justice system. [Consider the monikers given by the media to female serial murderers (Table 6.9).]

Historically, female offenders in this study received monikers that were either neutral or trivializing in their relationship to the crimes committed. The "Beautiful Blonde Killer," the "Giggling Grandma," and "Old Shoe Box Annie" are stereotypic, patronizing, and sexist. Conversely, males have received some of the most fear-inducing names imaginable, such as "The Strangler," "The Ripper," "The Night Stalker," "The Moon Maniac," and so on. The distinction appears to be based on the method of killing and the degree of violence and viciousness displayed by the killer. Even in those cases in which males were accomplices to females in serial murder the moniker seemed to be influenced: for instance "The Bloody Benders" and "The Lonely Hearts Killer." Apparently, not only are we less likely to suspect female offenders but also less likely to accord them the same degree of dangerousness as we do males. In reality some of these female offenders have killed several more victims than many of their male counterparts. Part

TABLE 6.9 Monikers of Selected Female Offenders

YEAR BEGAN KILLING	NUMBER OF VICTIMS	NAME
1864	12–42	Queen Poisoner/Borgia of Connecticut
1872	14	The Bloody Benders/The Hell Benders
1881	8+	Borgia of Somerville
1901	27	Sister Amy
1901	16–20	Belle of Indiana/Lady Bluebeard
1914	11+	Mrs. Bluebeard/Polish Borgia
1920	3+	Old Shoebox Annie
1925	11–16	Giggling Grandma
1925	3	Borgia of America
1931	15	Beautiful Blonde Killer
1932	14	Suicide Sal
1949	3–20	Lonely Hearts Killer
1964	5	Grandma
1975	2+	Black Widow

of this disparity in treatment of offenders can be traced to the writings of Pollak (1950) and W. I. Thomas (1907, 1923). Women were observed to be accorded differential treatment because of the "chivalry" of a system dominated by men. Women were also treated more "humanely" because they were not considered dangerous. From these earlier writings there appears to have been some confusion about the assignation of causes. Women were viewed as being deceptive, manipulative, void of emotion. Stereotyping women in general with these qualities was overkill to say the least. Closer to the truth, we may attribute these qualities to some women and some men as psychopathic tendencies. Regardless of gender, those people who manifest psychopathic qualities are much more likely to inflict harm on society than are members of the general population.

The perception of violence may play an important role in our treatment of female offenders. We seem to be much more uncomfortable and less willing to execute women than men. Table 6.10 indicates by percentage the adjudication of women in this study. No more than 15% of the female offenders were executed or await execution. Forty percent received life in prison, whereas 27% received shorter sentences or were sent to mental institutions. My intent here is not to point out a lack of punishment but to underscore the apparent preferential or discriminatory treatment experienced by female offenders.

Summary

We have examined the cases of several females identified as serial killers. Although they appear to be increasing in absolute numbers, they still represent only a small portion of serial murder cases. In America, this type of offender was noted even in the early nineteenth century but has only recently begun to receive media attention.

TABLE 6.10 Adjudication of Female Offenders*

STATUS	PERCENTAGE
Never apprehended	12
Killed by police	3
Confined in mental hospital	9
Given some prison time	18
Given life in prison	40
Death row	3
Executed	12
Pending	3
	100

*$N=33$

Most female serial killers acted alone. Those who had male partners were much more likely to use violence in killing their victims, whereas those who acted alone often used poisons. Females in this study appear to kill more victims on the average than their male counterparts. Because of the relatively small number of female offenders, however, such findings are more likely to raise suspicions than encourage agreement. The women, on the average, tended to be slightly older than the male offenders. The most likely occupational category for females was homemaker, which earned them the dubious moniker of "black widow." Several offenders were also categorized as nurses, or "angels of death." Very few females were known to have criminal records and, with one exception, all were white.

Over the past few years, female offenders killed fewer family members while increasingly targeting strangers. Female offenders who acted alone were more likely to kill hospital and nursing home patients than female offenders with accomplices. Husbands were the primary target of offenders who targeted family members. Most offenders murdered at least one adult, and a majority also killed at least one child. Female children were more prone to be victimized than male children. Since 1975, at least half of all female offenders were considered to be place-specific, which may help explain why they remain relatively obscure. Historically, poison has been the most commonly selected mode of killing for female offenders, who were less inclined to employ violent methods than male offenders were. Most females had experienced various forms of abuse as children, including sexual abuse and broken homes. Many appeared to be motivated to kill for financial gain, yet the literature suggests more complex explanations of psychopathology. Similar to their male counterparts, several of these females appeared to have developed socio-psychopathic personalities. Compared with male offenders, female serial killers in this study appeared to have been differentially treated by the media and the criminal justice system.

CHAPTER 7

The Male Serial Murderer

Victims of female serial killers continue to be found in boarding houses, homes for the elderly, hospitals, and private homes. However, more victims will be found in wooded areas, ravines, and other isolated areas—victims of male serial killers. Usually these victims die much more violently. The personalized violence inflicted on helpless victims has no boundaries or limitations to which offenders subscribe. For example, during 1990, a supposed male serial killer in San Diego, California, murdered at least five young women. One of the victims, a 20-year-old San Diego University student, was stabbed more than 50 times. That same year five students were stabbed to death in Gainesville, Florida, with a surgical instrument. One of the women was decapitated. Male serial killers wage their own personal wars against humanity, indifferent to the lives of others in their constant quest for control. Charles Starkweather, after his killing spree, casually observed "shooting people was, I guess, a kind of a thrill. It brought out something" (Reinhardt, 1960, p. 78). Edmund Kemper, reminiscing about the start of his killing career, remarked "I just wondered how it would be to shoot grandma."

Male serial killers represent the darkest, most sinister side of human existence, yet we are fascinated to read about them, to watch them portrayed in movies and learn of their obscenities. They are especially dangerous because we understand so little about their actual motivations, their lives and personalities. We search for "commonality" to help create descriptive parameters and taxonomies, yet the horror they create distorts their profiles, actual body counts, and inevitably our perception of them. What sort of person can quietly live with the knowledge that 25 decomposing bodies lie under the floor boards of his house? Masters (1986) chronicled the life of Dennis Nilsen, a British serial killer and necrophile, and described how involved the murderer became with his victims after death. They were a source of company for him. In one instance, Nilsen stored the body of a young male under his floor and frequently would retrieve him for an evening's entertainment. This included propping the boy in a chair next to Nilsen, who carried on conversations, bathing him, watching television "together" and performing sexual acts on the decomposing child.

Other serial killers have sex with their victims just before or immediately after death. Some are known for their habits of collecting trophies or souvenirs. For example, when the police arrived, Gary Heidnik was found to have several pounds of human flesh stored in his freezer while other body parts were simmering in a stew pot. Others collected lingerie, shoes, hats, and other wearing apparel. Some serial killers do not have any apparent sexual involvement with the victims, but their method of killing is so bizarre one can only speculate as to their actual motivations.

It is these bizarre killings that have contributed to the often distorted caricaturizations of serial offenders during the past 100 years.

Emergence of Male Serial Murderers

Intrigue and horror have generated several peculiar and chilling monikers for male killers since the mid 1800s. The following names are a sampling of monikers given to male offenders who acted alone.*

Monikers Given to Male Serial Killers in the United States

1846–1871	Edward H. Rulloff	The Educated Murderer
1874–1909	James P. Miller	"Deacon" Jim
1879	Stephen Lee Richards	Nebraska Fiend
1890–1905	Johann Otto Hoch	Bluebeard
1892–1896	Harry Howard Holmes	The Torture Doctor
1895	William H. T. Durrant	Demon of the Belfry
1910–1920	James P. Watson	Bluebeard
1910–1934	Albert Fish	The Cannibal The Moon Maniac
1911–1919	Joseph Mumfre	New Orleans Axeman
1921–1931	Harry Powers (a.k.a. Herman Drenth)	American Bluebeard
1926–1927	Earle L. Nelson	The Gorilla Murderer
1933–1935	Major Raymond Lisemba	Rattlesnake Lisemba
1942–1947	Jake Bird	Tacoma Axe Killer
1945–1946	William George Heirens	The Lipstick Murderer
1949	Harvey Louis Carignan	The Want Ad Killer
1957–1960	Melvin David Rees	Sex Beast
1958–1983	Richard F. Biegenwald	The Thrill Killer
1962–1964	Albert Henry DeSalvo	The Measuring Man The Green Man The Boston Strangler
1964–1965	Charles H. Schmid	Pied Piper of Tucson
1964–1973	Edmund Emil Kemper III	Coed Killer

(continued)

*Monikers for team killers are given in Chapter 8.

Monikers Given to Male Serial Killers in the United States *(continued)*

1965	Posteal Laskey	Cincinnati Strangler
1967–1969	John N. Collins	Coed Murderer
1970	Richard Macek	The Mad Biter
1970–1987	Donald Harvey	Angel of Death
1972–1978	John Wayne Gacy	Killer Clown
1974–1975	Vaughn Greenwood	Skid Row Slasher
1974–1978	Theodore Robert Bundy	Ted
1976–1977	David R. Berkowitz	Son of Sam .44-Caliber Killer
1977–1978	Carlton Gary	Stocking Strangler
1977–1980	Richard Cottingham	The Ripper Jekyll/Hyde
1980–1981	David Carpenter	Trailside Killer
1980–1982	Randall Woodfield	The I-5 Killer
1981–1982	Coral Eugene Watts	Sunday Morning Slasher
1984	Cleo Green	Red Demon
1985	Richard Ramirez	Night Stalker
1987	Richard Angelo	Angel of Death

One third of all males since 1800 in my study earned some type of moniker. Unlike the monikers for female serial killers, most names for males were designed to create an aura of mystery and fascination. Some male serial killers, due to extended killing careers or notoriety, earned more than one name.

Male serial killers have murdered men, women, children, the elderly, prostitutes, hitchhikers, transients, and patients. Each case brought with it unique situations, methods, weapons and motivations. Following World War II an increase in serial murders began that sharply accelerated during the late 60s and 70s. This rather dramatic "emergence" began to attract national attention in the mid to late 1970s. During the 1980s serial murder became an increasing concern for law enforcement professionals and an important research area for social scientists. Of the 169 male offenders in this study, 88% began their killings since the year 1900 (Figure 7.1). Between 1900 and 1924, 7% of offenders appeared; 8% between 1925 and 1949; 36% between 1950 and 1974; and 37% between 1975 and 1988. More offenders were identified in the 13-year time frame between 1975 and 1988 than during any previous 25-year span.

The causes have yet to be determined as to the actual reason for the sharp rise in serial homicides. In brief, some of these causes include (1) a belief in the emergence of a new breed of predatory criminal, (2) previous underreporting of such homicides, (3) self-fulfilling prophecy—you find what you expect to find by focusing specifically on serial killing, (4) incon-

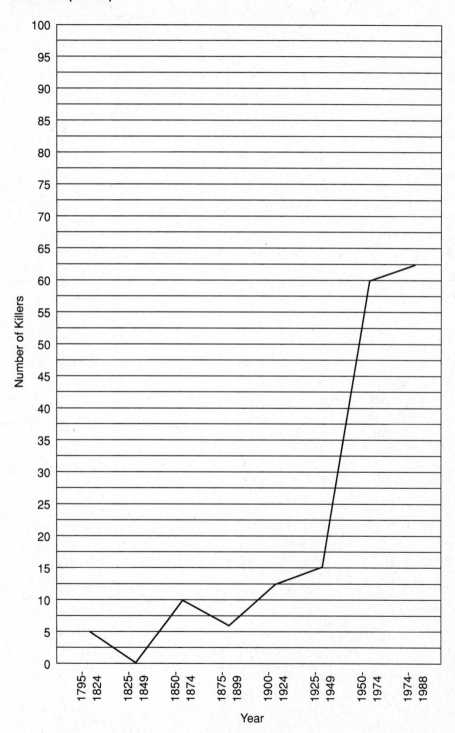

FIGURE 7.1 Frequency Distribution of Male Serial Murderers in the United States, 1795–1988 (N=169)

sistency in defining the phenomenon, (5) the media's proliferation of "splatter" and "snuff" movies, (6) pornography depicting violence and other sadoerotic material, (7) a belief that changes in the economy are connected to surges of violent behavior, and (8) a feminist belief that serial killing is an extreme form of male domination of women based on patriarchy. Whatever the reasons for the apparent surge, we still must sort through and evaluate each one.

The proliferation of serial murder cases has been experienced in varying degrees by most states. It is unlikely that any states have not dealt with at least one or two cases in the past two decades. As far as male offenders in this study are concerned, Maine, South Dakota, Hawaii, and Iowa were not found to have any particularly noted cases of serial murder (Table 7.1). However, in all probability, cases have occurred in these states but were not officially recorded, or they required a more thorough search to identify them.

California by far surpasses any other state in identified cases. This high number may be explained in part by the pattern of high mobility of people relocating to or exiting the state. Also, many serial killings occur in densely populated areas. Note that the second category of states includes some highly populated areas. As mentioned earlier, serial murders can occur anywhere, but anonymity is more likely among crowds of strangers, and the

TABLE 7.1 Rank Order Distribution of Cases Involving Male Offenders Across the United States, 1795–1988

STATE			NUMBER OF CASES IN WHICH ONE OR MORE VICTIMS WERE KILLED
California			47
New York Illinois Florida Ohio Washington			10–19
Oregon Georgia Michigan Tennessee Pennsylvania Utah Indiana	Louisiana New Jersey Colorado Virginia Alabama Kansas Kentucky		5–9
Massachusetts Connecticut Wisconsin Oklahoma Nevada Maryland Alaska Arkansas	Missouri Arizona Vermont New Hampshire Nebraska West Virginia Mississippi New Mexico	Idaho Delaware North Dakota Minnesota Wyoming South Carolina Rhode Island Montana District of Columbia	1–4

probability is greater for more randomized killings in large cities than in small ones. Even these explanations, however, do not fully explain the wide disparity between California and other states.

In this study, males were responsible for 88% (140 cases) of all serial murder cases. In examining the age of offenders at the start of their killing careers, male offenders tended to be in their late 20s, with the average age at approximately 28.5 years. Eighty-five percent of male offenders were white, 13% black, 1% Hispanic, and 1% Asian ($N = 163$ offenders).

Most of the 21 cases involving male black offenders were documented in recent years. Given the growing concentration of blacks in several major U.S. cities coupled with the plight and blight of urbanization that has especially affected black people, we should not be surprised to see the "emergence" of the black serial killer. Some of the outward motivations for killing may appear different for blacks, including poverty and various forms of discrimination, but the final product will be the same. Given the amount of "lag time" between the time a phenomenon begins and the time it is recognized by the community, eventually black serial killers may be as common as white male serial killers.

Serial murder in this study generally remained intraracial, but recent cases such as the Stocking Strangler (see Profile 7-1) in Columbus, Georgia, and the black serial killer in Jackson, Mississippi, who murdered whites, suggest that racial boundaries are not sacred. Rarely, however, do blacks and whites team up as accomplices in serial killing.

PROFILE 7-1: CARLTON GARY
1977–1978

Between September 16, 1977, and April 20, 1978, seven elderly white females were strangled to death in their homes in Columbus, Georgia. Two attempted murders of elderly women also occurred during this period of time. Eventually Carlton Gary, 34, "The Stocking Strangler," was arrested and charged with three of the homicides. Initially, Gary admitted he was involved in all seven cases, but later he insisted that he was only present and did not participate in the murders. He was simply there to burglarize the residences, claimed Gary, but his history of crime seemed to suggest otherwise. His police record revealed a history of crimes involving robbing fast food restaurants and steak houses in South Carolina, Georgia, and Florida. In 1970 he had been charged with the rob-

bery, rape, and murder of an elderly woman in New York. He plea bargained his way out by testifying against his partner.

Gary is described as a charmer, a ladies' man, very intelligent, and a "chronic talker." It was not until 1984 that police received a tip about a stolen gun that eventually linked Gary to the homicides. After his arrest he seemed to enjoy the notoriety he gained so quickly. Eventually he attempted escape and when that failed he tried to kill himself. As the trial date drew closer Gary attempted to feign mental illness but was unable to convince anyone.

Raised in a home without a father and then sent to his grandmother's house when his mother left, Gary had little home life. He dropped out of school

CARLTON GARY continued

in 1966, married, and was soon arrested for auto burglary. He and his wife moved to New York and started raising two children while Gary worked as a janitor and played drums in a band. By 1970 Gary had deserted his wife and children. His former wife described Gary as "gentle, kind, and dangerous." Gary traveled around under several aliases until he became involved in the murder of 74-year-old Nellie Farmer in New York.

Gary escaped from prison in New York one month before the stranglings began in Georgia, where he had moved to hide out. In 1979, after the killings in Georgia had ceased, he was arrested for a series of robberies in South Carolina and sent to prison for 21 years. Gary again escaped from prison in 1984, when he walked away from Goodman Correctional Institute in South Carolina, and headed to Florida to see his wife. Shortly afterward, Gary was arrested as the "Strangler."

Gary was found guilty of three of the Stocking Strangler cases, although a definite pattern had been established in the other cases and some palm prints had been found. He was convicted of murder, rape, and burglary in all three cases and sentenced to death for the crimes.

Carlton Gary's Victims

DATE OF MURDER	NAME	AGE	MARITAL STATUS	METHOD	SEXUAL ASSAULT
9/16/77	Mary F. Jackson	59	Widow	Strangulation	Possible
9/25/77	Jean Dimenstein	71	Single	Strangulation	Yes
10/21/77	Florence Scheible*	89	Widow	Strangulation	Yes
10/25/77	Martha Thurmond*	69	Widow	Strangulation	Yes
12/28/77	Kathleen Woodruff*	74	Widow	Strangulation	No
2/12/78	Mildred D. Borom	78	Widow	Strangulation	Possible
4/20/78	Janet T. Cofer	61	Widow	Strangulation	Possible

*Gary officially charged with the murders.

Mobility and Victimization

Half of all male offenders were categorized as local serial killers—those who stayed within the general area of a city or county but did not carry on their killing patterns in more than one state (Table 7.2). Less than one third of all male offenders killed victims in more than one state, and 20% used their own homes or places of employment as killing sites. These data refute the stereotype that serial killers are men who primarily travel across the country in search of victims. Based on cases examined here, most offenders (70%) never killed outside the state in which they began their killing careers.

By narrowing the time frame to the most recent years, when traveling would be expected to be at its highest rate, the percentage of offenders

TABLE 7.2 Victims of Male Offenders in the United States 1795–1988 by Mobility Classification

MOBILITY CLASSIFICATION OF KILLERS	(1795–1988) PERCENTAGE OF VICTIMS (N=1322–1847)	(1795–1988) PERCENTAGE OF OFFENDERS (N=169)	(1975–1988) PERCENTAGE OF VICTIMS (N=392–540)	(1975–1988) PERCENTAGE OF OFFENDERS (N=63)
Total	100	100	100	100
Traveling	36–42	30	34–38	24
Local	31–34	50	47–49	62
Place-specific	27–30	20	16–17	14

moving from state to state actually decreased. Similarly, the number of male killers identified as place-specific declined noticeably. In contrast, the number of offenders killing locally increased markedly from 1975 to 1988. Again, this increase may be in part due to rapid urbanization and a lessening need to travel in order to maintain anonymity. Finding, killing, and disposing of victims in and around cities may appeal to offenders in their quest to avoid detection.

Overall, the greatest percentage of victims were killed by traveling offenders, but the difference between this number and that killed by local killers is not large. Similarly, the difference between numbers of victims of local offenders and place-specific killers is relatively small. In recent years, nearly half of all victims were murdered by local killers. A slight decrease was noted in the number of victims of traveling offenders. The greatest decline in victims involved place-specific offenders. Proportionately, a shift appears to have occurred in the mobility type of offender responsible for the greatest percentage of victims. Male offenders who roamed the streets of U.S. cities and towns and remained relatively close to their killing sites appear to have been the most common type of serial murderer in recent years (see Profile 7-2).

PROFILE 7-2: ROBERT JOE LONG
1984

During an eight-month period in 1984, at least ten young women ranging in age from 18 to 28 were abducted in the Tampa Bay, Florida area. Each victim was bound, sexually assaulted, and then murdered. The victims, most of whom were prostitutes, were strangled, although one had her throat cut and another died from gunshot. The per-petrator, Robert Long, 31, generally drove his car around an area frequented by prostitutes and then lured his victims into his vehicle. Long, who was on probation for assault, was divorced and unemployed. He experienced sadistic pleasure from fashioning a collar and leash from rope and using them on his victims. Shortly before his capture, Long

ROBERT JOE LONG continued

abducted Lisa McVey from a doughnut shop in Tampa. He took her to an apartment and subjected her to 26 hours of sexual assault and then released her. The information she provided allowed police from three jurisdictions to "zero in" on Robert Joe Long. The impressive forensic work involving the comparison of his clothing fibers, carpet fibers, semen, tire treads, ligature marks, and rope knots influenced Long to make a full confes-

sion. Fiber evidence alone linked most of Long's victims to his vehicle. Long pled guilty in a plea-bargain arrangement to eight of the homicides and the abduction and rape of Lisa McVey. He received 26 life sentences, seven requiring no parole for 25 years. Long then received two separate death sentences for the murders of Virginia Johnson and Michelle Simms. He now sits on death row in Florida (Terry and Malone, 1987).

Robert Long's Victims

DATE VICTIM MISSING	DATE VICTIM FOUND	NAME	AGE	OCCUPATION	METHOD	MUTILATION
5/10/84	5/13/84	Ngeun Thi Long	20	Exotic dancer	Strangulation	Bludgeoned
5/25/84	5/27/84	Michelle Simms	22	Prostitute	Cut throat	Head bludgeoned
6/8/84	6/24/84	Elizabeth Loundeback	22	Factory worker	Unknown	Unknown
10/1/84	10/7/84	Chanel Williams	18	Prostitute	Gunshot wound to head	Neck puncture
10/13/84	10/14/84	Karen Dinsfriend	28	Prostitute	Strangulation	Head bludgeoned
9/31/84	10/31/84	Kimberly Hopps	20s	Prostitute	Unknown	Unknown
10/15/84	10/16/84	Virginia Johnson	18	Waitress/ prostitute	Strangulation	Unknown
11/9/84	11/12/84	Kim Swann	21	Student/ nude dancer	Strangulation	No
9/7/84	11/16/84	Vicky Elliot	21	Waitress	Strangulation	Unknown
3/28/84	11/22/84	Artis Wick	18	Unknown	Unknown	Unknown

Data on offenders were also examined relative to mobility and the average number of victims killed by each offender (Table 7.3). Overall, male offenders identified as place-specific were reported to have killed on the average more victims each than other mobility types did. This suggests that killing at home or work offered perhaps a greater degree of "invisibility." Another explanation for the high body counts of place-specific male serial killers may involve the type of victims targeted by these killers.

TABLE 7.3 Average Number of Victims by Mobility Classification of Male Offenders, 1795–1988

MOBILITY	(1795–1988) AVERAGE NUMBER OF VICTIMS PER OFFENDER (N=169)	(1975–1988) AVERAGE NUMBER OF VICTIMS PER OFFENDER (N=63)
Traveling	9–15	9–14
Local	5–7	5–6
Place-specific	12–15	7–9

Traveling offenders, on the average, killed nearly as many victims as place-specific offenders. By contrast, local offenders each killed relatively few numbers of victims. In recent years, as illustrated in Table 7-3, the victim-offender averages remained relatively stable for both traveling and local mobility types. Place-specific offenders, however, appeared to have killed fewer numbers of victims in recent years than in earlier ones. This could simply mean that reporting of body counts in recent years has become more accurate. For example, in several historical accounts H. H. Holmes was reported to have killed at least 200 women in Chicago in his "Murder Castle" during the late 1800s. However, a report citing police investigations indicated a body count of 27 victims. Clearly, cases with large body counts should always be critically examined. Often high victim counts are more the result of sensationalism than what actually occurred. Certainly high victim counts are possible but they should always be questioned.

In summarizing the connection between mobility and victimization, it appears that traveling offenders in recent years killed the greatest number of victims each. This helps explain the media stereotype of serial killers in recent years—a male who is extremely mobile. Although traveling offenders were responsible for many victims, on the average most serial killers in recent years have been local offenders. These killers were much more common than traveling killers but did not appear to have each killed as many victims. Those few offenders who were categorized as place-specific since 1975 appear to have killed more victims each than the local types but fewer than killers classified as traveling types. Also, the data in this study indicate that local offenders as a group are responsible for the greatest total number of victims.

Place-specific cases often receive limited press coverage unless they involve high body counts and the victims died violently. For example, most Americans know who Ted Bundy was but have never heard of Donald Harvey (Profile 7-3). This can be partially explained by the types of victims selected. Harvey quietly poisoned and suffocated male hospital patients, whereas Bundy brutally tortured and sexually mutilated young females.

PROFILE 7-3: DONALD HARVEY
1970–1987

Donald Harvey, "The Angel of Death," started killing when he turned 18 and began working as a nurse's aide at Mary Mount Hospital in Laurel County, Kentucky. He first killed an aunt, then committed what he referred to as "accidental homicides" followed by ten more patient deaths—a total of 13 dead in ten months. Some were suffocated, others had their oxygen supply shut off, and one victim died when Harvey shoved a wire coat hanger up his catheter tube, tearing his bladder.

Harvey then joined the Air Force where he attempted suicide on two occasions. Unable to cope, he was discharged after only nine months of service, but he continued to receive psychiatric care. In 1975 he joined the nursing staff at the Veterans Administration Hospital in Cincinnati, Ohio. During a two-year period he is believed to have murdered another 17 patients. The remaining eight years at the hospital were spent working as an autopsy assistant in the morgue. Being exposed to death and corpses seemed to satisfy Harvey, and apparently he killed no one during this time. In 1985 he was asked to resign on discovery of a gun, books on the occult, syringes, and slides of human tissue in his hospital locker.

He then joined the staff at Drake Hospital, also in Cincinnati, without anyone ever checking his references. Most of the patients at Drake were the elderly and the terminally ill. Using cyanide, arsenic, and sometimes injections of cleaning fluids, Harvey was able to kill at least 21 victims in a two-year period. When he had no poison for their food or IVs, Harvey suffocated his victims. Harvey later referred to his actions as mercy killings. He had become the angel of death and held the power over who would live and who must die. He finally confessed when investigators discovered large amounts of cyanide in the stomach of a victim. This final victim brought Harvey's total number of homicides to between 54 and 58. Almost all his victims were male; among his possessions police discovered a list of victims yet to be killed by Harvey. One of his female co-workers had hepatitis serum poured into her coffee by Harvey but miraculously survived her ordeal. Harvey also slowly poisoned his roommate only to nurse him back to health.

During his confession, Harvey explained that during a 13-year period, starting when he was five years old, he had been subjected to sexual molestation by an uncle and a male neighbor. He did not believe that this frequent molestation had anything to do with the fact that almost all his victims were helpless males, older than himself; nor did he feel it had anything to do with the fact he was a homosexual. He claimed to be a compassionate, caring person, which seemed to be validated by his fellow workers. They found Harvey to be dedicated, polite, and a good colleague. The courts found Harvey to be sane under law and competent to stand trial.

Harvey gave his confession only after being allowed to plea bargain and thereby escape the death penalty. Dozens of bodies were exhumed, and the victims were found to have died as Harvey described. Without remorse or guilt, Harvey received three consecutive life sentences and will not be eligible for parole until he has served at least 60 years. He was also fined $270,000 and received a life sentence for the murders in Kentucky.

Victims

As mentioned earlier, findings from this study support the belief that serial murder involves primarily stranger-to-stranger violence. Overall, over two thirds of all male offenders since 1975 killed at least one stranger (Table 7.4). The killing of family and acquaintances by male serial killers all but disappeared in recent years, Although male offenders killed a large variety of strangers, they appeared to have their preferences. Table 7.5 provides a rank order (according to frequency of victimization) of strangers, acquaintances, and family victims sought out by offenders.

Young females, especially if they were alone, ranked the highest in general preference of offenders. Of this category, prostitutes appeared to be the most readily accessible victims who could also be easily disposed of. However, many women who never engaged in prostitution were also victimized. Hitchhikers, students walking alone, women living alone or seeking employment, and women engaged in certain professions and jobs (such as nurses, models, and waitresses) sometimes or frequently increased their risk factor by associating with total strangers. Females who had lifestyles or employment that tended to bring them into contact with strangers appeared to increase their chances of being victimized. (Prostitutes and hitchhikers were at the highest level of risk.) In some cases the community was aware that a serial killer was operating in the area. Yet, some women would continue to take risks because, as Edmund Kemper, serial killer "extraordinaire," pointed out, "They [the victims] judged me not to be the one" (Profile 7-4). This does not mean that female victims should bear culpability but that in most cases women are much more vulnerable to men than men are to women by nature of physical strength and perceived motivation to kill.

TABLE 7.4 Percentage of Male Offenders Murdering Family, Acquaintances, and Strangers in the United States, 1795–1988

RELATIONSHIP	(1795–1988) PERCENTAGE OF OFFENDERS (N=167)	(1975–1988) PERCENTAGE OF OFFENDERS (N=62)
Strangers	69	84
Strangers/acquaintances	16	15
Acquaintances	5	0
Strangers/family	3	1
Family	3	0
Acquaintances/family	2	0
All	2	0

TABLE 7.5 Rank Order of Types of Victims Selected by Male Serial Killers

A. Strangers	B. Acquaintances

1. Young females alone
    Prostitutes
    Hitchhikers
    Students
    Women at home selected randomly
    Women seeking employment
    Nurses, models, waitresses
	Young women
	People in community
	People in own group/co-workers/employers
	Neighbors
	Children
	Visitors, transients
	Schoolmates
	Patients
	Roommates

A. Strangers

1. Young females alone
    Prostitutes
    Hitchhikers
    Students
    Women at home selected randomly
    Women seeking employment
    Nurses, models, waitresses

2. Children alone
    Boys
    Girls

3. Travelers
    People in cars
    Campers

4. Young males alone
    Hitchhikers
    Skid row derelicts
    Laborers
    Military

5. Employers/business
    Gas stations
    Fast food outlets

6. Elderly alone
    Female
    Male

7. Patients
    Elderly
    Infants
    Others

8. Police

9. Racial Targets
    Blacks
    Whites

B. Acquaintances

Young women
People in community
People in own group/co-workers/employers
Neighbors
Children
Visitors, transients
Schoolmates
Patients
Roommates

C. Family

Wives
Inlaws
Children
Mothers, brothers, grandparents

Male serial killers also frequently targeted children as victims (category A2 in Table 7.5). Primarily, the majority of victims were the powerless being exploited by the more powerful. (As one researcher pointed out, you don't ever hear of these offenders going after body builders.) The rest of the categories also include victims who were easily isolated and taken by surprise.

The next largest group of target victims, after strangers, was acquaintances. Again, young women were the most frequent victims identified. Finally, in the category of family victims, wives were most likely to be killed, followed by inlaws and children. Although we often hear of serial killers who hated their mothers, mothers were rarely victims. A myth has been created and perpetrated about serial offenders killing their mothers because such cases tend to be frequently dramatized (for example, Lucas and Kemper).

PROFILE 7-4: EDMUND EMIL KEMPER III
1964–1973

"I just wondered how it would feel to shoot grandma," Kemper, a boy of only 15 years of age, explained to police. His confession was calm and very matter of fact. He walked up behind his grandmother and shot her in the back of the head, shot her two more times in the back, and repeatedly stabbed her. Then he waited for grandpa to come home and shot him to death on the porch.

Born in 1948, Ed was raised by a domineering mother who frequently berated him in public. His parents were divorced when he was nine. When he was eight, his mother had forced him to sleep in the cellar of the house for nearly eight months, his only exit through a trap door that usually had the kitchen table on it. Ed would later claim a deep love-hate relationship with his mother, which for him was a constant source of frustration. His mother married several times while Kemper was young, preventing him from ever drawing close to male role models.

As a child Ed sometimes acted out his own death through mock executions. His younger sister would act as the executioner, and Ed would role play a person in the death throes in the gas chamber. He later admitted to fantasizing about killing his family, especially his older sister, who he believed received more love and attention. His sister remembered receiving a doll for Christmas only to find it a few days later with the head and hands cut off. Kemper's fantasies became more violent, and he killed the family cat by burying it alive and then decapitating it. He placed the head on a spindle and prayed over it. One day his sister teased him about the fact that he liked his school teacher and wanted to kiss her—to which he replied, "If I kissed her I'd have to kill her first." Years later this statement proved to be extremely insightful.

At 13, Ed ran away to see his father but was then quickly sent to live with his grandparents. Ed's mother warned her ex-husband that sending Ed to his grandparents could be very dangerous. A year and a half later Ed killed them. Kemper turned himself in and was subsequently placed in Atascadero mental hospital for sex offenders. During his incarceration he behaved as a model patient and impressed one psychiatrist so much that he allowed Kemper to administer psychological tests to other patients. Kemper learned the requisite psychological jargon and therapeutic skills to convince a parole board, against the advice of psychiatrists, to release him after only five years. Kemper returned to live with his mother and soon became embroiled in their usual fighting. However, Ed was now fully grown—280 pounds and 6 feet 8 inches tall. His IQ had been measured at 136, but he could manage only holding a job as a flagman for a construction company. At this point, his outward interests appeared normal for a young man, yet inwardly his violent rages and fantasies continued to grow.

In 1970–1971, Kemper began picking up young female hitchhikers, psychologically preparing himself for his mission. At the age of 23, Ed started killing again, a task that would entail nearly a year and eight more victims. He shot, stabbed, and strangled them. All were strangers to him, and all were hitchhikers. He cannibalized at least two of his victims, slicing off parts of their legs and cooking the flesh in a macaroni casserole. He decapitated all of his victims and dissected most of them, saving body parts for sexual pleasure, sometimes storing heads in the refrigerator. Ed collected "keepsakes" including teeth, skin, and hair from the victims. After killing a victim he often engaged in sex

EDMUND EMIL KEMPER III continued

with the corpse, even after it had been decapitated.

On one occasion Kemper visited at length with psychiatrists who stated at the conclusion of the interview that Ed was now safe and would not harm another person. They agreed at the meeting to have Kemper's juvenile record sealed to allow him to lead a normal life. Only Ed knew that at that very moment, the head of one of his victims was in the trunk of his car. Kemper finally decided to kill his mother; early one morning on Easter weekend, he entered her bedroom carrying a hammer and a large hunting knife (which he called "General"). After smashing her in the head, he slashed her throat, cut out the larynx, and placed it in the garbage disposal. Severing her head, he had sex with the corpse.

Ed would later explain that he was killing his mother all along, and once she was dead he could stop the murder spree. Perhaps as a final insult to his mother, he invited her best friend over for Sunday dinner. When she arrived, Kemper also strangled her and severed her head. Leaving a note for the police, Ed drove east to Colorado where he had thoughts of climbing up a hill near the highway and shooting travelers as they drove by. Instead he called the police and, after being told to call back several times, convinced them he was the "Coed Killer," so named by the news media. Hours later, while Kemper was still waiting at the pay phone, police arrived and placed him under arrest.

In his confession Kemper stated five different reasons for his crimes. His themes centered on sexual urges, want-

Edmund Kemper's Victims

DATE OF MURDER	NAME	AGE	RELATIONSHIP	METHOD	SEXUAL ASSAULT	CORPSE MUTILATION
8/24/64	Maude Kemper	66	Grandmother	Shooting/ stabbing	No	No
8/24/64	Edmund Emil Kemper I	72	Grandfather	Shooting	No	No
5/7/72	Mary Ann Pesce	18	Stranger	Stabbing	Body parts	Decapitated, dissected
5/7/72	Anita Luchessa	18	Stranger	Stabbing	Body parts	Decapitated, dissected
9/14/72	Aiko Koo	15	Stranger	Suffocation, strangulation	Necrophilia	Decapitated, dissected, severed hands
1/8/73	Cindy Schall	19	Stranger	Shooting	Necrophilia	Decapitated, dissected
2/5/73	Rosalind Thorpe	23	Stranger	Shooting	Possible	Decapitated
2/5/73	Alice Liu	21	Stranger	Shooting	Necrophilia	Decapitated, severed hands
4/20/73	Clarnell Kemper	40s	Mother	Hammer/ cut throat	Necrophilia	Decapitated, dissected
4/20/73	Sara Hallet	40s	Mother's friend	Strangled	No	Decapitated

EDMUND EMIL KEMPER III continued

ing to possess his victims, trophy hunting, a hatred for his mother, and revenge against an unjust society (Leyton, 1985, p. 70).

Elliot Leyton insightfully integrated Kemper's often bizarre reasoning into one single theory for his murderous behavior:

> As he slipped into the social niche of celebrated multiple murderer, he cured society's indifference to him and did so while exacting his fearful revenge and indulging all his repressed sexuality. . . . He had

come to terms with that "total frustration," which all our multiple murderers remedy in their crusades. . . . This should not be any surprise, for he has confronted all the major issues in his life and resolved them. Kemper has, in his own terms, rewritten his personal history and, in the lunacy of destruction, created himself [1986, p. 72].

Edmund Kemper was sentenced to life imprisonment. He was denied parole at his first parole hearing in 1980.

Patterns in victimization should also be examined for additional insight into the mind of the murderer. Over one third of male offenders targeted females only, whereas one fifth killed males exclusively (Table 7.6). Less than half of offenders killed both males and females.

As expected, males were more likely to kill females than males. Four fifths of offenders killed at least one female victim. Surprisingly, however, approximately two thirds of male offenders killed at least one male victim. Often the primary targets were females, but frequently males were killed,

TABLE 7.6 Percentage of Male Serial Killers Murdering People in Specific Victim Age and Gender Categories, $N = 167$

AGE		GENDER	
Only:		**Only:**	
Children	5%	Females	36%
Teens	3%	Males	21%
Adults	48%	Both	43%
At least one:		**At least one:**	
Child	27%	Female	79%
Teen	39%	Male	64%
Adult	88%		
Elderly	16%	**Variations:**	
		One or more adult females	70%
Combinations:		One or more adult males	53%
Adults and children	11%	Both adult males and females	36%
Adults and teens	21%		
Teens and children	4%	One or more female teenagers	25%
All age groups	5%	One or more male teenagers	16%
		Both male and female teens	5%
		One or more female children	16%
		One or more male children	16%
		Both male and female children	5%

which suggests that a person's gender often did not preclude victimization. Nearly half of all offenders killed only adults, whereas only small percentages of offenders specifically targeted children or teens.

Approximately one in four offenders killed at least one child, nearly 40% killed at least one teenager, and nine out of ten offenders killed at least one adult. In addition, one in six offenders murdered at least one or more elderly people. If we account for only the past few years, the elderly were increasingly being selected by male serial killers.

Female adults were victimized by over two thirds of these offenders, whereas only half reported killing at least one adult male victim. Only one third of offenders was found to have killed at least both male and female adults. Often offenders killed both adults and teens, but they rarely killed both adults and children. In short, adult victims appeared to be the most frequent targets sought out by male serial killers. Children were frequently victimized, but not as often as adults. The elderly appeared to be picked as victims more frequently in recent years, possibly as a result of their rapidly increasing numbers, as well as their accessibility to offenders.

Table 7.7 gives the percentages of victim facilitation. Overall, most victims did not place themselves in particularly vulnerable positions at the time they were targeted, but this appears to have changed slightly in recent years. Since 1975 at least one fourth of offenders attacked victims who facilitated their own deaths by placing themselves at risk.

TABLE 7.7 Degree of Victim Facilitation in Being Murdered by Male Offenders, 1795–1988

FACILITATION	(1795–1988) PERCENTAGE OF OFFENDERS ($N=160$)	(1975–1988) PERCENTAGE OF OFFENDERS ($N=59$)
Low	73	68
High	19	24
Both	8	8

In cases of serial murder, seldom do we perceive of victims as having precipitated their own deaths through acts of provocation. Most victims were unaware of the immediate danger when first they met their killers, especially in cases where males targeted females. In addition, not all offenders concerned themselves with the easiest target. In one case, the offender felt the urge to kill and tried to abduct a woman who was sitting in her car at a street intersection waiting for the light to change. Another just moved around neighborhoods, knocking on doors, until he found somebody at home.

The element of surprise is particularly operative in serial murder. Consequently, offenders take time to stalk a victim without giving warning signals.

Thus, a "selective" hitchhiker—one that is careful about getting in with "just anybody"—probably incurs the same risks as anyone else who hitchhikes. One investigator described serial killers as "charming" people; however, once they get you into their "comfort zone" it's too late to back out (see Profile 7-5).

PROFILE 7-5: ALBERT HENRY DeSALVO
1962–1964

Perhaps he could have been stopped, but the signs were ignored or missed, and Albert DeSalvo—also known as "The Measuring Man," "The Green Man," and "The Boston Strangler"—murdered thirteen innocent women. Born in Chelsea, Massachusetts, in 1931, DeSalvo was forced to live in extremely impoverished conditions. Often hungry and cold, he was subjected to cruel beatings at the hands of his alcoholic father. He was also forced to watch while his father abused and beat his mother. On one occasion he watched as his father broke each of his mother's fingers one after the other. On another occasion his father sold him and his sister into slavery to a farmer for several months. In 1944 Mrs. DeSalvo took her six children and divorced her husband.

His love for his mother and his hatred for his father seemed to bring out the worst in Albert. He remembered later how much he enjoyed shooting cats with his bow and arrow, especially when the arrows protruded through their bellies. His father had trained him well in stealing from stores, and Albert became proficient at the task. He gradually developed a liking for breaking and entering homes, which he began to do frequently.

By the time he was 12, Albert had been arrested twice, once for larceny and once for breaking and entering. He was incarcerated at Lyman School for delinquent boys where he learned a great deal more about burglary. After his release he began to apply himself full time to break-

ing and entering homes. Albert seemed to constantly try to bridge the gap between himself and those who had money and possessions. He was no more able to attain middle class respectability than he was able to satisfy his apparently enormous sex drive. He became sexually active with both girls and homosexuals in the neighborhood and gained a reputation for his remarkable sexual capacity. At 17 he joined the military and served with the occupation forces in Germany. Before returning, he won the U.S. Army middleweight boxing championship and married his wife, Irmgard. In 1955, at age 23, Albert was charged with his first sex offense, involving the molestation of a nine-year-old girl. The charges were dropped when the parents refused to proceed with the case. In 1956, he was honorably discharged from the military.

In 1958 Albert's first child was born and he briefly ceased his breaking and entering activities. However, his wife refused to submit to his excessive sexual demands, and his financial status seemed to be worsening. Albert shortly received two separate suspended sentences for breaking and entering. Before long, Albert earned the nickname "Measuring Man" by conning his way into scores of apartments by explaining that he represented a modeling agency and was in search of talent. Producing a measuring tape, he would take occupants' personal measurements, touching them inappropriately whenever possible. He later would claim that most of his victims

ALBERT HENRY DeSALVO continued

were quite willing to have their measurements taken, that few complained and a few even removed their clothing. He never attacked or harmed any of them

but promised they would soon be hearing from his agency.

Eventually Albert was arrested again for breaking and entering and was

Albert DeSalvo's Victims

DATE OF MURDER	NAME	AGE	METHOD	SEXUAL ASSAULT	CORPSE DESECRATION	APARTMENT SEARCHED
6/14/62	Anna Slesers	55	Blow to head/ strangulation	No	Bow under chin	No
6/28/62	Mary Mullen	85	Strangulation	No	No	No
6/30/62	Helen Blake	65	Strangulation	Yes	Bite marks; legs apart; bow under chin	Yes
6/30/62	Nina Nichols	68	Strangulation	Yes	Bottle in vagina; legs apart; bow under chin	Yes
8/19/62	Ida Irga	75	Strangulation	Yes	Legs apart and propped up on chairs; bite marks; twisted pillowcase around neck	Yes
8/20/62	Jane Sullivan	67	Strangulation	Yes	Body left in kneeling position, face down in bathtub; exposed	Yes
12/5/62	Sophie Clark	20	Strangulation	Yes	Legs apart; gag in mouth; bow under chin	Yes
12/30/62	Patricia Bissette	23	Strangulation	Yes	Bow under chin	Yes
3/9/63	Mary Brown	69	Fractured skull/ stabbing/ strangulation	Yes	Table fork embedded in breast	Yes
5/6/63	Beverly Samans	23	Multiple stab wounds to throat and breast	Yes	Gagged; legs apart tied to bed posts; bow under chin	?
9/8/63	Evelyn Corbin	58	Strangulation	Yes	Underpants stuffed in mouth; bow tied on ankle	Yes
11/23/63	Joann Graff	23	Strangulation	Yes	Bite marks on breast; bow under chin	Yes
1/4/64	Mary Sullivan	19	Strangulation	Yes	Legs apart; broom handle in vagina; bow under chin; Happy New Year card	?

ALBERT HENRY DeSALVO continued

sentenced to two years imprisonment. He earned his release in 11 months. According to police, at that time DeSalvo was still known only as a breaking and entering criminal. He returned home to again be rejected by his wife until such time that he could prove he had mended his ways. Overwhelmed with frustration, Albert began changing from the harmless "Measuring Man" to an aggressive, violent personality. He began tying up some of his victims and raping them. He always wore green pants during these forays and was soon dubbed "The Green Man." Police estimate he attacked several women. Feelings of rejection, sexual frustration, and inferiority to others became intolerable by June of 1962, when he attempted his first murder of a woman in her apartment. Apparently, during the attack he saw himself in a mirror by the bed and it jolted his sensibilities, so he stopped. A week later he began killing in earnest.

Most of DeSalvo's victims were strangled and sexually assaulted. Over 60% were older women, although most of his last few victims were young women. He seemed to enjoy desecrating the corpse and then ransacking the apartment.

Although DeSalvo was unsure of his motives for killing, he was even less sure why he suddenly stopped in January, 1964. Perhaps he felt he had given the supreme insult to society through the explicit humiliation of his last victims. DeSalvo continued to enter the homes of unsuspecting women as "The Green Man," tying them and raping them, but he no longer killed his victims. Eventually, after a description had been given to the police by one of his victims, Albert was arrested as "The Green Man" and was linked to sexual assaults in Massachusetts, Connecticut, New Hampshire, and Rhode Island. He was sent to Bridgewater, a mental institution, for evaluation, but not until the spring of 1965 did he confess to being the "Boston Strangler."

DeSalvo's confession, however, was given under special circumstances that protected him from prosecution for the murders. He never came to trial for the murders but instead was sent to prison for his many sexual assaults committed as "The Green Man." In 1967, he entered Walpole State Prison to serve a life sentence. Six years later Albert DeSalvo was stabbed to death by a fellow inmate.

Offenders' Backgrounds and Occupations

The male serial killers in this study came from a wide variety of backgrounds and occupations. Educational attainment was often only high school or less, some vocational training, or a year or two in college. Very few offenders held college degrees. Offenders generally held blue collar jobs, but a few managed to secure professional work as teachers, doctors, musicians, and ministers.

Table 7.8 provides an overview of various types of employment held by male offenders before or during their killing careers. Some offenders held responsible positions that provided regular employment. Some used their employment to facilitate victim selection: for example, a building contractor

TABLE 7.8 Occupations of Male Offenders Before or During Their Career of Murder

Skilled:
  Aircraft company
  Shoemaker
  Car upholstery
  Electrician/carpenter
  TV repairman
  Plumber
  Electronics technician
  Building contractor
  Computer operator
  Mechanic
  Nurse

Semiskilled:
  Woodsman
  Truck driver
  Warehouse employee
  Bartender
  Boiler operator
  Farmer
  Nurse's aide
  House painter
  Barber
  Factory worker
  Construction worker
  Motel clerk
  Store clerk

Unskilled:
  Laborer
  Hotel porter
  Gas attendant
  Garbage collector
  Kitchen worker

Criminal:
  Thief
  Conartist
  Pimp
  Burglar
  Robber

Government/professional:
  Security, auxiliary police
  Military personnel
  Minister
  Business owner: Hotel, plantation, ranch, bakery
  Lecturer
  Physician
  Clerk
  Salesman
  Musician
  Social worker
  Postal worker
  Accountant
  Photographer

Other:
  Transient/drifter/vagrant
  Cult follower
  Student
  Former mental patient

lured boys in search of work; a nurse's aide killed patients; a bartender killed his female employees; a farmer killed his laborers; a hotel clerk killed tenants; a physician killed his patients; a few salesmen killed their customers. Other offenders did not connect their employment in any way to their victims, and still other offenders were transients, unemployed, or recently out of jail or prison.

Contrary to popular opinion, male serial killers in this study generally were not highly educated nor did they commonly hold professional or even skilled careers. Occasionally an offender did appear to be extremely intelligent or had a prestigious occupation, but this type of offender tended to be the exception, not the rule. Due to the sensational nature of the serial murder phenomenon, it is not surprising that we tend to seize on unsubstantiated evidence, especially if such information tends to create further distortion of offender profiles. Indeed, offenders' ability to kill reportedly without detection appeared to be more a function of cunning and deceit than intellectual abilities or academic attainments. Commonly, offenders have been profiled as the "law student," the "lecturer," or the "businessman" when in reality they have had very little exposure to those roles. This appears to happen most often in the more sensationalized cases. For example, Ted Bundy was portrayed as a law student, but he never completed any course work. "Law student" was merely a status symbol that Bundy used to more easily infiltrate the communities in which he roamed. In short, we have perpetuated a myth about male serial killers that is based on only a few sensational cases. Blue-collar work and unskilled labor were found to be much more common among male offenders than higher level employment.

Two of the most important factors in construction of the stereotypical serial killer were found in the methods and motives of offenders. Table 7.9 provides a breakdown of methods used by offenders to kill their victims. In contrast to typical homicides, domestic or otherwise, male serial offenders

TABLE 7.9 Methods and Motives of Male Serial Murderers in the United States, 1795–1988

METHOD (N=159)		MOTIVE (N=160)	
Some mutilation[1]	55%	Sex sometimes[2]	58%
Some firearms[2]	45%	Enjoyment sometimes	38%
Some strangulation/suffocation	33%	Money sometimes	36%
Some bludgeoning	25%	Personal sometimes[3]	27%
Firearms only	19%	Perverted acts sometimes	21%
Some torture	18%	Sex only	21%
Some poison	10%	Money only	16%
Mutilation only	9%	Revenge	11%
Strangulation/suffocation only	8%	Perverted acts only	11%
Some drowning	4%	Personal only	10%
Poison only	4%	Cult inspired	7%
Bludgeoning only	3%	Mental problems	3%
Other	2%	Enjoyment only	2%
Combinations of the preceding methods	61%	Combinations of the preceding motives	48%

[1] Includes one or more of the following: stabbing; hacksaw; axe; decapitation; scalping; dissection; throat slashing.
[2] "Some" or "sometimes" denotes that offenders killed one or more victims by a specific method or for a specific reason.
[3] Includes: an urge to kill; belief that women are evil; heroism; hatred of women or elderly; racial hatred; curiosity; felt threatened; children are a burden.

did not commonly use guns as their sole means of killing. Firearms were used in nearly half the cases, but not as the main mode of death. Autopsy reports specify the exact cause of death as well as other contributing factors, including nonlethal injuries. In serial killing we are often faced with a *process* of murder rather than a brief act. Consequently, offenders were frequently found to have used a variety of nonlethal, potentially lethal, and lethal attacks on the victim.

Victims in this study may have actually died from strangulation, a bullet to the head or a stab to the heart, but these often were the final acts committed after the victim had been successfully tortured, mutilated, and/ or beaten by the offender. Conversely, a few offenders, such as necrophiles, would kill their victims as quickly as possible before they began their sexual assaults, mutilations, and trophy collecting. Other offenders engaged in physical assaults before, during, and after the death of the victim. In one case the offender tortured his victims for several days before finally killing them. The fact that such acts of torture, beatings, and mutilations often preceded the act of murder means that they should be viewed as part of the methodology of serial killing. One offender stated in an interview with me that "the response of the victim was everything." This meant that without torture, killing a victim was merely going through the motions (see Profile 7-6).

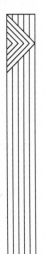

PROFILE 7-6: ROBERT HANSEN
1973–1983

Robert Hansen, 44, admitted having a "severe inferiority complex with girls." To compensate, he began raping women and inevitably started torturing and murdering them. Hansen, considered to be Alaska's worst mass murderer in history, confessed to killing 17 prostitutes, nude dancers and other women whom he resented. Hansen described to police how he—while working as a baker in Anchorage—abducted young women over a ten-year period. Hansen later worked as a respected businessman and was nationally known for his big game hunting. He explained how he abducted over 50 women and took them in his plane to his mountain retreat. If they gave him free sex, he would spare their lives, but any demand for money sealed their doom. Hansen would often strip his victim naked and then give her a head start to escape from him in the wilderness. He explained how much he enjoyed hunting victims down with his .223 caliber Ruger mini-14 rifle, a weapon used by big game hunters. He usually kept his victims tied up in his cabin for several days of sadistic rape and torture before sending them naked into the woods to be hunted.

Another commonly held myth about male serial killers is that their primary motivations for murder are sexually rooted. Consequently, the typical stereotype of the offender is the "lust killer" who is driven to kill for sexual gratification. Most serial killings we hear and read about involve lust murders. Thus, it becomes that much easier to view sex as the primary motivating force behind the serial offender. Some serial killers, however, never become sexually involved in any way with their victims. Some experts may argue, however, that "enjoyment" is related to sexuality.

Sexual motivations were found to be the most common explanations of serial murder, but only one fifth of offenders gave it as the sole reason for killing. Similarly, offenders frequently stated that they enjoyed killing but rarely killed for enjoyment only. Money was a factor for approximately one third of the offenders, yet infrequently did they kill for money only. Even those who killed in order to engage in perverted sexual acts seldom committed the murders to carry out perverted acts only. As discussed in Chapter 4, sex may serve much more as a vehicle to degrade and destroy. Ultimately, by depriving a victim of things she or he holds sacred, such as dignity and self-respect, the offender achieves his most important goal, which is to have complete control over the victim. In short, many of offenders' stated "motivations" may actually have been methods by which they achieved ultimate power and control over other human beings. One offender pointed out how good it made him feel to completely control another person's life. To have that control over life and death, he noted, gave him a special thrill.

Another area of research pertaining to the male offender is his prior history of violent, criminal, or abnormal behavior. We tend not to think of male serial killers as having criminal records but rather as embarking on a unique form of criminal activity.

After careful examination of the lives of 58 male serial killers, I compiled data that indicated that two fifths of them had prior incarceration(s) in prison(s) or mental institutions (Table 7.10). One third were found to have

TABLE 7.10 Percentage of Male Offenders Reporting a History of Violent, Criminal, or Abnormal Behavior

HISTORY	PERCENTAGE OF OFFENDERS ($N=58$)
Prior incarceration in prison or mental institution	43
Sex-related crimes	35
Theft/stealing	24
Robbery	23
Burglary	21
Psychiatric problems	18
Assault	15
Homicide	7
Illegal drugs	5
Forgery, impersonation, bigamy	5
Other: child abuse, animal abuse, arson	5
Combination of the preceding behaviors	58

histories of sex-related crimes, whereas one fourth had been convicted of thefts and robberies. One fifth had also been arrested for burglaries, and another fifth were found to have histories of psychiatric problems. Less than one tenth had prior homicide records, and even fewer offenders were discovered to have had illegal drug involvement or have been charged with child abuse or arson. Nearly 60% were found to have a history of a combination of criminal activities. In short, at least one half of the offenders examined were found to have some form of criminal history. Instead of being faced with a new breed of offender, we may have failed in our criminal justice system to adequately deal with the "old" criminal before his career of serial killing began (see Profile 7-7).

Another important area of background research is the killer's childhood history. In 52 cases of male offenders, various degrees and types of traumatization occurred while they were young (Table 7.11). This does not preclude the possibility that other offenders also may have had similar experiences. Trauma was defined as rejection, including being abandoned by parent(s), being neglected by parent(s), and being rejected by significant

PROFILE 7-7: PAUL JOHN KNOWLES
1974

Paul Knowles had history of criminal behavior long before he started his killing spree. As a teenager and an adult, Knowles had spent time in jails for petty theft, car theft, and burglary. By the time he was released from prison, the 28-year-old Florida resident suffered from loneliness, rejection, and failure. Sandy Fawkes, a woman he met (but chose not to kill), described Knowles as a man who could be thoughtful and even protective. He also appeared to be confused as to his sexuality. Some of the rapes he confessed to were never completed because of his sexual inadequacies. One of his male victims appears to have been associated with homosexual behavior. Knowles met him in a gay bar and was invited to spend the night at his home but killed him following an argument. Knowles decided to make his mark on society and began a four-month killing rampage that would cover seven states and include at least 18 victims. He later claimed to have killed at least 35 people; the admissions were never confirmed.

Knowles's killings were generally random; he often murdered someone to conceal detection or to rob him or her. Some of his victims he simply killed for enjoyment. He murdered children, teenagers, adults, and elderly persons. Most of his victims died by strangulation, although at least five were shot to death. Most of them were female, but he raped or attempted to rape only a few. He managed to elude law enforcement through cunning and sheer luck as he drove thousands of miles, killing along the way.

Finally he abducted a police officer and another male traveler, handcuffed them to a tree, and shot both in the head, killing them instantly. After running a road block he smashed his car into a tree and fled into the woods. He surrendered moments later when confronted by a local resident pointing a shotgun at him. After his arrest Knowles reveled in the notoriety and gave several interviews. He made a point of telling the press he was the "only successful member of his family." The next day Knowles was shot and killed as he attempted to escape from the police.

PAUL JOHN KNOWLES continued

Paul Knowles's Victims

DATE OF MURDER	NAME	AGE RANGE	GENDER	STATE	METHOD	SEXUAL ASSAULT	AREA OF KILLING OR BODY FOUND	ITEMS STOLEN
7/74	Alice Curtis	Elderly	F	FL	Suffocation	No	Home	Money/car
7/74	Mylette Anderson	Child	F	FL	Strangulation	—	Swamp	—
7/74	Lillian Anderson	Child	F	FL	Strangulation	—	Swamp	—
7/74	Marjorie Howe	Adult	F	FL	Strangulation	—	Home	TV
8/74	Hitchhiker	Teen	F	FL	Strangulation	Rape	Woods	—
8/74	Kathie Pierce	Adult	F	FL	Strangulation	No	Home	—
9/74	William Bates	Adult	M	OH	Strangulation	Possible	Woods	Car
9/74	Emmett Johnson	Elderly	M	NV	Shooting	No	Camper	Credit cards/car
9/74	Lois Johnson	Elderly	F	NV	Shooting	No	Camper	Credit cards/car
9/74	Unidentified woman	Adult	F	NV	Strangulation	Rape	Car	—
9/74	Ann Dawson	Adult	F	AL	—	—	—	—
10/74	Dawn Wine	Teen	F	CT	Strangulation	Rape	Home	Records/ tape recorder
10/74	Karen Wine	Adult	F	CT	Strangulation	Rape	Home	—
10/74	Doris Hovey	Adult	F	VA	Shooting	No	Home	—
11/74	Carswell Carr	Adult	M	GA	Stabbing	No	Home	—
11/74	Miss Carr	Teen	F	GA	Strangulation	Attempt	Home	—
11/74	Officer Campbell	Adult	M	GA	Shooting	No	Woods	Car
11/74	James Meyer	Adult	M	GA	Shooting	No	Woods	Car

others. Rejection was far the most common theme surrounding the lives of these killers as children. However, most people have experienced rejection to lesser or greater degrees than serial killers have, yet they do not become violent killers. Many people have lost their parents; experienced divorce, poverty, and unstable homes where parents drink heavily; used drugs; or been involved in prostitution or sexual abuse. However, most people who have had such experiences do not turn to homicide. Serial killers may be different in that they were not prepared or able to cope with the stresses the trauma created (see Chapter 4). Such an explanation will require more extensive research but may eventually provide us with greater insight into causation. For the present, it appears that early childhood trauma can and will influence future behavior to the extent that some individuals will become violent offenders.

TABLE 7.11 Percentage of Male Offenders Who Experienced Forms of Traumatization as Children

TRAUMATIZATION	PERCENTAGE OF OFFENDERS ($N=52$)
Rejection	60
Unstable home	29
Parents deceased	23
Divorce	23
Poverty	23
Corporal punishment	17
Adopted	13
Sexual abuse	10
Illegitimate	8

Disposition of Serial Killers

There has been considerable concern about the disposition of serial offenders. Given the facts that some states do not have capital punishment and that several serial killers were removed from death row when capital punishment was struck down by the U.S. Supreme Court in 1972, many offenders are spending the rest of their lives in prison instead of waiting to be executed (Table 7.12).

Of the 157 male offenders examined for sentencing, one fifth have been executed as of this writing. Another 14% reside on death row, and a few committed suicide or were killed before a trial could be held. In total, 43% of all offenders are now dead or currently await execution. At least half of all

TABLE 7.12 Disposition of Male Serial Killers after Apprehension

DISPOSITION	PERCENTAGE OF OFFENDERS ($N=157$)
Life in prison	25
Executed	20
Sentenced to a specific number of years in prison	16
Currently on death row	14
Pending in courts	10
Suicide	5
Killed before trial	4
Confined to mental institution	4
Escaped	1
Now free	1

male offenders spent or will spend the rest of their lives in prison. The chances of parole or early release for any of these offenders is at present extremely small, if not nonexistent (see Chapter 10).

Men Who Kill Women: The Solo Killer

Given the variations among types of serial killing, cases can also be sub-divided into a number of taxonomies, subgroups, or categories. These subgroups may also provide valuable information about the methods, motives, victim selection, or mobility patterns of particular serial killers. Examination of different subgroups may, in the final analysis, provide in-sight into the mind and behavior of serial killers, as well as generate new areas of research. This section focuses on male serial offenders who pri-marily killed young women. This subgroup was selected for a number of reasons: (1) the public tends to associate the phenomenon of serial murder with young women as victims; (2) young women are the most likely targets of serial killers; (3) these murderers generally receive more extended media coverage than some other groups of serial killers; (4) these offenders display habits and traits that tend in some ways to set them apart from other serial offenders.

These are the types of killers we so often hear or read about in the media. These are the rapists who enjoy killing and often indulging in acts of sadism and perversion. These are the men who have engaged in necrophilia, cannibalism, and the drinking of victims' blood. Some like to bite their victims; others enjoy trophy collecting—shoes, underwear, and body parts, such as hair clippings, feet, heads, fingers, breasts, and sexual organs. Offenders in this subgroup have earned monikers like "Bluebeard," "The Torture Doctor," "Demon of the Belfry," "Sex Beast," "The Thrill Killer," and "The Coed Killer," which are designed to evoke our disgust, horror, and fascination.

The subgroup in this study consisted of 42 solo male serial killers, which constituted 25% of all male serial killers. The number of these types of offenders appearing since 1960 was relatively stable, with about 9–10 new cases each decade, or one per year. Given the intensity of media coverage of such crimes, it is unlikely these figures were significantly underreported.

California and Illinois showed the greatest frequency of cases (8) from this subgroup. These two states were followed closely by Florida (6 cases), New York (5 cases), and Oregon (5 cases). The age of most offenders ranged in the twenties; the youngest was 16 years and the oldest 48 years. (These figures represent the age at which the offender first began killing, regardless of the time span between victims.) The average age for the offenders in this subgroup was 28. Of 40 cases, 13% of offenders were black and all others were Caucasian. This subgroup was responsible for 27%–29% of all victims claimed by male serial killers in general. Compared with serial killers who pursued victims other than young women, these 42 offenders on the average each tended to kill more victims. Other male solo offenders murdered on the average 8–10 victims, whereas offenders in this subgroup killed 9–13 victims per case. A number of possible explanations exist for this discrepancy, all of which need further investigation beyond the scope of this study. Perhaps males who target young women are more devious, more obsessed, and more intelligent than other males who kill solo. Or young women may simply be the easiest targets and more accessible.

In this subgroup, 70% of offenders killed young women. The majority of these women-killers (62%) were classified as traveling offenders. These are the offenders who have been known to travel thousands of miles in a month eluding police, in search of easy victims. However, like other types of information regarding serial murder, this has been subject to exaggeration. For example, Henry Lee Lucas, a self-confessed serial killer in Texas, said he had killed in nearly every state and claimed he sometimes drove his car 100,000 miles in a month. This means he would have averaged 3,225 miles per day, in a 31-day month, if he drove nonstop, maintaining a speed of 134 m.p.h. for the entire month. Obviously, such statements are ludicrous, but it is exactly this type of misinformation that helps create stereotypes. Some serial killers do travel throughout the United States and Canada, and a few even travel overseas. They commit crimes in several different law enforcement jurisdictions, which they often use to their own advantage. In such situations, poor interagency communications, as well as limited cooperation among agencies, can keep a strong police response from ever developing. As you will see in Chapter 10, efforts are being made to deal with the particular problems created by the traveling serial killer.

The remaining serial killers in this subgroup maintained their territoriality by staying local (21%) or place-specific (17%). Few of these types were strictly stay-at-home killers; some waited for victims to come to their homes, but they also roamed locally in search of prey. Jerry Brudos, about whom Ann Rule wrote *The Lust Killer* (1983), would return to his home with his captured victims; however, he also victimized women who made the fatal mistake of knocking on his door.

This subgroup of killers was also slightly more inclined to seek out strangers (71%) for victims than other solo male offenders (65%). This trend was confirmed by the fact that, since 1970, more than 95% of this offender subgroup targeted primarily female strangers. Overall, 88% of offenders identified in this group killed at least one or more female strangers. Generally the women were prostitutes, hitchhikers, or students. Sometimes nurses, models, or waitresses were targeted. Although a few offenders randomly selected women who were at home alone, most victims succumbed to the ruses and con games played by offenders in both public and private areas. One offender, who now resides at the Florida State Prison in Starke, Florida, was able to talk his way into anyone's trust. Charismatic, irresponsible, unfaithful to his wife and family, he always blamed others for his problems. He felt completely invincible as he stalked his prey. After talking an attractive 38-year-old real estate agent into showing him some very expensive property, he led her into a wooded area in the backyard, where he beat and stabbed her to death.

Compared with other male offenders who acted alone, this subgroup similarly often targeted women who placed themselves at risk, including those who hitchhiked, worked as prostitutes, or walked alone at night. The majority of these offenders (71%), however, sought out women who generally did not perceive themselves at risk. Swimming at a crowded beach, shopping in a mall, and walking home are not activities one generally considers to be risky, yet there are potential dangers in practically all public and many private activities. For serial killers like Ted Bundy (Profile 7-8), the challenge is to exploit situations in which the risk of danger appeared so remote that the victims never felt a need to be on guard.

PROFILE 7-8: THEODORE ROBERT BUNDY
1973–1978

In the end, society gave Ted what he so eagerly sought throughout his life: infamy, notoriety, and the attention of millions of people. Even though the lives of 30 to 50 young women, including several teenagers and a 12-year-old girl, were sacrificed, the final price paid by Ted was never a real issue for him. Like some other serial killers, Ted Bundy found his fortune in the recognition and celebrity status he acquired through his involvement with the judicial system of the United States.

Ted was born out of wedlock in Burlington, Vermont, 1946, to Louise Cowell. During the next few years, Ted and his mother lived with Louise's parents. Some relatives believed it was during this period of time that Ted was deeply traumatized by his violent grandfather.

At age four, Ted and his mother Louise relocated to Tacoma, Washington. In short time his mother married an army cook, Johnnie Bundy. Ted was forced to live a meager lifestyle and grew up deeply resenting not having money or respectable social class affiliations. He nurtured feelings of inadequacy, of being unable to compete with others who possessed upper-middle-class standing. Michaud and Aynesworth (1983), who later interviewed Bundy, discovered: "Even the Little Teddy was deeply class conscious." As Leyton (1986) explained

in his profile of Bundy, "The status anxiety seemed particularly intense in his relationships with women" (p. 98). He dated infrequently while in high school and, as Leyton points out, "he ultimately captured and killed sorority girls, or their idealized models, for it was an obvious way in which his class-scarred soul could conceive of the possession" (p. 99).

His quest for identity served as a catalyst for constantly presenting himself, especially in physical disguises, to be somebody else. One person he truly did not want to be was Ted Bundy, the Nobody. Yet Ted seemed to lack the ability to comprehend the dynamics of social life, of being able to fit in, and admitted to his interviewers: "I didn't know what made people want to be friends. I didn't know what made people attractive to one another. I didn't know what underlay social interactions" (Michaud & Aynesworth, 1983, p. 68) Consequently Ted created a series of social fronts and disguises to help him blend into the "right groups."

His decision to begin killing, however, was spurred only in part by his social-class paranoia. Ted later explained, using the third person, that he was eventually overcome by an internal force or an "entity" that constituted a "purely destructive power." In essence, Ted began to delve deeper into a world of

THEODORE ROBERT BUNDY continued

sexual fantasy that became increasingly violent in nature. He consumed quantities of pornographic material depicting sexually violent acts. Bundy explained pornography "as a vicarious way of experiencing what his peers were experiencing in reality. Then he got sucked into the more sinister doctrines that are implicit in pornography—the use, abuse, the possession of women as objects" (Winn & Merrill, 1980, pp. 116–117).

He fed his sexual fantasies through voyeurism. For years he peeped through windows to watch women undress. Combined with his increasing appetite for alcohol, Ted was gradually preparing himself to begin his killing career. During this time he established what appeared to be an impressive record. He had been in Boy Scouts, worked as an assistant programs director at the Seattle Crime Commission and wrote, ironically enough, a booklet for women on rape prevention. He was even accepted to law school but attended only a few classes.

He continued to struggle to fit in but perceived each setback as devastating, regardless of its true magnitude. Like some other serial killers, Bundy began to act out his fantasies by first stalking his women and then attacking them. As Leyton observed, "He decided to commit himself to another career . . . having failed at social mobility" (p. 106). Like Ed Kemper, Bundy had already picked out some dumping sites for his victims. It is unlikely we will ever know exactly how many victims Bundy accrued, but there exists sufficient evidence to link him to at least 30 homicides, though many people believed he killed nearly 40.

The victims were all young, attractive females who appeared to come from middle- or upper-middle-class families, and many were students. He killed victims in at least five different states between 1973 and 1978, usually leaving the bodies in secluded wooded areas.

Several bodies were not found until all that remained were a few bones scattered by animals. Some victims were never recovered. Robert Keppel, a former detective who investigated eight Bundy killings in the Seattle area, believes he may have murdered over 100 victims. Ted was usually able to lure the intended victim to his car by asking them for assistance. He was always polite and friendly and sometimes wore his arm in a sling to appear as a harmless, well-bred young man simply in need of help. At other times he was known to lurk in dark shadows and attack women who were alone. An early victim was abducted from her basement apartment where she was sleeping.

Ted usually attacked his victims with a blunt instrument, such as a tire iron or a wooden club, and rendered them unconscious. Some of them died quickly from having their skulls crushed, whereas others would linger for hours or days until Ted strangled them. Once Ted had maneuvered his victim into a position that allowed him to be in control, the woman's fate was inevitable. Only one victim managed to escape death after he had placed her under his control. He raped most if not all of his victims; several were subjected to sodomy and sexual mutilation. Some of the victims had vaginal lacerations caused by foreign objects. In the Chi Omega sorority house killings in Tallahassee, Florida, Bundy left teeth marks on the breast and buttocks of at least one victim. In some instances Bundy would keep the body for days and is believed by some investigators to have shampooed the hair of and applied makeup to more than one victim.

Ted also liked to match wits with law enforcement personnel, and on two occasions was able to escape from a jail and a courthouse in Colorado. Ted was able to avoid apprehension because of his de-

THEODORE ROBERT BUNDY continued

gree of mobility. Moving from state to state, he drew in dozens of police agencies all wanting to capture him.

In the end, Ted's own psychopathology appeared to have caused his downfall. Before his last kill, Bundy drank heavily and resorted to frequent thefts of wallets and sprees of shoplifting. In his last few days of freedom he was overcome with desperation, paranoia, and the inability to make and act on decisions that would allow him to remain free. His frequent and excessive use of stolen credit cards and his impulsive purchases of clothing, especially socks, were not the actions of the "old" Ted who had been in control. Fueled by his paranoia, fetishes, and constant intake of alcohol, perhaps he foresaw or even wished his inevitable capture. Bundy's final victim, Kimberly Leach, whom he randomly selected from a grammar school, was only 12 years of age. A few days later after murdering her, Ted was pulled over by a suspicious patrol officer, and eventually police discovered that he had been placed on the FBI's Ten Most Wanted list.

Bundy was convicted of three murders and sentenced to die in Florida's electric chair. Reveling in the notoriety, he defended himself in court and used his trial to bask in the light of national TV and newspaper coverage. He finally gained the prominence and self-validation he so desperately sought. In an interview with Dr. Ron Holmes of the University of Louisville, Bundy discussed the classic characteristics of serial killers but could not recognize those traits in his own personality (author's files). He continued to the very end to employ legal maneuverings to avoid the electric chair. His trial and appeals cost approximately $9,000,000. Bundy's court record was one of Florida's longest in history, more than 28,000 pages, or about the size of the *Encyclopedia Britannica*. For

Ted that was also a way to satisfy his desire for revenge on a society he believed maligned him. For Ted there was no guilt, and as he declared on one occasion, "I don't feel guilty for anything. . . . I feel sorry for people who feel guilt" (Winn & Merrill, 1980, p. 313). As his interviewers, Michaud and Aynesworth, came to realize, Ted did not act under some irresponsible uncontrollable urge; rather he consciously used his free will, his agency, to create the killer within himself. Bundy's fame attracted many young female followers who continued to send him letters of love and support. During his incarceration in Florida, Ted married and even managed to father a child. He had absolutely no remorse for his crimes. As Ted so aptly observed, "I'm the coldest mother-fucker you'll ever put your eyes on. I don't give a shit about those other people." But in the end Ted decided to confess his crimes, possibly to buy additional time for himself. His confessions, his efforts to show he was insane, and that he did not receive a fair trial, all faltered.

As Bundy's execution date drew near, the nation watched with increasing interest. Talk shows, newscasters, and newspaper editors all began exploring the life of Ted Bundy and the phenomenon of serial murder in general. Some individuals and groups eagerly awaited his last moments. T-shirts with slogans such as "Fry-Day" and bumper stickers that read "I'll buckle up when Bundy buckles up" were common in Florida and other states where the killer had killed young women. Radio stations played a song parody, "On Top of Old Sparky," and an Indianapolis station held a "Bundy countdown" one hour before his execution. Dances and cookouts called "Bundy-Cues" were held in several locations. The execution in many respects took on the atmosphere of a circus. Even those strongly opposed to

THEODORE ROBERT BUNDY continued

Ted Bundy's Victims

DATE OF MURDER OR DISAPPEARANCE	NAME	AGE	OCCUPATION	LOCATION	METHOD
1/31/74	Lynda Ann Healy	21	Student	WA	Clubbing
3/12/74	Donna Gail Manson	19	Student	WA	?
4/17/74	Susan Rancourt	18	Student	WA	Clubbing
5/6/74	Roberta K. Parks	22	Student	OR	Bludgeoning
6/1/74	Brenda C. Ball	22	Unemployed	WA	Clubbing/strangulation
6/11/74	Georgeann Hawkins	18	Student	WA	?
7/14/74	Janice Ott	23	Probation officer	WA	Bludgeoning
7/14/74	Denise M. Naslund	19	Secretary/student	WA	Bludgeoning
8/2/74	Carol Valenzuela	20	—	WA	Strangulation/clubbing
8/2/74	Unidentified victim	17–23	—	WA	?
10/2/74	Nancy Wilcox	16	Student	UT	?
10/18/74	Melissa Smith	17	Student	UT	Strangulation/fractured skull
10/31/74	Laurie Amie	17	Student	UT	Strangulation/fractured skull
11/8/74	Debbie Kent	17	Student	UT	?
1/12/75	Caryn Campbell	23	Nurse	CO	Fractured skull
3/15/75	Julie Cunningham	26	Ski instructor	CO	Fractured skull
4/6/75	Denise Oliverson	25	—	CO	—
1/15/78	Lisa Levy	20	Student	FL	Fractured skull
1/15/78	Margaret Bowman	21	Student	FL	Clubbing/strangulation
2/9/78	Kimberly Leach	12	Student	FL	Strangulation/slashed throat

Bundy also confessed to, or is believed by investigators to, have also murdered:

1973	Rita Lorraine Jolly, 17, Clackamas County, OR
1973	Vicki Lynn Hollar, 24, Eugene, OR
1973	Katherine Merry Devine, 14, Seattle, WA
1974	Brenda Joy Baker, 14, Seattle, WA
1975	Nancy Baird, 21, Farmington, UT
1974–1975	Sandra Weaver, 17, UT
1974–1975	Sue Curtis, 17, UT
1974–1975	Debbie Smith, 17, UT
1975	Melanie Suzanne Cooley, 18, Nederland, CO
1975	Shelly K. Robertson, 24, Denver, CO

THEODORE ROBERT BUNDY continued

capital punishment were few in number at the Florida State Prison in Starke as dozens of people anxious to see him die cheered, set off firecrackers, and chanted "Burn, Bundy, Burn" as the appointed hour approached. Indeed, it was a disgusting end to a disgusting life. On January 24, 1989, at 7:00 A.M., Theodore Robert Bundy died in the electric chair. His last words before a black hood was placed over his head were "Give my love to my family and friends."

The following statements by Bundy attempt to add a rational note to his murderous career.

- "Sitting there in a cell, I could convince myself that I was not guilty of anything."
- "Walking right up to the edge [regarding confession] is a thrill, but I can't do it. I haven't allowed myself to choke."
- "They [society] will condemn Ted Bundy while walking past a magazine rack that contains the very things that send kids down the road to being Ted Bundys."

Offenders in this subgroup were also found to be relatively more violent toward their victims than other males who killed alone. For example, they were much more inclined to use a combination of methods of killing (67%, compared with 47% for other males). There did not appear to be any one clear-cut method employed as the preferred manner to kill victims. Although strangling and suffocation were common methods, they were used as the sole method by only 15% of the subgroup offenders. Whereas only 27% of other solo male killers ever strangled or suffocated their victims, 59% of offenders in this subgroup chose this method in killing some or all of their victims. Guns were used as the sole means of death by only 8% of subgroup offenders; bludgeonings, 3%; mutilations, 5%; and poisons, 3%. Compared with other solo male killers, this subgroup used firearms in similar proportions (36% and 37%) but contrasted in all other methods. Poisons were used less often by this subgroup (8%) than other solo male killers (17%). Torture was common among the subgroup (21%) but not among the other solo males (5%). Mutilation was used frequently by all solo killers, but this subgroup of women killers used it more (54%) than other solo offenders (42%).

It is especially this subgroup of killers that reinforces the belief that sex is the primary driving motive behind the murders. Because of these offenders' sexual abuse of their victims, the public believes that serial killers are motivated by particularly bizarre and perverted sexual urges. Certainly they experience a degree of sexual arousal and gratification in what they do, but this does not mean that sexual gratification is the primary motive for killing. When we begin to evaluate sexual acts as vehicles to gain control, maintain power, and degrade and inflict pain on the victim, we inevitably are making headway toward understanding the mind of the serial killer.

Most offenders in this subgroup can be described as "lust killers" because sexual acts and associations are both overtly and subtly interwoven into their assaults. The need for control was never more manifest than in this particular group of male offenders. Post mortem acts of mutilation and desecration were common, as were repeated and prolonged acts of sexual sadism and torture. Necrophilia also was very common. The fear of rejection appeared to be so powerful that some offenders would have sex with the victim only after she had died. In the perception of the offender, a corpse permits him to be intimate without risk of rejection.

In summarizing motives for this subgroup, sexual acts usually were methods of killing, not reasons for killing. The primary motive was control; such offenders must control others in order to feel that they themselves are in control of their own lives. The vehicle to achieve control for this subgroup was through sexual acts. Other male killers may use different methods, such as guns, to achieve a similar sense of control. Offenders in this subgroup were much more prone to carry out acts of rape (75%) than other male solo offenders (44%). They were also more likely to express enjoyment or pleasure (48%) about the murders than other male offenders (25%). Financial gain was seldom (13%) found to be a motive for the subgroup offenders, whereas other male solo offenders (56%) often cited money as a factor in the killing process. Also, the subgroup offenders cited personal reasons (38%) more often than others (22%) for the murders. For example, 20% of all offenders in this subgroup explained the reason for their crimes as an "urge to kill," whereas other male offenders were more likely to kill for revenge (17%). Offenders in this subgroup were also twice as likely (65%) to have a variety or combination of motives in comparison with other male offenders (31%).

Another important characteristic of these lust killers was the "perversion factor." This subgroup was nearly three times more likely to carry out bizarre sexual acts (33%) than other male offenders (12%). These acts most commonly included necrophilia and trophy collection. Jerry Brudos (Profile 7-9) severed the breasts of some of his victims and made epoxy molds. Brudos, like others, also photographed his victims in various poses, dressed and disrobed. The photos served as trophies and a stimulus to act out again.

The backgrounds of these lust killers also contrast somewhat with those of other male serial offenders. Other offenders appeared to have had slightly more involvement in theft, robbery, or burglary (23%) than this subgroup (15%). The lust killers had a more frequent history of sex-related crimes (44%) and time in prison or mental institutions (41%) than other male offenders (35% and 23%). Again, offenders in the subgroup were much more likely to have had more than one previous social or psychological problem (67%) when compared with other male solo killers (45%). This may suggest that lust killers are influenced to violence as a result of such problems. Another explanation, and probably more accurate at this point in the development of serial murder research, is simply that lust killers receive more attention from both law enforcement and researchers. Consequently, we are probably going to find more information on the sensational cases, especially if research is based primarily on the more gruesome statistics and facts, paying less attention to other details.

Regardless of the subgrouping of male serial killers who act alone, a recurrent problem noted in most of them was feelings of low self-esteem and worthlessness. These feelings, according to offenders, appeared to stem

PROFILE 7-9: JERRY BRUDOS
1968–1969

At an early age, Jerry Brudos developed a particular interest in women's shoes, especially black, spike-heeled shoes. As he matured, his shoe fetish increasingly provided sexual arousal. At 17 he used a knife to assault a girl and force her to disrobe while he took pictures of her. For his crime he was incarcerated in a mental hospital for nine months. His therapy uncovered his sexual fantasy for revenge against women, fantasies that included placing kidnapped girls into freezers so he could later arrange their stiff bodies in sexually explicit poses. He was evaluated as possessing a personality disorder but was not considered to be psychotic.

Jerry completed high school, served in the military, and then became an electronics technician. His sexual fixations carried into marriage; he insisted his wife, Ralphene, stay nude while in the house. He would take pictures of her naked, and, according to his wife, he occasionally dressed in her panties and bra. He continued to collect women's undergarments and shoes. Prior to his first murder, he had already assaulted four women and raped one of them. At age 28, Jerry was ready to start killing. His first victim came to his home quite by accident looking for another address. On January 26, 1968, Linda Slawson, 19, working in book sales, knocked on Jerry Brudos's door. He took her to his garage where he smashed her skull with a two-by-four. Before disposing of the body in a nearby river, he severed her left foot and placed it in his freezer. He often would amuse himself by dressing the foot in a spiked-heel shoe.

His fantasy for greater sexual plea-sure led him, on November 26, 1968, to strangle Jan Whitney, 23, with a postal strap. After killing Ms. Whitney, he had sexual intercourse with the corpse, then cut off the right breast and made an epoxy mold of the organ. Before dumping her body in the river, he took pictures of the corpse. Unable to satisfy his sexual fantasies and still in the grasp of violent urges, he found his third victim, Karen Sprinker, 19, on March 27, 1969. After sexually assaulting Karen, he strangled her in his garage, amputated both breasts, again took pictures, and tossed her body into the river. Four weeks later, on April 23, 1969, he abducted his last victim, Linda Salee, 22, from a shopping mall. He sexually assaulted Linda, and, after strangling her in his garage, he shocked her torso with electric charges and watched her body jerk with spasms. Investigators also found needle marks on her body.

All of Brudos's victims were young, white, female strangers, whom he methodically killed in his garage under the special mirrors he had installed to help feed his fantasies. He later confessed that he enjoyed the killing, especially how his victims looked once they were dead. Brudos was sent to Oregon State Prison for the murders.

Twenty years later, Brudos is now granted a parole hearing every other year under Oregon's old parole system. He has adjusted to prison life and has turned his energies to his personal computer and printer, which make life in a cell much more meaningful. It is unlikely he would ever be paroled, but Brudos has not given up hope.

from periods of rejection or denial by loved ones, especially parents, or by society in general. This subgroup seemed to have experienced unstable homes (33%) more than other male offenders did (3%). This instability in the home included fathers or mothers who were alcoholics; mothers who were prostitutes; parent(s) being confined to mental institutions or prisons; a history of mental problems in the family; and repeated separations from parents when the offender was a child.

Although these descriptive data appear to point out commonalities among serial killers of a specific type, much more research is necessary to measure their validity and reliability. In the meantime, efforts need to be made to collect more complete and accurate data.

Men Who Kill Men: The Solo Killer

Serial killers select a variety of victims contingent on their own perceived needs and abilities. Given the apparent reality that male solo offenders prefer to attack women, what types of men would elect to kill males? During the settlement and expansion of U.S. territories, men killing men was a common phenomenon, especially during the taming of the "Wild West." Gunslingers and other outlaws were a constant threat to those wishing to establish order and preserve the peace. By definition, gunslingers who roamed the country in America's early days meet some of the criteria of what a serial killer was and is supposed to be. However, given the fact that carrying guns was established as the rule of law for many years, it is not surprising that men frequently killed men. Most people carried weapons, especially guns, for protection. Others carried guns in order to commit property crimes, and some killed during the completion of such crimes. The term "cold blooded killer" was commonly affixed to outlaws such as the members of the Dalton gang, Jesse James, and other robbers because they often killed men who tried to interfere with their pursuit of criminal activity. But these men are not the types of offenders generally thought of as serial killers, even though they killed over time. Generally, they are excluded from the definition of serial killers because their primary objective was to rob, not kill. However, the question could be asked: How do we know the exact intent of their criminal activity? Some outlaws who robbed may have also looked forward to killing innocent bystanders. The same question could be asked about organized crime figures, military personnel, or even police officers.

As with other subgroups of serial killers, efforts were made to identify offenders of earlier eras using the contemporary definition of serial murder. Even by omitting most outlaws, certain offenders were identified who fit the intended definition of serial killers. These men were identified as serialists because their primary objective was clearly to kill others. It was not until the twentieth century that information began to surface about the sexual involvement of serial offenders who killed men. This may have been more a function of limited record keeping than a puritan spirit. Eventually, as record keeping became more complete and crimes of sexual nature were more openly discussed, cases of men killing men began to document an array of perversities.

In this study, serial killers who murdered men came from a wide spectrum of educational levels and social classes, including transients and local politicians, farmers and racists. The most common thread among this particular subgroup, which also sets them apart, appears to be that offenders were involved homosexually with their victims or killed as a result of homosexual liaisons. Lust killers use sex as a vehicle to destroy their victims; often men who kill men use sex in a similar fashion. Some of the offenders in this subgroup committed their crimes while traveling; others searched for victims locally or used their own homes or places of employment for the killing sites. For the most part, these offenders were single, lower/middle-class, and had histories of deeply troubled lives (see Profile 7-10).

PROFILE 7-10: JOHN WAYNE GACY
1972–1978

Few other serial killers have attracted as much attention as John Wayne Gacy, "The Killer Clown," one of the most prolific murderers of all time. Born on March 17, 1942, he appeared to have experienced a rather normal childhood, but there were a few dark sides. His father, Gacy Sr., was an alcoholic and frequently mistreated the family by beating his wife, abusing John, and terrorizing his daughters. John could never seem to gain the approval of his father regardless of the efforts he made. As a child, John was accidentally struck in the head by a swing. For five years he experienced blackouts until a blood clot was diagnosed and dissolved by medications. He dropped out of high school in his senior year and left home for a short time, working in a mortuary in Las Vegas. But Gacy had been strongly influenced by his mother since childhood, and, succumbing to that influence, he returned home to live. After finally graduating from a business college, he began selling shoes. His friends found him to be a braggart, because he frequently talked about his time in the military. However, Gacy had never served time in the military.

In 1964, Gacy, now 22, married and went to work for his father-in-law as a worker for, then manager of, a chain of Kentucky Fried Chicken establishments.

Gacy joined the local Jaycees and became chaplain of the Waterloo, Iowa, chapter and chairman of the group's first citywide prayer breakfast. In 1967 he was named outstanding vice president and honored as the best Jaycee club chaplain in the state of Iowa. In the spring of 1968, Gacy started his downward spiral, a trip that would take ten years before ending. A grand jury indicted Gacy for handcuffing an employee and trying to sodomize him and also for paying a youth to perform fellatio on him. He had also hired someone to beat up the youth when he testified against Gacy. He pled guilty to one charge and was incarcerated at the Psychiatric Hospital, State University of Iowa. After being diagnosed as a bisexual with a personality that was "thrill-seeking or exploratory," Gacy was sent to prison. Because of being a model prisoner and an active community member, Gacy was paroled after serving only 18 months.

Gacy's first wife, who had two children by John, had divorced Gacy during his trial. Upon his release from prison, Gacy went back to Chicago to live with his mother again. For a while he worked as a cook and then told his mother he had decided to buy his own home. In 1971 he was arrested for picking up a teenager and attempting to force the youth to engage in sex. The case was

JOHN WAYNE GACY continued

dismissed when the youth failed to appear on the court date. Gacy was now living in Des Plaines, near Chicago, and had begun his own construction business. He married again to Carol Hoff, who remembered how John started bringing home pictures of naked men. After four years the marriage ended because of a lack of sexual relations between the couple and because John would often stay out very late at night in his car. John's wife had also learned not to ask questions about personal items she found while cleaning. Gacy had become enraged when she asked him about her discovery of some wallets belonging to young men.

Gacy had begun to add onto his home, and part of the construction included building a large crawl space under the addition. He frequently had some of his young employees help in digging a trench in the crawl space. During this time Gacy was actively involved in the community. In 1970 he had become a Democratic precinct captain and even had his picture taken with First Lady Rosalynn Carter shortly before his arrest in 1978. He also became a local celebrity, dressing up as Pogo the Clown and performing at children's parties and at hospitals. He also frequently held summer parties at his home, inviting local dignitaries and neighbors. Sometimes people would comment about the peculiar smell, but John simply explained that there was a lot of dampness in the crawl space that created the odor.

Only Gacy knew that the crawl space held his personal collection of bodies of young males whom he sexually tortured to death. Some of his victims were young males who worked for Gacy; others were male prostitutes he picked up late at night at "Bughouse Square," a well-known locale in Chicago frequented at night by homosexuals and male prostitutes. Gacy would lure the victim to his home promising money or employment. When they arrived at Gacy's home, he would talk his victim into participating in his "handcuff trick." Once he had the youth in handcuffs, he would chloroform the victim and then sodomize him. Next followed the "rope trick," usually when the victim was conscious. Gacy would tie a rope around the victim's neck and, after fashioning two knots, would insert a stick and proceed to twist it slowly like a tourniquet. The terrifying deaths sometimes were accompanied by Gacy reading passages from the Bible.

John managed to bury 29 victims in the crawl space and cement driveway. Four other victims, for want of space, were discarded in the Des Plaines River. Police were led to Gacy after one of his intended victims escaped and reported him. Investigators eventually demolished Gacy's house and dug up most of his yard in search of bodies. Gacy confessed at least five times, only to later recant his statements. He now claims other people must have put the bodies there. "Where the hell could I have found time? I was working 16 hours a day, and the rest of my time was devoted to the community, charity affairs, and helping you people." During the determination of Gacy's sanity, he was described as a veritable Jekyll-and-Hyde. His defense attorney, Mr. Amirante, cited passages from Robert Louis Stevenson's *The Strange Case of Dr. Jekyll and Mr. Hyde*, quoting Dr. Jekyll: "If I am the chief of sinners, I am the chief of sufferers, also. Both sides of me were in dead earnest." The prosecution, however, described Gacy as having an "antisocial personality," as "a psychopath, a person who commits crimes without remorse."

In 1980, John Wayne Gacy was found guilty of all counts of murder and

JOHN WAYNE GACY continued

sentenced to die in the electric chair at Menard Correctional Center in Chicago. Three years after his trial, Gacy stated he was opposed to capital punishment on religious grounds: "Let he who is free of sin cast the first stone." He believes the lengthy appeals process will save him from execution. Today Gacy claims to be a quiet and kind person. He blames some of the parents for the deaths of their children because their sons were prostitutes. He says he is incapable of violence and continues to receive letters every day from "kind people," most of them women. "Ninety percent of the writers are women, and I have 41 people on my visiting list. I'm allowed three visits a month," explains Gacy. Although the prosecution portrayed Gacy as a skillful, competent torturer and killer who enjoyed the "God-like power" of life and death, Gacy says it's a lie: "How could I live on top of those bodies?" (Simon, 1983). Yet in a 1986 interview with author Tim Cahill, he remarked that if he could spend 15 minutes in a room with the parents of the people he killed, "they would understand."

Men Who Kill Children

Over one fourth of all male serial killers researched had killed at least one child, whereas about 5% killed children only. Although male offenders in this study targeted primarily children only relatively rarely, the effects of those who did were devastating to the community as well as the families of the victims. Nearly all offenders in this subgroup were in some manner involved sexually with their child victims, either before or after death occurred. Like other offenders, these men (and one teenager) demonstrated a need to control their victims and have power over them. Some carried on their killings for many years. Given the amount of publicity and attention crimes against children generate, especially those shrouded in ritualistic abuse, we naturally can expect the media to focus on such cases.

In these particular child murders, ritualism was not as evident as with some other serial killers. However, there appeared to be a high degree of emotionalism among some offenders in this subgroup, including hatred expressed through acts of sadism. Some offenders looked forward to killing more children, whereas other offenders expressed deep regrets for their crimes. Like other serial killings, the murders in this subgroup tended to be intraracial. Wayne Williams of Atlanta was the most publicized case of a black offender killing black children (Profile 7-11). Offenders usually presented themselves as nice, normal, trustworthy people, thus gaining the trust of their child victims. The more normal they appeared and the more caution they exercised and premeditation they engaged in, the greater their homicidal longevity appeared to be.

PROFILE 7-11: WAYNE B. WILLIAMS
1980–1981

For 22 months the residents of Atlanta lived in growing fear and outrage as a serial killer methodically hunted their children. The body count reached 30 victims before the killer was apprehended. They ranged in age from seven to 28, and most were young males. Some were shot or strangled; others were stabbed, bludgeoned, or suffocated. All the victims were black. The deaths of so many black young people gave rise to a variety of theories and accusations, including belief in a plot by white supremacists to systematically kill all black children. Others began to think the children were being killed by Satan worshippers, blood cultists, or even copycat murderers. The Ku Klux Klan came under close scrutiny, but no link could be made between their members and any of the murders. Atlanta became like a city under siege and inevitably attracted the attention of the entire country, including the resources of the federal government.

It appeared the murders would never stop until one night, as police staked out a bridge over the Chattahoochee River, they heard a car on the bridge come to a stop, followed by a distinct splash caused by something being dropped into the river. They pulled Wayne B. Williams, 23, over for questioning and finally arrested him as a suspect in the child murder cases. Williams was found to be a bright young black man who lived with his retired parents and involved himself in photography. A media and police "groupie," Williams would often listen on his shortwave radio and respond to ambulance, fire, and police emergency calls. He would then sell his exclusive pictures to the local newspapers. At age 18, he was arrested for impersonating a police officer. He spent one year at Georgia State University but dropped out when he felt his "rising star" was moving too slowly.

Wayne's freelance work as a cameraman was never steady, and he began to focus his energies on music. As a self-employed talent scout, he eventually lured his victims into his control. He was known to distribute leaflets offering "private and free" interviews to blacks between the ages of 11 and 21 who sought a career in music. At his trial, Williams was depicted as a man who hated his own race and wanted to eliminate future generations. He was described as a homosexual or a bisexual who paid young boys to have sex with him. A boy, 15, claimed he had been molested by Williams, and several witnesses testified they had seen him with some of the victims.

Williams denied everything, and the prosecution had only elaborate forensics on which to base their case against him. The forensic evidence suggested a distinct link between Williams and at least ten of the homicides and indicated a pattern surrounding the murders. The judge ruled the evidence admissible, and Williams was found guilty of murdering two of his older victims, Nathaniel Cater, 27, and Ray Payne, 21. Due to the nature of circumstantial evidence, the judge sentenced Williams to two consecutive life sentences. He was eventually named as being responsible for 24 of the Atlanta slayings, although some believe the child killings have not ended with Williams's arrest.

Men Who Kill the Elderly

This subgroup includes 12 cases of male offenders who primarily murdered elderly persons. The most publicized case was that of the Boston Strangler. People tend to think of Albert DeSalvo as a man who raped and strangled young women; however, he attacked mostly older women: eight of his 13 victims (62%) were 55 years of age or older. As mentioned earlier, rape is not necessarily motivated by sexual desire. The reality of these killings suggests that raping women has much more to do with power, control, and desecration than it does sexual desire. A 30-year-old man raping and sodomizing a 96-year-old woman is not only disgusting, vicious, and perverted but also forces us to reconsider our perceptions of exactly what motivates rapists.

Most of the cases in this subgroup involved men who killed older women. In these cases, most of the women had been sexually assaulted. The pattern killing of these elderly victims was just as distinct as pattern murders of young women. The sexual assaults and tortures rivaled those inflicted on younger victims. The theme of control was pervasive throughout these cases of elderly serial killings.

The victims generally lived alone or were institutionalized. Either way, offenders could obtain relatively easy access to their intended victims. In addition, most older victims were completely powerless against these offenders. As America "grays," more elderly people become potential victims. Although young women are still the most frequent victims, cases of elderly serial murder appear to have increased from 1975 to 1988. Future policies of the health care industry will undoubtedly focus on the aged. As of 1990, little has been done to provide better security for the elderly at home, at the hospital, or in the nursing home. Elderly people who are alone and unprotected unknowingly provide accessible targets for serial offenders (see Profile 7-12).

PROFILE 7-12: CALVIN JACKSON
1973–1974

Calvin Jackson, 26, worked as a porter at the Park Plaza Hotel, a run-down building in New York City. Many elderly and those on fixed incomes lived there trying to make ends meet. They did not realize that their porter was an exconvict who had a long history of robberies and burglaries. He also was a regular drug user and had been involved in several assaults. On one occasion Jackson had plea bargained a robbery charge, and, instead of getting a 15-year sentence, he served 30 days. For years he moved from one dilapidated hotel to another. On his arrival at the Plaza, he decided to start burglarizing apartments there, except this time he would kill the occupant. He ransacked each victim's apartment and stole radios and television sets along with other items of small value. He attacked and killed at least nine women, most of them older. He usually strangled or suffocated his victims, although at least one was stabbed to death. All the

CALVIN JACKSON continued

victims were sexually assaulted, some after death, and, except for his final victim, they all lived in the Plaza Hotel.

Jackson was finally captured after he was seen carrying a TV set down a fire escape at 3:00 A.M. He confessed to all the pattern killings and was judged sane by the courts. His defense argued that Jackson would often make something to eat after he had killed his victim and sit and watch her, sometimes for an hour, to make sure she was really dead. The defense believed that only an insane person could do that. The courts did not agree and convicted Jackson on nine counts of homicide. He was given 18 life sentences, making him eligible for parole in the year 2030.

Calvin Jackson's Victims

DATE OF MURDER	NAME	AGE	RESIDENCE	METHOD	SEXUAL ASSAULT
4/10/73	Theresa Jordan	39	Plaza Hotel	Suffocation	Raped
7/19/73	Kate Lewisohn	65	Plaza Hotel	Strangulation/ crushed skull	Raped
4/24/74	Mabel Hartmeyer	60	Plaza Hotel	Strangulation	Raped
4/28/74	Yetta Yishnefsky	79	Plaza Hotel	Stabbing	Raped
6/8/74	Winifred Miller	47	Plaza Hotel	Strangulation	Raped
6/19/74	Blanche Vincent	71	Plaza Hotel	Suffocation	Raped
7/1/74	Martha Carpenter	69	Plaza Hotel	Suffocation	Raped
8/30/74	Eleanor Platt	64	Plaza Hotel	Suffocation	Raped
9/12/74	Pauline Spanierman	59	Building next to Plaza Hotel	—	—

Men Who Kill Families

Most serial killers are portrayed as offenders who seek out individual victims. Occasionally some killers elected to abduct two victims at the same time. However, few offenders attempted such abductions because dealing with more than one victim tended to weaken their control. Serial killers, especially the "lust killers," often wanted "private" time alone with the victim. Team killers tended to be the exception (Chapter 8). A few offenders killed several victims at once, including entire families. However, such occurrences appear to be rare in serial killing; also, these types of murders by male offenders occurred mostly before 1940. Some of these cases involved "Bluebeards," or men who killed one spouse after another (Profile 7-13). Most of these cases did not include sexual attacks, and often money appeared to be a primary motivating factor in the killings. Guns and poisons were more likely to be used, with less emphasis on torture and strangling.

PROFILE 7-13: JAMES P. WATSON
1910–1920

Like many con artists, James P. Watson, "Bluebeard," went by several aliases. When asked by police for his real identity, he simply replied "I don't know." His last official residence was in California, but Watson operated from Mexico to Canada. A very bright individual but not without his own peculiar sexual quirks, Watson was married to at least 18 women and possibly as many as 26, several of them at the same time. He frequently placed ads in newspapers luring women into marriage.

> *Personal*: Would like to meet lady of refinement and some social standing who desires to meet middle-aged gentleman of culture. Object matrimony. Gentleman has nice bank account, as well as a considerable roll of government bonds.
>
> H. L. Gorden
> Hotel Tacoma.
> [Pearson, 1936, p. 132]

There were always several women who eagerly responded and happily accepted the fact that he worked for the secret service and would need to be on the road frequently. He was very careful to marry women of wealth, which he quickly maneuvered into his control. He began to act out his fantasies of killing women, because he believed they were the root of all evil. He murdered at least seven and possibly as many as 15; the exact count was never established. Some of them he drowned, others he beat to death with a hammer. They died in Washington State, Idaho, California, and probably other states. His fantasies led him in at least one murder to sexually mutilate his victim. He would later confess to investigators:

> "All I felt after killing seemed largely, in each instance, some kind of relief, yet unexplainable. The sensation experienced was a sensation of ease as if I had been relieved. Instead of remorse, I had passive satisfaction or passive pleasure. I had no sexual sensation at the time but maybe for a day or two afterwards feeling more that way than normal. The greater sexual desires shortly after was from a memory of the killing. Sometimes I have looked at the body in a way of satisfaction, a kind of pleasure. Yet there was no reason why I should do that because I had seen the same person in married relations" [Ellis & Gullo, 1971, p. 20].

Watson agreed to lead them to the body of one of his victims in return for a guarantee he would receive a life sentence and not death row. The courts agreed, and he went to San Quentin, where he eventually died.

Men Who Kill Men and Women

The final subgroup in this chapter includes 13 cases of serial murder in which the offender killed both men and women. Some of the cases could be referred to as "spree serial killings" because they occurred within a relatively short time frame. Anger, revenge, greed, madness, sadism, and delusions of heroism were often associated with these killers' homicidal actions. This subgroup includes some well publicized cases, including "Son of Sam"

(Profile 7-14), Charles Starkweather, and the "Night Stalker" case in California. In several of these cases, guns were used as the sole means of killing the victims. Some of the killers were extremely violent in their attacks, whereas others quietly poisoned or suffocated their victims. In contrast to the lust killers, most offenders in this subgroup were not involved in sexual attacks, or particularly perverted acts. This type of serial killer tended to resemble the profile of the mass murderer, who kills all his victims in a few minutes or hours. Most of the cases lasted less than one year, and some lasted only a few weeks. Although some of the offenders had developed a distinct pattern in their murders, several cases involved a high degree of randomness in victim selection. Except for the "Night Stalker" case, which was allegedly connected to some form of self-styled satanism, most of the cases were less ritualistic and more impulsive and spontaneous than other types of male solo serial killers.

PROFILE 7-14: DAVID RICHARD BERKOWITZ
1976–1977

For 13 months David Berkowitz, "The Son of Sam," or "The .44-Calibre Killer," was able to hold the attention of millions of people in New York City and across the country. During that time he shot 13 young men and women on eight different occasions. Six of his victims died, and seven others were severely injured after he fired on young women or couples parked in their cars at night. Investigators finally tracked him down through a parking ticket placed on his car while he was in the area looking for someone to kill. They expected to find "The .44-Calibre Killer" to be a monster but instead found a well-mannered, 24-year-old postal worker who lived alone. His apartment was filthy, littered with liquor bottles and the walls scratched with graffiti. On one area of the wall he had scrawled: "In this hole lives the wicked king."

To those few who knew him, he lived a rather uneventful life. Born out of wedlock, he had been placed for adoption. He was an exceptional student who frequently was taunted by his classmates for being Jewish. He served three years in the U.S. Army, worked as a security guard, and once worked as an auxiliary New York police officer. His main character trait seemed to be that he was introverted and liked to roam the streets alone at night. On July 29, 1976, two young women, Donna Lauria, a medical technician, and Jody Valenti sat talking in their car when David walked out of the shadows and fired five shots through the windshield. Donna died quickly; Jody was wounded in the thigh. In October, he fired on a young couple through their rear windshield, wounding the young man. In November David walked up to two women sitting in their car in Queens and, as he asked for directions, pulled out his .44-calibre gun and fired at both women, paralyzing one of them. On January 30, 1977, a young couple were saying goodnight to each other when the windshield shattered with gunfire. Christine Freund died a few hours later of her injuries. On March 8, 1977, an Armenian student, Virginia Voserichian, was approaching her mother's house when David met her on the sidewalk and shot her directly in the face, killing her instantly. On April 17, 1977, in the same area as some of the other attacks,

DAVID RICHARD BERKOWITZ continued

David shot to death Alexander Esau and Valentina Suriani as they sat in their automobile. A note was found at the scene that read in part: "I love to hunt. Prowling the streets looking for fair game—tasty meat. The women of Queens are prettiest of all." The .44-Calibre Killer had identified himself as "Son of Sam" in letters he had sent to a New York columnist, James Breslin. By now the city was beginning to panic, but David still easily found victims. In June he shot out the windshield of another car but only wounded the two occupants.

In July David decided to relocate his killing to the Brooklyn area in order to throw off the police. At 1:30 A.M. he fired four shots through the windshield of a car, striking a young couple. Stacy Moskowitz died a few hours later, and her friend Robert Violante was blinded for life. It was here that David's car was ticketed and shortly thereafter linked to the killings. David was arrested exclaiming "You finally got me!" But there had been several clues during the long year's ordeal. David had sent threatening notes to his Yonkers neighbors. Sam Carr had made reports to police that David was out to get him because his dog barked too much. Carr's dog had been shot by David with his .44-calibre gun on April 27, shortly after David sent him the letters. David's capture proved to be providential for several young New Yorkers. He told police that he was planning a raid on a Hampton discotheque that night and that authorities "would be counting bodies all summer." Police found a submachine gun and a note to authorities lying on the seat of his car (Leyton,

1986a, Ch. 5).

At first Berkowitz claimed he committed the killings because demonically possessed dogs commanded him to do so. Years later, he would recant those claims publicly by saying that it was the need to justify those shootings in his own mind that caused him to fabricate the demon story. He said he simply wanted to pay back his neighbor, Sam Carr, for all the noise his dog made, so he created the story that Sam was telling him to kill by using the dogs as a medium. In a letter he sent to David Abrahamsen, a psychiatrist who determined Berkowitz to be competent for trial, he conceded: "I will always fantasize those evil things which are part of my life. I will always remain a mental pervert by thinking sexual things, etc. However, almost everyone else is like me, for we commit numerous perverted sexual acts in our minds day after day. I will always think of violence, for only a monk, perhaps, could ever succeed in eliminating these desires and thoughts. But what I hope to do is mature to such a point in which I will develop a deeper respect for human life and an increased respect and appreciation for humanity" [Abrahamsen, 1985, p. 23].

David Berkowitz received three 24-year sentences for the murders to which he confessed, with a recommendation that he never be paroled. New York passed a "Son of Sam" statute prohibiting criminals from profiting financially from their crimes. Thus, Berkowitz will not be able to profit from any books or movies written about his time as The .44-Calibre Killer.

CHAPTER 8

Team Killers

The primary catalyst for serial murder victimization stems from a perceived need to acquire power and control over others. Of course, human nature, practically by definition, includes a drive for power of some type, in some degree. For some people, however, the road to power is strewn with human sacrifices. Power can be all-consuming and justifies every means and method to obtain it.

In the drive for domination, the intensity, the frequency, and the subsequent interpretation of murder are more fulfilling for some killers than for others. The lust for power is the chameleon of vices and as such can be perceived and experienced in many different ways. For some multiple killers, murder must be simultaneously a participation and a spectator endeavor; power can be experienced by observing a fellow conspirator destroy human life, possibly as much as by performing the killing. The pathology of the relationship operates symbiotically. In other words, the offenders contribute to each other's personal inventory of power.

In the mid 1960s, Walter Kelbach and Myron Lance went on a killing spree for several days. In some of the murders, the killers would toss a coin to see which one would get to stab the victim to death. Alone, they may never have killed. What they could never become alone, they could aspire to collectively. Inhibitions and fears were dissipated by the interaction of the two men. History is replete with examples of the destructive forces of group behavior.

In groups of people who kill, there are often a few who play subservient roles. They provide an immediate audience "privileged" to experience or witness the destructive power of the main actors. Serial killing groups are frequently masterminded by one person—for example, Buono, in the "Hillside Stranglings" in California; Douglas Clark in the "Sunset Strip" killings in Hollywood; Charles Manson and his "Family"; and Gary Heidnik, "The Fiend of Franklinville" in Philadelphia.

Like other subgroups of serial offenders, team killers, or those who kill with one or more accomplices, have been documented for many generations. They have generally been considered anomalies that occur infrequently; thus little attention has been given to the nature of team killing.

Identifying Team Killers

Thirty-two cases, comprising 76 offenders, represented the base for the analysis for this subgroup of serial killers. Thirty-eight percent of the cases involved one or more female offenders. Sixty-three percent of the cases involved less than one-year time frames, and the remaining cases involved more than one year before the killings ceased. The average age of offenders was approximately 30 for males and 28 for females. Eleven percent of offenders were black, and an additional 2% were other racial minorities. Eighty-one percent of cases involved only two offenders, whereas the remaining cases had three or more offenders in each group. The largest group was identified as having five offenders. Several of the cases or offenders involved were labeled by the media, the community, or by themselves with creative monikers, such as those in the next table.

Several of these cases attracted public attention and have inspired books and movies, including *The Hillside Strangler* and *Helter Skelter*, both of which were popular at the bookstore and the box office.

Monikers Given to Selected Team Killers in the United States

1870–1873	The Bender Family	The Bloody Benders The Hell Benders
1901–1908	Belle Gunness	Belle of Indiana Lady Bluebeard
1920	Mary E. Smith	Old Shoebox Annie
1932–1934	Clyde Barrow Bonnie Parker	Texas Rattlesnake Bonnie and Clyde Suicide Sal
1949–1950	Raymond Fernandez Martha Beck	The Lonely Hearts Killer
1969	Charles M. Manson	Charlie
1972–1977	Patrick Kearney	Jigsaw Murders
1973–1974	Manuel Moore Larry C. Green Jessie Lee Cooks J.C. Simon	Zebra Killers
1974–1975	Joseph Kallinger	The Shoe Maker
1977–1978	Gary James Lewingdon Thaddeus C. Lewingdon	The .22-Caliber Killers
1977–1978	Kenneth Bianchi Angelo Buono	Hillside Stranglers
1980	Douglas D. Clark	Sunset Strip Killer
1986–1987	Gary Heidnik	Fiend of Franklinville

FIGURE 8.1 Frequency of Cases of Serial Murder Committed by Team Killers in the United States, 1800–1988*

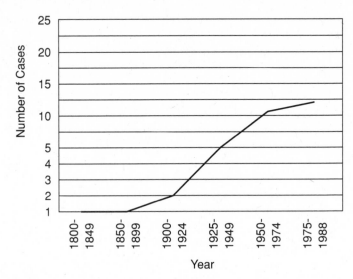

* 32 cases, 76 offenders.

As indicated in Figure 8.1, the emergence of team killers has mirrored the rise of solo offenders. Although predicting criminal behavior has never been the forte of researchers, assuming that such cases will continue to appear as they have during the 70s and the 80s, we will likely see a continued sharp rise in such cases. First, law enforcement is becoming educated about serial killings and is more likely now to recognize patterns of serial murders. Second, fluctuations in the stability of the U.S. economy have a profound effect on the psychological well-being of some individuals. Third, desensitization of portions of our communities toward the value of human life is continuing as a result of violence portrayed in the movies, on TV, and in the media. Fourth, the elderly are a fast-growing group of particularly accessible, potential victims.

Only time will prove the accuracy of the gloomy predictions of an increase in serial murders. In the meantime, understanding some of the characteristics of team killing may assist in unraveling its etiology. As briefly discussed earlier, relationships between or among team killers can reveal a great deal about the offenders and the motivations for murder. Table 8.1 indicates that approximately one third of all team offenders were legally or blood related (see Profile 8-1). The relationships were widely distributed, including several sibling and parent-child combinations. Nonrelated team killers were subdivided into four groups, two of which involved offenders who were intimately involved. The remaining two groups had either males or females who provided leadership to the group.

TABLE 8.1 Relationship of Team Offenders to Each Other

RELATIONSHIP	PERCENTAGE OF OFFENDERS ($N=25$)	
A. Relatives		
1. Husband/wife	24	
2. Father/son	20	
3. Brothers	16	
4. Mother/son	16	
5. Father/mother/daughter/son	16	
6. Cousins	8	
	Subtotal	34
	PERCENTAGE OF OFFENDERS ($N=52$)	
B. Nonrelatives:		
7. Male-dominated teams	65	
8. Male/female lovers	15	
9. Homosexual lovers	15	
10. Female-dominated team	5	
	Subtotal	66
	Grand Total	100

PROFILE 8-1: KENNETH BIANCHI AND ANGELO BUONO 1977–1978

October 18, 1977, the nude, strangled body of Yolanda Washington was discovered in Los Angeles. She had been a part-time waitress and prostitute who worked the streets of Hollywood. On October 31st, the body of 15-year-old Judith L. Miller, a runaway, was found along a roadside, strangled and sexually abused. The child had been severely tortured. There would be at least eight more victims of Bianchi and Buono, "The Hillside Stranglers." Except for Yolanda Washington, who was killed in a car, all the victims were taken to Buono's house where they were bound, gagged, raped, sodomized with instruments, beaten, and finally strangled to death. The corpses were dumped along the highways and hillsides of Los Angeles and

Glendale, except for Cindy Hudspeth, who was found in the trunk of her car in a ravine.

Buono, age 44, and Bianchi, 26, were cousins who decided to kill someone just to see what it would feel like. Each killing, sexual attack, and torture session became easier for them, a game that they looked forward to with excitement. Lauren Wagner was burned with an electrical cord placed on her body. Kristina Weckler was injected with a cleaning solution so they could watch her convulse and then was gassed by having a bag placed over her head with a hose attached to a stove. The killers abducted not only prostitutes but school girls like 12-year-old Dolores Cepeda and 14-year-old Sonja Johnson. In a span of

KENNETH BIANCHI AND ANGELO BUONO continued

five months, at least ten homicides had been linked to the Hillside Strangler.

Bianchi relocated to Bellingham, Washington, and the murders ceased in Los Angeles. A year later, the bodies of Karen Mandic and Diane Wilder, college roommates, were found raped and strangled, and Bianchi, a prime suspect, was arrested. The similarities in the killings and other circumstantial evidence linked Bianchi to the Hillside killings. Bianchi first tried to convince authorities he suffered from multiple personalities and was not responsible for his actions. When that failed, he agreed to plea bargain and testify against Buono in order to avoid the death penalty. Although they both had developed a taste for killing, Buono and Bianchi were quite different in personality. Bianchi was a bright, smooth-talking ladies' man, a con artist, who had nearly mastered the art of lying. Buono, much less articulate, remained silent throughout his trial. He had been married three times and fathered at least seven children. With only a ninth-grade education, Buono began his own upholstery business and also pimped for prostitutes. He enjoyed sex with pain and had abused many women

sexually. Bianchi, who was married at the time of some of the murders, concealed his actions from his wife and newborn son, Sean.

It was California's longest criminal trial at the time and was very costly. Several witnesses spoke on behalf of the killers, especially Buono, but there were always those who knew of his dark side as well. In 1984, Buono received life in prison without parole, and Bianchi is required to spend 26 years and eight months in prison before his first parole hearing can be scheduled. Judge George, who had remained impartial throughout the long trial, commented to the two sadistic killers, "I'm sure, Mr. Buono and Mr. Bianchi, that you will only get your thrills by reliving over and over the tortures and murders of your victims, being incapable, as I believe you to be, of ever feeling any remorse."

In 1986, in a brief ceremony at Folsom Prison, Angelo Buono, then 52 years old, married Christine Kizuka, 35, a supervisor at the Los Angeles office of the State Employment Development Department. His conviction in nine murders apparently did not lessen his appeal (Levin & Fox, 1985, Ch. 11).

In the nonrelative category, males almost exclusively assumed leadership. Cases were extremely rare in which nonrelated females masterminded multiple homicides. This also tended to be true for cases of male/female lovers. In short, although women frequently became involved in serial murder as a part of team killing, they generally were not the decision makers or main enforcers. These findings support the contention that female "Rippers" have yet to make their mark in the United States. They do not, however, refute the fact that women can be as deadly as men. The females in this subgroup, with a few exceptions, tended to be followers, not leaders. Some of these followers quickly learned how to kill and participated directly in some of the bloodiest murder cases ever chronicled (see Profile 8-2).

Without exception every group of offenders had one person who psychologically maintained control of the other members of the team. Some of these leaders were Charles Manson types who exerted a mystical control

PROFILE 8-2: ALTON COLEMAN AND
DEBRA D. BROWN
1984

A man with an explosive temper and ready to fight, Alton Coleman had committed a long list of violent crimes and sex offenses by the age of 28. He was living with Debra Brown, whom he frequently beat and threatened. Alton was raised in the black slums of the Midwest, the son of a prostitute who died while Alton was a teenager. Having no father and being rejected by his mother while still an infant, Alton went to live with his grandmother. She apparently provided a good home for Alton, who nevertheless was characterized as an unhappy, bitter child who was called "Pissy" by schoolmates because he wet his pants so often. As he grew older, he became more aggressive. He gambled frequently and began to hustle women whom he usually abused through beatings and sexual assaults. He spent at least three years in prison, where he was known for his aggressive homosexual behavior. His brutality with women and his fascination for bondage, violent sex, and young women ended his first marriage after only six months. He is believed to have raped several women and young girls before his murder spree.

His first victim was nine-year-old Vernita Wheat, whom Coleman abducted from an acquaintance. She was raped, strangled, and stuffed into a small closet. While police investigated her disappearance, Alton and Debra left the area. Three weeks later they attacked two girls, ages seven and nine. The youngest, little Tamika, was kicked in the face and chest and strangled until she died. Alton then beat and raped the second child and left her unconscious. For the next several weeks, the couple traveled back and forth through five different states, including Ohio, Indiana, Illinois, and Michigan, where they murdered, raped, and robbed several more

people, both black and white, young and elderly, male and female. A mother, Virginia Temple, and her ten-year-old daughter were beaten, raped, and strangled and left in a basement crawlspace. Coleman possessed a real talent for gaining the trust of strangers and eluding the police, who placed him on the FBI's Most Wanted list. One psychiatrist, who was familiar with Coleman, described him a 'pansexual,' a person who enjoys sex with anyone—man, woman, or child. His sexual enjoyment was surpassed only by his ability for sadism and viciousness.

Debra Brown was described as a high school dropout, from a family of 11, who was easily influenced and dominated. On meeting Coleman, she almost immediately broke off her engagement to another man. Her ability to kill seemed to come easily. In one instance Coleman and Brown attacked a husband and his wife, who lived in suburban Cincinnati, using an array of devices including a four-foot wooden candle stick, a crow bar, vise-grip pliers, and a knife. The wife, Marlene Waters, died after being bludgeoned to death. Other victims were shot to death.

After eight weeks, the two killers were captured without a struggle while watching an outdoor basketball game in Evanston, Illinois. Bond for Coleman was set at $25 million, full cash, and $20 million cash bond was set for Brown. They are believed to be guilty of at least eight murders in addition to a variety of abductions, beatings, robberies, thefts, and sexual assaults. Brown remained loyal to her lover; moments before his first sentencing they signed legal documents creating a commonlaw marriage. Perhaps in efforts to save Coleman from the death penalty, Brown stated in court regarding one of the victims, "I killed the

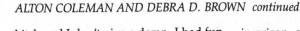

bitch and I don't give a damn. I had fun out of it." When the courts finished with Coleman, he had received four separate death sentences and more than a hundred years in prison. Debra Brown, after receiving her second death sentence, life in prison, and dozens of additional years in prison, apologized for her part in the killing and wrote "I'm a more kind and understandable and lovable person than people think I am." They are currently awaiting execution (Linedecker, 1987, Ch. 2).

over their followers; others used coercion, intimidation, and persuasive techniques. In team murders, not all the participants shared equally in the "thrill" of the kill. As one offender pointed out, *real* serial killers are people who make it their *life's* work. Certainly not all team offenders in this subgroup shared exactly the same motivations or abilities for killing. Given time, however, several became molded to the task.

Truman Capote, in his acclaimed *In Cold Blood* (1965), described the relationship between two killers, Dick Hickock and Perry Smith. In the aftermath of the vicious murders of the entire Clutter family, Perry begins to question the normality of people who could do such a thing. Dick's response reaffirms in Dick's own mind his superiority over Perry: " 'Deal me out, baby,' Dick said. 'I'm a normal.' And Dick meant what he said. He thought himself as balanced, as sane as anyone—maybe a bit smarter than the average fellow, that's all. But Perry—there was, in Dick's opinion, 'something wrong' with Little Perry to say the least" (p. 108).

Such relationships tend to be built on deception, bravado, and intimidation. Often in the aftermath of apprehension by police and eventual incarceration, the leaders of some groups tend to go through a process of self-abdication and place culpability for the murders on the followers. In one case the group leader, denying absolutely any involvement in a series of horrific mutilation murders, contended that his exgirlfriend conceived and executed the murder plans. From his perspective, he was always just a bystander. The case involving Douglas Clark and Carol Bundy (Profile 8-3) also illustrates this point.

Parents and children as well as husbands and wives have also been serial killers. Imagine the dynamics of a family whose mom, dad, son, and daughter systematically killed 14 victims! In one case, the wife had never been involved in any form of violent criminal behavior. By the end, she helped in luring victims to an automobile that she then drove while her husband raped, beat, and strangled them in the back seat.

At what point does a person acquiesce and agree to assist in murdering victims? What enables someone to convince others that murdering people is the direction to follow? It appears unlikely that some male and female offenders ever would have indulged in such crimes had they not been exposed to group dynamics and the power of persuasion and manipulation. Some of those who led groups of team offenders experienced a sense of power and gratification not only through the deaths of victims but also

TABLE 8.3 Distribution of Cases and Team Killers by State, 1795–1988

STATE	NUMBER OF CASES	NUMBER OF OFFENDERS
California	12	31
Texas	5	11
Florida	4	9
Ohio	4	8
Oregon	3	5
Illinois	3	8
Washington	3	5
Utah	2	5
Pennsylvania	2	4
New York	2	4
Michigan	2	4
Indiana	2	4
Kansas	1	4
Colorado	1	3
Arizona	1	2
New Jersey	1	2
Louisiana	1	2
Tennessee	1	2
Montana	1	2
Oklahoma	1	2
Missouri	1	2
Virginia	1	2
Arkansas	1	2
Kentucky	1	2
Nevada	1	2
Alabama	1	2

case in Manhattan Beach, California, seven people were accused of the ritualistic torture of children. After the longest trial ever in United States history, charges against most of the defendants were dropped because of insufficient evidence, and the key suspects were acquitted. Similar cases have surfaced in Bakersfield, California; Jordan, Minnesota; and Annawaakee in Douglasville, Georgia. On April 11, 1989, a mass grave was unearthed near Matamoros, Mexico, just south of the Texas border. The grave contained 15 corpses, many of which appeared to have been ritualistically sacrificed. Cauldrons with animal remains mixed in a broth of human blood and boiled body parts were found not far from a bloodstained altar. Suspects arrested said the victims were "killed for protection." This group of drug smugglers was practicing a form of black magic in which sacrifices to the devil, both human and animal, were believed to provide protection from bullets and criminal prosecution (Fox & Levin, 1989, pp. 49–51). Kahaner, in his book *Cults That Kill* (1988), noted that Satanism and murder are increasing and that an epidemic of youth violence is sweeping the country. The Robin Gecht case supports this claim (Profile 8-5).

Such cases continue to surface and ignite public outrage, especially those that center on families and children. Marron, in his book *Ritual Abuse* (1988), described the complexity of a case in which parents allegedly performed ritualistic tortures on their own children. By the time the courts, investigators, and social service agencies had all been involved, affixing blame and determining culpability had become extremely difficult.

In attempting to sort out the connection, if any, between Satanism, cult activities, and serial murderers, investigators should recognize that many murders in general are carried out by nonstrangers. Also, acts of Satanism or cult worship are much more likely to be self-styled than part of any organized effort. In one case, that of Robert Berdella, a serial killer involved in the murders of several young men was accused of Satan worship. Indignant, Berdella requested an interview with the press and, although he admitted to the murders, he categorically denied any association with cultists, Satan worship, or occult activities (author's files). In only a few cases of team offenders who targeted children were there any hints of Satanism, rituals, or other cult-like activities.

The connection of satanic worship and child sacrifices never fails to generate near hysteria in a community. The reality, however, is that people are much more likely to be killed in a domestic argument, by an intoxicated driver, in an accident, or by disease than by Satan worshipers. The cases of those few who do fall prey to such bizarre practices generate such publicity that people believe the problem has suddenly become epidemic. To add to the confusion, some serial killers may give the appearance of killing children for cult-related purposes. Such self-styled "Satanism," in which each offender adapts rituals to his or her own purposes, appears to be more common than organized satanic sacrifices.

Victim Selection

In more than half of the cases involving team killers, offenders murdered both male and females. When offenders sought out a specific gender, females were more likely than males to become victims. Overall, in 80% of the cases, at least one female was murdered, and in 70% of cases, at least one male was killed.

As indicated in Table 8.4, very few cases or offenders were identified that specifically targeted children or teenagers. Nearly one fifth of all cases included one or more female children, and 16% included one or more male children. Nearly half of all cases included both male and female adult victims, with the latter being the most common. Females were also the most

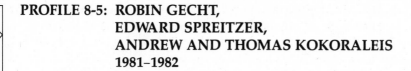

PROFILE 8-5: ROBIN GECHT, EDWARD SPREITZER, ANDREW AND THOMAS KOKORALEIS 1981–1982

Robin Gecht, 28, could be described as charismatic in his ability to draw others to him, especially those who were easily led. Raised on the north side of Chicago, he went to live with his grandparents after he allegedly molested his sister. He eventually became a carpenter-electrician in order to provide for himself, but his strongest skills were his abilities to manipulate and use others. Gecht also had a developing interest in Satanism, cults, and secret rituals. On one occasion he remarked to a friend that through his study of ancient torture practices, he discovered that some female victims were mutilated and their breasts removed to be used later as tobacco pouches. But Robin seemed to be a harmless individual, and no one suspected him, at least not those who knew him, to be involved with the wave of female abductions in the city.

Meanwhile Robin sought out those who might help him realize his sexual fantasies. He had already hired Ed Spreitzer to work for him and eventually met the Kokoraleis brothers, who joined his group. They were all young men: Andrew Kokoraleis, 19; Thomas Kokoraleis, 22; and Ed Spreitzer, 21. One investigator described the three as "classic followers" and "generic nobodies." Using a van belonging to Gecht, they roamed the city, usually at night, hunting for female victims. Police confirmed eight murders carried out by the group, although some of the killers claimed between 10 and 12 victims, and others went as high as 17. The victims were raped, beaten, stabbed, or strangled to death and often sexually mutilated. Following Gecht's arrest for slashing an 18-year-old prostitute, police began to probe deeper into the assail-

ants' backgrounds. They undoubtedly became more suspicious when they discovered that Gecht had worked for John Gacy, the killer of 33 males. Gecht had commented to a friend that Gacy's only mistake had been to bury the bodies under his house. In one place where Gecht had recently lived, police found crosses painted in red and black on the walls of the attic. Thomas Kokoraleis admitted that the room had contained an altar on which cult members dissected both animal and human parts as sacrifices.

As the probe continued, police found a common trait among the victims whose bodies had not completely decomposed. In each of the cases the victim's breasts had been mutilated and cut off with a knife or piano wire. At least one of the killers admitted that they had been told by their leader Gecht to "bring a breast back to the house." Apparently the trio wanted to do Gecht's bidding in order to please him. Once a victim had been found and killed, her breasts would be placed on the altar. Gecht would then read Bible passages while the group engaged in cannibalism.

After five years, the four were convicted of various offenses. Gecht, whom prosecutors described as being similar to Charles Manson, has yet to be convicted of any murders even though the others testified against him. Instead he received a 120-year sentence for the attack on the 18-year-old prostitute, on the evidence of one eyewitness. His lengthy sentence includes time for attempted murder, rape, deviant sexual assault, armed violence, aggravated kidnapping, and aggravated battery. Police continue at this writing to collect more evidence against him. Ed Spreitzer pleaded guilty to six murders and received a death sentence. Some of

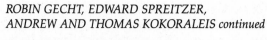

ROBIN GECHT, EDWARD SPREITZER,
ANDREW AND THOMAS KOKORALEIS continued

the victims included Lorraine Borowski, 21, a secretary; Rose Beck Davis, a housewife; Sandra Delaware; Linda Sutton, 28; Shui Mak, 30; and Rafail Tirads, 28, a male who had been shot from a car. Andrew Kokoraleis also received a death sentence for his part in the murders. Thomas Kokoraleis had his murder con-

viction reversed on technical grounds, and after a second trial and a plea bargain he received a 70-year sentence. It is unlikely that the remains of all their victims will ever be recovered, because many of them were buried in forested areas (Baumann, 1987).

TABLE 8.4 Percentage of Team Offenders Murdering Specific Victim Age and Gender Categories

	PERCENTAGE OF CASES (N=32)	PERCENTAGE OF OFFENDERS (N=76)
Gender:		
1. Females only	28	21
Males only	19	21
Both	53	58
	100	100
2. At least one female	81	79
At least one male	72	79
Age grouping:		
1. Adults only	34	37
Teens only	3	3
Children only	6	7
Gender and age grouping:		
1. Adults		
One or more females	69	70
One or more males	59	66
Both males and females	44	50
2. Teens:		
One or more females	25	27
One or more males	19	23
Both males and females	3	5
3. Children:		
One or more females	19	20
One or more males	16	18
Both males and females	6	7
4. Age combinations		
Adults and teens	31	28
Adults and children	9	10
Teens and children	3	4
All ages	13	11

common targets among teenage victims. Overall, team offenders targeted females more often than males, but the difference was not particularly great. In addition, when team offenders killed victims from more than one age category, adults and teenagers were the most likely targets. Conversely, team offenders, in all cases, were least likely to select both teenagers and children as victims.

The majority of cases involved stranger-to-stranger violence (Tables 8.5 and 8.6). Half of all female offenders and three fourths of male offenders

TABLE 8.5 Percentage of Team Offenders Murdering Family, Acquaintances, and Strangers in the United States, 1795–1988

RELATIONSHIP	PERCENTAGE OF CASES (N=32)	PERCENTAGE OF FEMALE OFFENDERS (N=15)	PERCENTAGE OF MALE OFFENDERS (N=61)	TOTAL NUMBER OF OFFENDERS (N=76) %
Strangers	66	53	74	70
Strangers/acquaintances	16	33	14	17
Strangers/family	6	—	5	4
Acquaintances	6	—	3	3
Acquaintances/Family	3	7	2	3
Family	3	7	2	3

TABLE 8.6 Rank Order of Types of Victims Selected by Team Killers

A. Strangers:
1. Females: Young females walking alone
   Hitchhikers
   Prostitutes
   College students
   Handicapped
   Responders to newspaper ads
2. Travelers/campers
3. People at random in homes
4. People at random on street
5. Young boys
6. Employees/business people
7. Children at play
8. Police officers

B. Acquaintances:
9. Neighbor children
10. Females: People on street
    Waitresses
11. Males: Group members
    Visitors
    People in authority

C. Family
12. Children
13. Wives/brothers/mothers

targeted strangers. Again, this reinforces the belief that strangers are preferred as victims by serial killers. Very few cases involved the killing of a family member or an acquaintance.

Stranger-to-stranger homicide facilitation was influenced by several circumstances, including time of attack or abduction, accessibility to victims, age and race of victims, and location of potential victim and offenders. Although research has yet to explore some of these factors, it would appear that not all strangers were equally at risk. Individual lifestyle appeared to be a critical factor in determining the types of strangers who fell prey to team offenders or any other serial killers. Risk-takers such as prostitutes and hitchhikers appeared to be at greater risk than those who avoided such lifestyles.

Table 8.7 compares cases and offenders with the degree of facilitation provided by the victims. Did the victim walk alone at night? Did he or she hitchhike or pick up partners in bars? Perhaps the person was too trusting of strangers instead of exercising caution. In any case, recent team offender cases appeared to involve more frequency of facilitation by victims than in earlier years. For example, overall since 1800, 59% of these cases were reported to have one or more victims rating low in facilitation. Since 1975, however, that number has dropped to 42%. This in turn raises questions of whether victims are actually taking more risks, taking greater risks, or whether offenders are merely exploiting a pool of risk-takers they had earlier ignored.

TABLE 8.7 Degree of Victim Facilitation in Being Murdered by Team Offenders

FACILITATION	PERCENTAGE OF CASES ($N=32$)	PERCENTAGE OF OFFENDERS ($N=76$)
Low	59	63
High	28	24
Both	13	13

Methods and Motives

Guns were commonly used by team offenders during the commission of their crimes (Table 8.8). However, guns were used in only one out of four cases as the sole method of killing. As in other serial murders, the purpose was usually not to dispose of victims quickly but to keep them alive so they could be subjected to tortures and mutilations. Consequently, more than two thirds of team offenders used two or more methods to kill their victims. Mutilations, including stabbings, dissections, and other forms of cutting, were particularly common. Several offenders expressed enjoyment in being

TABLE 8.8 Methods Used by Team Offenders to Kill Their Victims

METHOD	PERCENTAGE OF CASES ($N=32$)	PERCENTAGE OF OFFENDERS ($N=76$)
Firearms	56	58
Mutilation	47	45
Torture	28	26
Firearms only	25	21
Bludgeoning	25	30
Strangulation/ suffocation	22	22
Poison	9	8
Neglect	6	4
Drowning	3	4
Combinations of methods	69	67

able to perform acts of sadism. The case of Dean Corll and followers graphically illustrates this point (Profile 8-6).

Team killers were more likely than other offenders to kill for cult-related reasons. Nearly one fifth of all team offenders were involved in ritualistic torture of victims. Most of these offenders belonged to larger teams of killers and were not the planners and decision makers. As mentioned earlier, cult activities involved extensive torturing of victims and using human blood and body parts for altar offerings. Enjoyment of torture and killing was more frequently expressed by this group of team killers than other serial offenders. This, in part, may be due to the bravado some of the group members may have felt was necessary for the public to hear and see once they were apprehended.

Almost identical to other serial offenders, team killers most likely had motives of a sexual nature (Table 8.9). Rape, sodomy, fellatio, and so on were recurrent forms of sexual acting out. As discussed earlier, such "motives" appear to fall under the category of methods; the sexual assaults appeared to be methods of gaining control over victims. Money was found to be commonly cited as a motive for murder, although it was much less likely noted as the sole reason for killing. Similar to all serial killers, team offenders could rarely be legally classified as insane. Regardless of how obscene some of the murders were, insanity could not be established.

Offender History

Research data were sometimes limited regarding certain biographical information on team serial killers. In approximately half of team offender profiles, sufficient data existed to examine previous violent, criminal, or abnor-

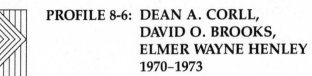

PROFILE 8-6: DEAN A. CORLL, DAVID O. BROOKS, ELMER WAYNE HENLEY 1970–1973

Born in Fort Wayne, Indiana, Dean Corll relocated to Houston, Texas, about the time his parents were divorced. A model student, he played trombone in the high school band and was never a disciplinary problem. He was often referred to as "good ole Dean." He became active in his family's candy business and eventually became vice-president. For a two-year period he left the Corll Candy Company to care for his widowed grandmother. He later served time in the military and received an honorable hardship discharge to return and help his mother with the family business. Dean's generosity and kindness became well known among the local children and they came regularly for candy handouts. The candy company dissolved in 1968, and Dean entered an electricians' training program. He began to move frequently, and in 1969 met David Brooks, who became attracted to Dean's personality.

Brooks' parents had also divorced. He had a short history of theft before he was sent to live with his grandfather, then his grandmother; finally he moved in with Corll. He always maintained to his friends that "Nobody can figure me out." He continued to steal, shoplift, and burglarize while Corll helped him purchase a Corvette. The two became sexually involved, and Dean began giving money to Brooks for sexual favors. Wayne Henley, 17, also began associating with Corll. He too had come from a broken home and helped support the family after his father left. As his grades dropped, Wayne left school in the ninth grade. He had tried to enlist in the Navy at 16 but was rejected. Life worsened for Wayne, and he was arrested for breaking and entering and assault with a deadly weapon. He began drinking heavily and

associating with Dean Corll, but unlike the bisexual Brooks, Wayne was not interested in any homosexual liaisons.

The two young men, however, were willing to procure young males for Corll to sexually abuse. They would later state in confessions that Corll agreed to pay them $200 for every boy they picked up. The two found male hitchhikers and brought them to Corll's apartment for glue-sniffing parties. When the boys passed out, Corll would molest them. Eventually Corll wanted more and began torturing and killing the boys. He would tie or handcuff them to a seven-by-three-foot board and then sodomize, strangle, and shoot the boys. Their deaths often were gruesome; Corll would sometimes chew off the victim's penis or assault the youth with a 17-inch double-headed dildo. Most of the victims came from the Heights area in Houston, and some were neighbors. The victims ranged in age from nine years to college age. Corll killed several of his victims in groups of two, and on at least two occasions he killed brothers. Henley seemed to enjoy the sadistic killing; on one occasion he fired a bullet up the nostril of one of the victims and then shot him again in the head. Brooks later testified that Henley "seemed to enjoy causing pain." The killing went on until Corll decided to kill Henley after they had had a disagreement. Henley managed to convince Corll not to kill him, and when Henley was freed, he grabbed a gun and shot Corll five times, killing him on the spot.

The story became public when Henley decided to call the police and tell the entire story. Police found 17 bodies of young white males under a boathouse near Pasadena, Texas. They had been placed in sheets of heavy plastic and cov-

DEAN A. CORLL, DAVID O. BROOKS, ELMER WAYNE HENLEY continued

ered with lime. Various smaller plastic containers held an assortment of body parts, primarily sex organs. Ten other bodies were exhumed at two additional sites under the guidance of Henley. Some observers believe police stopped searching for bodies once they had surpassed the existing number of homicide victims found in a single case at that time.

Elmer Wayne Henley eventually was found guilty of helping to murder six of the boys and sentenced to six sentences of 99 years each. A Texas appeals court in 1978 overturned his conviction as a result of a technicality. David Brooks was convicted of only one murder and sentenced to life in prison. Ironically, Dean A. Corll's coffin was covered in an American flag in keeping with the tradition that we honor those who have served their country honorably (Nash, 1981).

TABLE 8.9 Motives Reported by Team Offenders for Killing Their Victims

MOTIVES	PERCENTAGE OF CASES ($N=32$)	PERCENTAGE OF OFFENDERS ($N=75$)
Sexual	59	53
Money	50	40
Enjoyment	44	47
Personal reasons	28	27
Perverted acts	16	19
Cult expectations	9	17
Revenge	6	5
Insanity	3	4
Combination of motives	41	52

mal behaviors. Offenders having such histories were most likely to have been incarcerated in prison or a mental institution.

Team offenders appeared more likely to have prior records of incarceration than their solo counterparts (Table 8.10). They were also more likely to have criminal records for theft but were about as likely to have robbery, burglary, or child abuse records or histories of psychiatric problems as solo offenders. However, team offenders were less likely to have criminal records for sex-related crimes and assault than solo killers. Team offenders were likely to come in contact with one another as a result of prior incarcerations and criminal records. There appeared to be somewhat more interest in financial gain among team serial killers than solo offenders in considering past crimes. Indeed, some team killers grouped themselves together in almost businesslike ventures that culminated in murder. Such is the case of Leonard Lake and Charles Ng (Profile 8-7).

TABLE 8.10 Percentage of Team Offenders Reporting a History of Violent, Criminal, or Abnormal Behavior

HISTORY	PERCENTAGE OF CASES ($N=19$)	PERCENTAGE OF OFFENDERS ($N=37$)
Prior incarceration in prison or mental institution	74	64
Theft	42	33
Sex-related crimes	26	27
Robbery	26	24
Burglary	26	21
Psychiatric problems	21	27
Assault	5	6
Abuse of children	5	3

PROFILE 8-7: LEONARD LAKE AND CHARLES NG
1983–1985

On June 2, 1985, a man arrested in San Francisco was detained and charged with illegal possession of a weapon with a silencer. A few moments later the man swallowed a cyanide capsule and collapsed; he died four days later after being removed from life support systems. Fingerprints indicated his name was Leonard Lake, a 39-year-old Vietnam veteran who was described by neighbors as "quiet, strange and somewhat arrogant." He allegedly attended weekly Bible classes. It is also believed that he and an accomplice, Charles Ng, who fled to Canada, may have murdered 25 or more males and females in a specially constructed cinder block bunker located near Sacramento in a mountain retreat that was used as a torture chamber. Some victims were lured to the house by a promise of work, whereas others answered classified ads. Apparently, some of the earliest victims were relatives, friends, and neighbors because they were easiest to lure to the bunker. The goal was to seek out sexually attractive females who would then be used as sex slaves, subjected to sexual torture and often killed. Males were targets simply because they were companions of the women or because they had credit cards, cash, or desirable identification. It has been speculated that some of the men may have actually worked at the retreat prior to their deaths.

Some reports indicate that Lake was involved in clandestine cult meetings where human sacrifices were discussed. Some photographs show Lake wearing robes worn by modern-day witches and posing with a goat made up to look like a live unicorn. Police also discovered that Lake had skipped bail in 1982 after he was arrested on charges of possession of explosives and illegal automatic weapons. Shortly after this arrest, Lake's wife divorced him. Two years earlier Lake had been arrested for grand theft for stealing building materials from a low income housing project. Later he was arrested after police found an arsenal of bomb material, machine guns, silencers, and other weapons at a ranch where he worked as caretaker.

LEONARD LAKE AND CHARLES NG continued

Ng, a 24-year-old who also had many encounters with the law, had been involved in several incidents of stealing and shoplifting as a youth. Following a hit-and-run accident, Ng joined the Marines, where he was arrested for stealing a variety of weapons, including grenade launchers, machine guns, and hand guns. Ng escaped from marine detention, and after seeing an ad placed by Lake in a magazine for mercenary soldiers, he joined forces with Lake in a spree of killing.

When investigators went to the secluded ranch where the bunker was located they found a sign posted on a vehicle that read "If you love something, set it free. If it doesn't come back, hunt it down and kill it." Entries found in one of Lake's diaries indicated that some of the men brought to the ranch may have been used as game animals to be hunted down and executed. Wrote Lake, "Death is in my pocket and fantasy my goal" and "the perfect woman is totally controlled; a woman who does exactly what she is told and nothing else. There is no sexual problem with a submissive woman. There are no frustrations, only pleasure and contentment."

The diaries revealed graphic illustrations of sexual abuse, torture, murder, kidnapping, and cremation. Lake believed he would be a survivor of the nuclear holocaust in his concrete bunker filled with sex slaves, weapons, and food. Police found several tapes and pictures of women being sexually abused and tortured. Some of the tapes showed Lake and Ng raping and sodomizing their victims. When the two had finished they executed their victims by shooting or strangling them. It appears that victims may have been then cut up into pieces with power saws and tree trimmers found at the site and placed in metal drums for incineration. The remaining bones were then pulverized and buried. Police found 45 pounds of bone fragments, including many teeth. Some victims, including some campers, were buried around the ranch area. Lake had made a map of "buried treasure," which police thought meant grave sites. The exact number of the victims of Lake and Ng will never be known. Ng, at the time of this writing, waits in a Canadian prison while U.S. and Canadian officials negotiate his extradition. Lake was cremated but his brain was preserved for scientific research into the causation of homicidal behavior.

Another important area of biographical data concerned the degree to which team offenders had experienced traumatization while in their youth (Table 8.11). In comparing male team killers to male solo killers, several disparities were found. For example, team killers were twice as likely to come from unstable homes as solo killers. This included alcoholic parents, prostitution by mother, incarceration of parent(s) (Profile 8-8), periodic separation from parents due to troubles at home, and psychiatric problems involving the parents.

Although an unstable home was the most common factor noted among male team killers, only one third of them were found to have made particular reference to rejection by parents or friends. In contrast, most solo offenders frequently were found to have experienced specific forms of rejection by significant others. Nearly one third of team killers had parents who died

TABLE 8.11 Percentage of Male Team Offenders Who Experienced Forms of Traumatization as Children, Compared with Male Solo Offenders

TRAUMATIZATION	MALE TEAM KILLERS (N=21)	MALE SOLO KILLERS (N=31)
Unstable home	43	19
Rejection	33	77
Parents died/orphaned	29	19
Poverty	24	23
Divorce of parents	19	26
Sexual abuse	14	6
Beatings	14	19
Adopted	10	16
Illegitimate	10	6

PROFILE 8-8: GERALD A. GALLEGO, JR., AND CHARLENE GALLEGO 1978–1980

When Gerald Gallego, Jr., was born, his father, a 19-year-old convict, was doing time in San Quentin prison. Gerald Jr. was nine years old when in 1955 his father was executed in Mississippi for having killed two correctional officers. His father, whom Gerald Jr. thought had died much earlier in a car accident, wrote a letter telling others, especially youth, to avoid breaking the law. But less than a year later Gerald Jr. began getting into trouble with the law. At age 13, he was detained by the California Youth Authority for sexual involvement with a six-year-old girl. From that point on his life continued to gradually self-destruct.

By the age of 32, Gerald Jr. had been married seven times, one wife having married him twice. He was known to have been married to more than one woman at the same time, and when he married Charlene he did not bother to divorce his previous wife. By this time, Gerald was developing a real penchant for violence and sadism. By the time of his final arrest, Gerald had compiled an amazing history of murder, deviant sexual conduct, a jail escape, an armed robbery, and several other crimes.

Unlike her husband, Charlene apparently grew up in a family that provided love and support and had the respect of neighbors and friends. Why she decided to attach herself to an exconvict who referred to her as "Ding-a-Ling," is unknown, but she quickly accepted his lifestyle, including his bizarre and perverted sexual fantasies.

Gerald decided it was time to seek out young female virgins that he could keep in a secluded hideaway where he would be able to use them as his personal sex slaves. His first two victims, 17-year-old Rhonda Scheffler and 16-year-old Kippi Vaught, were abducted September 11, 1978, from a Sacramento shopping mall. Their bodies were later found badly beaten, both having been shot in the head with a .25-calibre handgun. Autopsies indicated both girls were sexually abused. On June 24, 1979, in Reno, Nevada, two more girls, 15-year-old Brenda

GERALD A. GALLEGO, JR., AND CHARLENE GALLEGO continued

Judd and 14-year-old Sandra Kaye Colley, were abducted from a crowded fairground. Their bodies were never recovered. On April 24, 1980, 17-year-old Stacy Ann Redican and Karen Chipman-Twiggs disappeared from a Sacramento shopping mall. In July, picnickers near Reno discovered the girls' bodies in shallow graves. They too had been beaten severely with a blunt metal object and sexually abused. June 6, 1980, Linda Teresa Aguilar, age 21 and expecting her first child, was abducted while hitchhiking from Port Orford, Oregon, to Gold Beach. She too was later found in a shallow grave, tightly bound with her skull crushed in by blows from a metal object. The autopsy report indicated she had been buried while still alive. The next victim, 34-year-old Virginia Mochel, mother of two, was abducted while walking to her car from the bar and grill where she worked as a waitress. Three months later her body was discovered outside Sacramento. On November 1, 1980, Mary Beth Sowers and her fiancee, Craig Raymond Miller, were kidnaped from a parking lot. Gerald had no particular interest in Craig, and on arriving in a secluded area he shot him in the head three times. Later Gerald raped and sexually abused Mary Beth and also shot her in the head three times.

Police were finally able to apprehend Gerald and Charlene after a friend of the engaged couple witnessed the abduction and was able to memorize the license number of the car driven by Gerald. After a difficult manhunt that took authorities to several states, the Gallegos were captured. After their return to California, the couple pleaded innocent to charges of murder and kidnapping. Because Charlene was not legally married to Gerald, she eventually agreed to testify against him in exchange for a plea bargain. She explained how she would help lure the girls to the car where Gerald could overpower them. She admitted sitting in the front seat while Gerald would rape, beat, and sodomize his victims and force them to perform oral sex and sometimes kill them. Charlene also admitted holding a gun on two of the girls while Gerald raped them. She described in detail the ten gruesome murders in her husband's quest for the perfect sex slave. She admitted watching while Gerald used a hammer to beat his victims to death. The Gallegos were convicted of murder, and Gerald was sentenced by the state of Nevada to die by lethal injection. Charlene is now serving two concurrent 16-year and eight-month sentences in Carson City, Nevada, for her part in the murders (Linedecker, 1987).

while the offenders were young. Other possible traumatizing factors included divorce of parents and poverty. Rarely were sexual or physical abuse experiences noted in the profiles of team killers.

Disposition of Offenders

Of this particular subgroup of team killers, one tenth have been executed (Table 8.12). Another 16% currently sit on death row. Ten percent were either killed before a trial could be held or committed suicide. In total, 36% of team offenders are dead or await execution. Another 35% were incarcerated for life, and 19% were sentenced to serve a specific number of years in prison. A

TABLE 8.12 Disposition of Male and Female Team Offenders after Apprehension

DISPOSITION	PERCENTAGE OF OFFENDERS ($N=69$)
Life in prison	35
Sentenced to specific number of years in prison	20
Death row	16
Executed	10
Killed before trial	6
Suicide	4
Pending in courts	4
Confined to mental institution	3
Escaped	1
Now free	1

few of these offenders are currently awaiting court dispositions. Occasionally an offender has been placed in a mental institution. Rarely has anyone convicted of such crimes escaped or been freed from prison. The problem, however, is not being able to keep these offenders incarcerated but rather freeing other convicted psychopathic felons every year who will go on to become some of America's most infamous serial murderers.

More than half of the serial killers in this study are destined to live out the rest of their lives in prison. What efforts, if any, are being made to study them or rehabilitate such offenders? What are the issues surrounding sentencing? Is capital punishment the best response to these offenders? Chapter 10 will explore these issues and what appear to be the future challenges and trends in criminal justice regarding the apparent increase in serial murders.

Chapter 9 explores serial killing through the mind of a serial murderer. The interview in this chapter shares insightful information about people who feel a need to kill. Chapter 9 also examines serial murders in other countries and the similarities they share with those in the United States.

CHAPTER 9

Interviews, Foreign Offenders, and Unsolved Cases

Scientific researchers have developed several methodologies for data collection and analysis. Typically, data gathered from random sample surveys or aggregate data collection allow researchers to perform comparative analyses of various social phenomena, based on information gathered from a large number of subjects. Researchers can also gather information from life history analysis. Diaries, autobiographies, and personal interviews can provide particularly insightful information unavailable through more empirically oriented research. The "trade-off," which may not always be equitable, permits researchers to focus exclusively on a few cases in order to allow in-depth exploration.

Obviously, gathering data about serial killers cannot be managed by simply mailing out questionnaires or conducting telephone surveys. Serial killers are not only relatively rare in numbers, but they also are not easily accessible. The Federal Bureau of Investigation undoubtedly has the easiest access to serial killers once they have been incarcerated. However, even those agents from the Behavioral Science Unit in Quantico, Virginia, do not receive cooperation from all multiple homicide offenders. Some killers do confess their crimes, but some serial killers continue to claim they are innocent long after they go to prison and, thereby, refuse to cooperate with police by giving them any information about the murders. In all likelihood, many of the myths associated with serial killers could be dispelled if and when researchers are able to have greater access to offenders. In short, the interview can become a critical tool in understanding serial murder.

Interviewing multiple offenders certainly is not without its limitations and problems. Given the nature of their offenses, offenders are often eager to gain the attention of the researcher, police, or anyone else who will help publicize the crimes. Many of these offenders have led insecure and emotionally truncated lives; they are at last receiving the attention they so desperately longed for. Sometimes, as in the case of Henry Lee Lucas, a convicted serial killer in Texas, offenders will confess to many more homicides than they actually committed in order to attract public attention. This in turn brings into question the validity of multiple homicide data. Researchers must be careful not to be drawn into the sensationalism of high victim counts in lieu of investigating the accuracy of those claims.

201

In addition, certain individuals who are attracted to offenders befriend and follow them through the criminal justice process. Such "groupies" have been common in cases of particular notoriety, including that of Ted Bundy. Several young women, similar in appearance to his victims, attended the court sessions and frequently corresponded with the killer. Some wanted to marry Bundy; others believed they could "help" Ted. Such "groupies" are often criticized because they contribute to the killer's notoriety. Similar criticism is sometimes leveled at researchers who spend time interviewing serial offenders, because the information can be easily manipulated and distorted.

In addition, a serial offender may tell interviewers exactly what he or she wants them to hear—or, conversely, what he or she thinks the interviewers want to hear. Some psychiatric units term such behavior as "gaming." Occasionally criminals who have been sent to a mental hospital for evaluation feel a need to live up to the expectation that they are indeed criminally insane. To prove their state of mind, the offenders will "bounce off the walls" for a few days, often in an isolation cell, until they calm down. Inevitably they realize that most people they see on the ward are not acting out and appear rather "normal." To some degree the serial killer, thrust under public scrutiny, may feel a need to fit the typical "mold" of such offenders.

Another criticism regarding interviews is that what offenders have to say, even if they believe it, may not reflect a realistic perspective. Hindsight can easily distort reality and mold it to the psychological needs of the offender. How objective, how truthful, can we expect serial murderers to be? One may expect a certain degree of distorted thinking in the mind of an offender who has mutilated 15 or 20 victims.

Although such criticisms certainly have merit, researchers recognize that, despite the stumbling blocks, interviews can be productive. The interview should be regarded as another source of information, another perspective into the murdering mind. Some offenders have acquired particular insight into their own distorted thinking or the mindset of other serial killers. For example, serial killers are stereotyped as persons without or incapable of remorse. While this appears to be true for many such offenders, there are also exceptions. One offender, the killer of five young boys in Utah, apologized to the victims' families and begged their forgiveness. On several occasions he expressed his deep regrets and sorrow. To prove sincerity and to show his willingness to do anything to help right the wrongs he committed, Arthur Gary Bishop stopped his appeals process to allow himself to be executed. While his remorse appeared to have been sincere, Bishop recognized that what he had become had completely engulfed him. Shortly before his execution, he commented that even though he was deeply sorrowful for his deeds, he knew that if he were released he would continue to kill.

Each murderer has an explanation of what may have caused him or her to commit terrible crimes. Researchers would be remiss if they did not take every opportunity to gather such information. However, researchers must be cautious about assuming they understand the mind of the serial killer simply because they may have interviewed two or three offenders. Also, some offenders believed to be linked to many deaths may be incarcerated for only one or two homicides and emphatically deny involvement in other killings. Several appear to have embraced the "Bundy Complex," or complete denial of responsibility despite overwhelming evidence to the contrary. However, these offenders can also provide researchers with insights to their personalities and psychological characteristics.

The following is an example of an interview I conducted with a male serial offender (O). The interview is published anonymously as part of the agreement in exchange for the interview. The offender, in this instance, does not wish to have any publicity regarding his crimes. He claims 12 victims.

AN INTERVIEW WITH A SERIAL MURDERER: 1990

H: How long have you been in the prison?

O: I've been here eight years now. It took about a year and a half to get me here, convicted, through the trial process.

H: You were convicted in what area?

O: Southern Arizona.

H: Are you in isolation?

O: No, I'm not—general population.

H: You've murdered children. Don't you find that to be a problem?

O: Absolutely. Not as much as when I first came here. I had a tremendous amount of publicity. It was that first six months to a year that was pure hell. But since then it's tapered off. It never stops completely. There is always somebody whispering and pointing and trying to stir some of the other convicts and make a name for themselves.

H: Have you ever been attacked?

O: Yes, I have.

H: By somebody who didn't like you because you were a child killer?

O: I think it was about six months after I got here, I was struck in the head from behind. Put me right out and I'd say that was one of the turning points for me in here in terms of my own outlook. That did a lot.

H: I bet it did.

O: I had to see what I could do to survive, and then I have been in a few fisticuffs here and there. But those have actually been a blessing in disguise. If you get into a fight you have one of two choices. You're either going to run or you're going to duke it out right there.

H: Do people run very often?

O: Yeah, you do. You have some people that do that usually. . . I've seen big guys run. I've seen little guys run, but when you do, you're running forever. You're marked. You're marked as a coward. You're marked as somebody who isn't going to defend himself.

H: Do you feel intimidated all the time? Always looking over your shoulder?

O: Yeah, in fact I have often thought this must be the way Vietnam vets feel, you know. You've heard of soldiers who hear backfire and dive for cover. I am constantly aware of my surroundings. I know who's out there in that visiting room right now. I know who's enemy and who isn't, even though we have never exchanged words. While I'm walking to work I know who's on the alley. They may not know that I know, but it's just something that has become a natural thing in life. When I got hit on the head I was hit by somebody who, as it turned out, had never even seen me. He had been in the bucket for as long as I had been here.

H: The bucket?

O: The hole. Segregation. We used to have these steel mop buckets here, now they use plastic or aluminum because of that. But he got me from behind and I felt the first one. He hit me three times, but the first one I felt it. The officer who had escorted me told me that this guy had just gotten out of the bucket. He knows of my crimes and so forth, but he doesn't know me. So that was put away in my head and for the first three or four weeks after that all I had was one friend who was a big six-foot-eight-inch guy, you know, muscular, former biker. I was walking to work one day, and all of a sudden I see this big arm coming at me. I thought, here it comes again, and I wheeled around and swung at the arm and crouched like a karate stance, but inside I almost fainted. I almost died right there, and prior to all of this, I had read about rape victims and how they live in...they have tremendous psychological problems, fear, afraid to get close to anybody, especially strangers, afraid of being alone, and I always thought that was hogwash. It was always just a small thing to me. Their reaction was, I always thought cowardly. But now here I am, that arm. That arm coming at me and thinking I've had it, and that was the first time that I started really looking at what I've done to others, the trauma, particularly to those whom I didn't kill and the first time I could experience first hand just how really black that was. I guess in a sense it was the first time I ever saw the truth.

H: As a serial killer, do you perceive that you will ever get out of here? Do you believe that if you do what is right, play the game they play here, follow the rules, do good time, that you'll get out with some life left?

O: Probably that'll never happen. The people in this state have pretty much made it clear that I am a state hazard.

H: If they abide by the sentencing structure you'll leave here 30 years from now...30 years from the time you came in.

O: 53–54. But I don't think that'll happen. It's certainly something that bothers me, that I may never leave, that I've squandered my life as well as the lives of others. But that's a waste, a tragedy. It's not something that I blame on anybody other than myself.

H: If you get out, what will you do?

O: Play softball without worrying about someone coming up behind me, taking my head off with a bat, being able to lay on the grass without having to worry about someone stomping me in the ribs. A burrito. Looking back on my past and all the things that were part of my lifestyle, the criminal lines, material things, attention, status symbols. That doesn't mean a damn thing to me anymore. I was rather young when I started working in a rehab center, and I thought I was really something, and then my father wanted a new car so I bought his off of him, a brand new sedan. I thought I was really something driving around in a nice little car, good job and money was in the pocket as well as my crazy violence on the side which I had glamorized. These things don't mean anything. What matters is being free inside. Knowing that those things don't make the man, that those things aren't really what make me, and that's what made me before. You know, I lived a lie. Surrounded myself with trappings. . . .

H: You feel that being in here is a form of justice?

O: Yes, absolutely.

H: Do you believe in God?

O: Yes, I believe that there is definitely a God.

H: Do you believe that you must face Him one day for what you've done?

O: Yes.

H: Do you feel that if you spend enough time in prison that that will compensate for what you've done?

O: No. I don't think that it will get by God. I believe that no matter how, regardless of the severity of the sin or the crime, they all must stand before Him. I guess what I'm saying is no one is capable of standing perfect before God. People out there have done very violent things to one another that certainly they regret. I can't answer for what I've done. How can I pay full retribution for what I've done?

H: If you can't pay for it now, do you think that you'll ever be able to pay for it? Do you feel you'll be in damnation for the rest of your life or eternity?

O: No, because I also believe that God is an understanding God. There's no way in the world when I started when I was a kid and started a lying lifestyle and thinking perversely, reading things that I should never have touched. . . there's no way in the world that I could have ever have known I was gonna kill at the end of the road, and I think that God knows that too, and that he knows it started in anger. Now that doesn't lessen my responsibility at all because I'm the one who made the choices all the way down the road even though I was blind where it would end. But I think he understands that. I mean he's aware of that, and I think that I can stand before him and say: God, you know that I didn't plan it this way, you know when I was more or less swept up.

H: But you feel responsible for what you did?

O: Sure, sure. You're still making the decisions. There were times when I could have stopped. There was one case in point. My father. . . I went and took his credit card one time and this is all again, living this distorted existence of extravagance. I'm number one. I can do anything I want. I want to appear like I'm really somebody so I get my father's credit cards, and I ran them up, and I used to take care of the bills so he didn't know what was going on for a while. Well, pretty soon I couldn't hide the bills anymore, you know. I used to just write the checks out for him and he'd sign them. Now this had gone on for months. They called him at work, and they asked him what had happened with the payments. When I say I ran them up, probably ten or fifteen, thousands of dollars, and my father, when he confronted me, at first he was upset, then he said you're gonna pay for this. And he says later, just tell me, tell me how many more there are, how many more I can expect, get them all together, I'll pay for it. You won't pay a cent. Just start your life over today. It was very attractive. That moment stands out. It was so full of meaning, so full of possibility. It wasn't just the bills but it was the whole lying existence that was on the line. The whole distorted thought line. I didn't have the guts, even though I was going to get caught anyway, I told him, "That's all of it." And, the next ones, naturally when another would show up at work he was disgusted.

H: Let's explore a little bit with your support system. You have Susan. Now, Susan has been coming to see you for four years?

O: Six years I think, five or six years, maybe seven. I believe that if she felt that, God, felt that this was not the right thing, she would walk away in an instant. I've told her this and it kind of gets her upset at times. Susan, I am really convinced that you really believe that you feel you're doing the right thing. At times I really think you're wrong. At times I think you're wasting your life. At times I feel that you should get on with your life, I'm going to be here forever. At least I believe I will be and it certainly looks that way. It's not an easy relationship.

H: She supports you in some way; she said she used to write letters. Now she comes to see you all the time.

O: Yeah, they changed the rules here and they allow a lot more visits.

H: You earn your own money. What do you do in here?

O: I work as an orderly inside. It's not an hourly job. Most prisons will only permit you to spend so much per month. That's to curtail the drug traffic, and here it's $120 per month. I make $95, right around there. They're paying for your job and your skills.

H: Do you have other people come and visit you?

O: Mike comes in once about every three to four months—when he can. I used to have another friend that used to come in fairly regularly every other month or so—she just died last month. She was an older lady. She was the only person I knew that started coming in that knew me before.

H: And your dad is?

O: Deceased.

H: And your mom?

O: She's living in a large city right now. I call her every other week.

H: So you are still close with your mom?

O: Yes. She is not aware—she is aware of these two murders. I had an assault with a deadly weapon, drunk drivings, she's aware that this wasn't the only crime I committed. It started from youth and it was cumulative. It wasn't something that happened overnight—it wasn't something that was like a man who woke up one day and said I'm gonna go out and do this. My brothers, when I was taken down to my home town, they all came and visited me. And I talked to another brother for the first time in a few years just a couple weeks ago. Now, my younger sister, we get along real fine. The oldest girl I get along with just fine. We don't talk much—I think that has to do with out of sight, out of mind. I could call them regularly if I wanted—I think it's just easier that way not to hate me, but they're embarrassed. And I think they feel enough for me that it is painful when we talk. Now for my older sister she won't have it—I have to call her and talk with her once in a while. And my mom insists on my calling every other week, and Henry I haven't spoken with him for five years.

H: Do you go to the college program?

O: I was for about a year and a half—then I became very discouraged. I have a life sentence in another state as well for kidnapping concurrent with what I'm doing up here. I went to that hearing—it was an especially long hearing and I talked to them just as I talked to you, and when I was all done, they just blasted me. You're nothing but a con, you vicious killer. I went back to my cell, I went back, and just sat there crushed. I was devastated. Not because I expected anything, because I told them, I don't feel like I have anything coming so I can live with whatever you folks say. I fully expected nothing but I didn't expect that. They'd ask why did you do this and what were you thinking? And I told them, there's no way to make the truth look pretty. And they took that and threw it back in my face.

H: Tell me about your education.

O: I flirted with it, you might say. I was there, I had a scholarship to go to a private university, and I dropped out. I was drunk most of the time—in fact I didn't finish out the year, the first semester.

H: What were you thinking about majoring in?

O: Psychology. I think that had more to do with my father's work. Working with mentally retarded and emotionally disturbed. I was basically living a double life. I was one thing to this person and another thing to that person, all lies. And the reason for that is just a low self-image. You're not happy with who you are. You're not comfortable with who you are. You don't have any self-confidence. I wasn't out committing crimes all the time. One day I'd be fine, and the next time I'd be out, I'd have this compulsion to go out and kill somebody, and so I started looking back at each instance, what was I thinking, and this is what I came up with, and it's kind of a higher stage process. The first stage is what I call distorted thinking. It's a distorted thought line, and I found that I was God's gift to earth, I'm the center of the universe. I'm perfect. I'm the smartest guy that ever lived. Nobody's as perceptive as I am. So long as nothing came against that self-image, I was fine. But the problem with that was that it, as I mentioned earlier, was all lies. Everything was a lie, and you know a lot of times the money that I had was my father's credit cards and it was a lie. I'd go on a date, and be living it up like this was mine. So long as I was living it out, I was all pumped up. I felt very important, just this immense personality, and that couldn't last because it was always based on lies. There was always going to be some challenge to this grandiose self-image. Sometimes it would be a lot of little things, sometimes it would just be the stress of having to live these little lies, having to always be looking over your back, and other times it would be a very definite event, a girlfriend leaves you or something like that. Whenever that happened, then there would be a fall. I was always way up here, and I think that's true of most serial types, serial offenders like I was, arrogant, maybe not outward, but at least internally. We're arrogant people, perceiving ourselves as almost godlike beings. All of a sudden we have this fall, psychological fall, and it's very debilitating, very disorienting, confusing, harrowing. It's a very scary feeling. I'm used to being perfect. I'm not about to put up with anything that tarnishes my own sense of perfection, so that would lead to internal negative response, and that's what I was saying to myself. I'm not gonna have this, and instead of being scared, frightened, knocked off balance, I wheeled into a retaliatory mode. I'm gonna fight this. I'm gonna stand up for my self-importance. The way to deal with that was simply to prove it. You're going to be a somebody, and my means of being a somebody was violence. To me violence had already been reinforced through time as a means of being the star, center stage in this drama. Up to this point I've had a fall, and I felt like I'm not in control. I'm not top dog.

H: The fall comes as a result of what?

O: Of any challenge to the feelings of superiority. If you live out in the real world, you're going to get them, at work, your relationships and so forth. That's why it's repetitive. That's why it always continues, and violence to me had been reinforced as a means of taking control, as a means of getting even, getting even with the world. It's reaffirming that I was all those things, and the actual deed, the victimizing, the brutalizing of another human being, was my proof, a seal, a seal of approval, self-approval, my evidence that I'm really a somebody, and the result of that would be a triumph, a restoration, I'm restored. I'm doing not what other people will, but what I will, and that would restore all those feelings of largeness, power, self-importance that strengthened the overloaded ego that I had in the first stage, and I'd be fine. The act done, it wasn't done so much for fun as it was for restorative gain. As long as I was back in that first stage, there really wasn't any desire to go out and kill. It wasn't like I had an ongoing insatiable lust for murder, and it really wasn't a lust for murder. It was a lust for self-importance at the expense of others, and that's basically the cycle. Sometimes it wouldn't take very much at all. I had a friend who owned a body shop, and I was working for him, and had no car and I get on a bus and I'm just filthy. I was just as filthy as can be, and I'm in distorted thinking. This gal gets on the bus, dressed up real nice and the seat next to me is the only one empty and she comes

over and she looks at that seat and the she looks at me—all covered with dust and smelly—and she just turns her nose up in the air, spins around, and walks up and grabs a bar. How can you sit there? Right away I become very conscious of all this. I'm on the run at this time.

H: You had committed some crimes?

O: Yes, I had committed a kidnapping.

H: Had you killed anybody at that time?

O: Yes. All these images of what I used to do which I always thought was so great and the cars—all those flashed alongside the image of this gal going uumph. And boom, I'm in the fall real quick and I just wanted to hide, okay? Wanted to hide and there's that confusion of the fall and then quickly into a negative response. That bitch, who does she think she is?...and so on. That wouldn't have mattered to me if that happened to me today. I'm a lot more confident in my own self now. That kind of thing doesn't bother me. I've gotten used to it.

H: Did you have a desire to kill her?

O: Yes I did. And I did—not her.

H: But you acted on somebody else?

O: Yes—shortly thereafter. And I hope you can see the cycle here...being way up here and then crashing down, sudden rejection, lonely, the retaliatory mode—the determination to set things straight.

H: To gain control?

O: Right, and then restoration. Yes, it's a very distinct cycle, very distinct.

H: So, what you're telling me...it means imbalance. In your case and other serial cases, you chose to go the very destructive path.

O: Right, because of what had been reinforced over the years as a means of coping with stress. From a young age you start imagining yourself as being special, beyond all other people in the world. You're going to have stress; you're going to have all these things because the world isn't going to cooperate with you. And that's what happens. I think from the time I was a youth, somehow or another I got it into my head that I was immortal, even from the time I was five years old, and smarter than anybody.

H: Where do you think you got that notion?

O: The banana incident, this one time in the middle of the night; I think one of my brothers got up—I'm four so they gotta be three and two—and took a banana out of the fruit bowl. My father loved bananas, grapes, and when he got up in the morning, the banana's gone. Well, it so happened that during the night I got up to use the restroom and they heard me and said who is that. I said − − − and they said okay so I went back to bed. Well, my father called me on the carpet in the morning. Now he's already told me honesty is the best policy and he asks me if I took it. I said no and he called me a liar. He told me I don't believe you. You were up in the middle of the night. He put me up against the wall with my nose to the wall, kept me there all morning until I copped it, till I told him I took this banana. To this day I can remember how long that was. It was like an eternity, and I remember from that age thinking, feeling a real contempt for truth, honesty. Honesty isn't going to save my butt—then the hell with you. I'll lie at every opportunity I get.

H: Did you hate your father for it?

O: No—as a matter of fact I didn't even remember it all that much. I just remembered the results.

H: What kind of victims did you select?

O: It was people like kids, usually attractive, just like the ones I was in high school with, and I had felt rejected [by].

H: Your victims, you say, were primarily white female teenagers.

O: Yes.

H: Did you ever attack males?

O: Only in one instance. I think the serial murder by virtue of the nature of the compulsion. . . If they don't find somebody in a reasonable amount of time they will take anybody. Incidentally, the two here were the only children. All the rest were at least in their teens or older.

H: I'm sure ten-year-olds are not going to be too much aware of what's going on.

O: And I think that's the reason. I've also heard the term "compartmentalization." I like kids. I always did. Back then it was perhaps self-serving. I used to take kids out to the ballpark. I got the praise and adulation of the parents. I enjoyed it, and here I killed two kids because I was in a frenzy—at that time I was in a fall and had been there for long enough and had failed to find somebody that fit the model. And there were these two victims of opportunity, like a wolf stalking.

H: Hunting humans?

O: Yes.

H: You say you killed approximately 12 victims. When you first began, until you were caught or until you did your last two, was there a greater space, time frame, between the first and second victim? Did they progressively get closer together? Did you notice you were escalating toward the end?

O: It was erratic. I mean, I just killed somebody and I'm infuriated because I didn't get done what I had to do, couldn't act out this ritual that accidentally killed this body, and within a matter of hours I had someone else. With this second victim it involved brutalizing, rape, and then killing. Actually rape ended the episode, killing was just getting rid of the witness. The first killing was not done that way. The first killing, the victim died before I had acted out even. . .

H: Were you erratic in your methods you used in killing? Did you have a pattern you used each time?

O: No. It was very specific, and yes I did have a pattern and most serial killers do.

H: By the time you got to the two girls you had killed several people. In some serial cases by the time they get to the last few victims they are really in a frenzy as you said you were, so to kill them is much more brutal, much more vicious.

o: Yes. I strangled one and I suffocated another with a pillow. It was a ritual. From the time I was a kid I used to go down to the garage and read these books. My father had a rather extensive library. In a room with all these books and reading about violence, and I'm already a liar, I'm already living this imaginary existence. I'm already a manipulator. The violence that I read was a means of getting even with people, you know, people who got in my way, who challenged me. You know, I'm reading all these books because they're the kind of things that turn me on, that I'm interested in, fascinated with, and I think when I entered puberty, that's when the switch overcame. That's when you have a natural enemy in females. You have perceived them as a natural enemy since the first time they challenge you. You call it rejected, but I, in my mindset, would call it the challenge against my sense of superiority.

H: You killed sometimes for what other people would perceive as trivial issues.

o: Yes. Very trivial. You're living on such a high plane, such a distorted plane, that trivial is very big.

H: How did you feel after you did a killing? What were your physical and psychological responses to it?

o: Relief. Kind of a mixture. It's a very intense feeling. Self-magnification is a very intense feeling, and sex is power, so was the assault.

H: There was a sexual component to most of the killings?

o: Yes. Sex was sort of a vehicle. So when that was done, climax was reached. You've already terrorized this person. You've already hurt them, beat them, whatever. But there would be a feeling of letdown. You're excited, and then all of a sudden you come down. Kind of like a ball game. All this had been acted out for years and in particular, it always involved stripping the victim, forcing them to strip themselves, cutting them, making them believe that they were going to be set free if they cooperated, tying them down and then the real viciousness started. The victim's terror and the fact I could cause it to rise at will...their pain didn't register. All I could relate to was the ritual and the sounds. All this was proof to me that, I'm in control, I am playing the star role here, this person is nothing but a prop. I'm growing and they're becoming smaller. Once both the violence and the sexual aspect were completed, then that was it. That was the end of an episode.

H: Do you think if you were out that you would kill again?

o: I don't know. I don't think so because the kind of mindset that was required for that is based on many lies. I sit in that cell and sometimes I just feel I'm so filled with frustration and rage toward myself because I didn't con anybody. I didn't con anybody at all. I conned myself.

H: Have you ever thought about suicide? Have you tried suicide?

o: No.

H: Do you feel some guilt that your father is dead?

o: Yeah, absolutely. I'll tell you why, because my father was the best friend I ever had but I didn't recognize that. On the very night he died, I wished he'd die. I hoped for him to die. I said boy if he dies he'll not be around to bother me anymore. I felt that right from Day One. There's no way that I can erase the fact that in his last week of life I was hoping and hoping, die on me, die on me cause he was a strict disciplinarian. He was blunt. He was straightforward, and I didn't like that.

H: Were you ever abused as a child?

O: No I wasn't. Growing up I saw myself as abused, hated my father, and he was public enemy number one to me. He did no more than what I had coming. The discipline I received was for things I did, and I just didn't want to accept it as such. The thing is that there are people who are psychologically less ready for failure than others. And I feel that when my father disciplined me, I was not ready for that, unwilling to accept that rather than take blame for what I did and accept my just desserts; instead I would just freeze up and deal with that by saying, no I'm not wrong, he's wrong. I'm right, and that became a pattern, a way of dealing with anything, any failure, any challenge, anything that might indicate imperfection in my life, and that's typical of the serialistic mind set, is that they are totally incapable of accepting anything that would tarnish their self-image of perfection.

H: You hated your father?

O: Yes I did.

H: Did you hate your mother?

O: No, I didn't. I always felt I could manipulate her.

H: Some serial killers abuse animals, or have abused animals when they were younger, or they wet the bed, or enjoyed setting fires. Did you have any of those types of things in your past?

O: I can only think of one instance where I abused an animal, and I didn't find it particularly satisfying. I think every child at one time or another has wet the bed, but I didn't. As a small child I had a little problem, and as for the fire setting, there was something. I kind of enjoyed it because it was destroying. It was model airplanes, you know, set them on fire in the back yard. It looked like a crashing plane, but there was a kind of reveling in it, seeing this whole being reduced to smoldering ashes.

H: Did you set fires later?

O: No.

H: You recognize what you've done, and you believe you wouldn't do it again. I've interviewed many people, and if they didn't comply, didn't say the right things, they were never going to get out.

O: I hear what you're saying and that's certainly possible. One never knows until it hits. I would think that certainly there is no way of knowing, absolutely no way of knowing. But, one, I've done this on my own. I've never seen a shrink as long as I've been in here, and aside from a 15-minute psychological evaluation that was done before my parole board hearing for my crime in another state, aside from that I've talked to no one. This is something that I chose to do on my own and it was not fun and it was not easy and it's taking years to reach the point where I can

admit these things let alone talk to you about them. In talking about maturing I think that's probably part of it. In some respects serial killers are nothing more than children in men's bodies.

H: Will you ever leave here?

O: My crimes were very brutal. There are people who have committed more brutal crimes but never had the publicity that I did, and that's basically what it's all about, public interest, public reaction. It is a legitimate concern for them, and myself, I really don't care one way or the other right now. I have more of a fatalistic outlook that if I ever get out, I'll get out when I'm supposed to. If I don't, well, that's not too bad either. That's fairly just. I don't file writs. I don't fight this thing in appeals. The prison Matrix calls for 10–15, but this coming Matrix, as I read it, it came in the paper the other day, calls for 121 months. That's ten years and one month, no range, that's it, 121. Since I have consecutive, that would be 242, 20 years and two months. Probably the only thing that I do have going for me is the fact that most everybody, the legislature, probably assumes that I was convicted of aggravated murder. Aggravated murder is not going to be affected by this new Matrix. Aggravated murder, you come in, you have a 30-year minimum. They were trying to execute me, and the death penalty statute at that time carried death penalty only for straight murder, not aggravated murder. They could have tried me for aggravated murder and given me two 30-year minimums, but they said no, let's fry this guy. Two weeks before I was sentenced, they threw the death penalty out.

H: In that respect you're very fortunate.

O: Yes.

H: Because you probably would have been sentenced to death.

O: Correct. No doubt. Since legally I was convicted of straight murder, I do fall under this Matrix, and it does carry a considerably lesser sentence than what I should have gotten. In the present Matrix, they would probably have set me for 30. Under the new Matrix the most they would give me is 20 years two months.

H: So minus the time you've done you could still get out when you're not an old man.

O: In my forties. I'd love to have a second chance at life, a chance to do it right this time and to contribute rather than take away, and contribute even if it's just contributing by not bothering people. That would be a change from the past. I've got a sister who is an alcoholic, who has really taken a lot of heat from Harry, who is now the eldest, and my mom, and I don't think they look at her with a compassion, and I want to be there to do that. I've got a lot of making up to do, and I fear I may never get that chance.

H: But you'd really like to have that opportunity?

O: Oh yes, I used my family. I stole from them. I cheated them and lied and embarrassed them and then betrayed them in the worst possible way. I'd like the opportunity to be the eldest son, the responsible son that I should have been.

H: When you killed the two girls, was that the first time that you ever killed two together? That you did two victims at the same time? Did you always do them individually before?

O: It was the first time I ever abducted two at once, not the first time that I murdered two in the same day. I saw them out walking across a field. I was wandering. I was kind of in a controlled frenzy. I was certainly aware of what I was doing, in control, but inside I was desperate and I would not have taken them had I not been there, anywhere else but there, I would have let them go. There was no reason. It was a cold day, no one was around. There was a secluded area nearby. In other words, it was a killing site, and I was in a very remote part of town. There were houses there but there was also fields off to one side. I had no vehicle there.

H: How old were you then?

O: Twenty-six. They had their rackets and were going to play badminton. Somehow or another I conned them to go into a secluded area. I can't remember exactly what I said. Had it not been for their age, they probably would not have complied.

H: They were naive enough.

O: Right.

H: So they just went with you, voluntarily, up to the secluded area?

O: Yes. I pulled a knife on them, forced them to sit down, tied them together, cut their clothes away, then separated them. I took one girl here and...there was that ritual. That act, now. Had I had a vehicle, usually it was my home.

H: You're alone with one of the girls and you raped her at that time?

O: The first girl, no. What I did, well I tied her up, and I had bound her with her legs spread wide open.

H: So she was staked down, the ritual that you were talking about?

O: That was the ritual. That was something that had been in my head since I was a kid. I had read it in this book that my uncle had.

H: So here is an 11-year-old girl that is very cold, and you have her staked out...

O: She was very cold, in a catatonic state. I found a rock, and my intention was to elicit some kind of response. It was big, about that long. I pushed it up inside of her. Now, one of the reasons that they called it a mutilation murder was that the girl was on her stomach at some point, and the claim was that I had slashed her nipples. I hadn't done anything there, but I guess they tried to say that I cut them off or something. It was a very rough floor.

H: She was conscious?

O: Very unresponsive, and it was getting me angry because there was no response. At least what I'm looking for is a response, what I'm reacting to is a response, what spelled success for me is a response. I'm terrorizing this person. I'm controlling them.

H: And the other girl?

O: She's just sitting there not doing anything. And I should say that I hopped. You know I went over here, and I should point out that the girl I took with me, the one that is over here on the side was more attractive, was more physically mature than the other girl, so there in my head, I'm not seeing a child.

H: What were you doing when you were going back and forth?

O: Doing the same thing to her.

H: The one on the other side, she was also tied down?

O: Right, and she's suffering better than the first one.

H: She is responding more?

O: Right.

H: What are you doing to the one on the other side?

O: Same thing, staking her down, beating her, just terrifying her with the knife, and I came back and I killed the first one. I strangled her, and she was, I'm sure she was dead but then I . . . It was strictly to kill the witness. In my effort to terrify her, I had run the knife like this, but they were just scratches. In fact, I don't even think they drew blood. I think I burned her right here with a cigarette.

H: She didn't scream?

O: Neither one of them ever did. I don't think they realized what was going to happen. I took the other girl, and I said come on, we're going. And she says, well what about my friend? And I say your friend is okay, follow me, and do as I say, or I'll come back and hurt your friend, something like that. She came, and I've always wondered . . . you heard of the Stockholm Syndrome?

H: She's a kidnap victim, and she kind of identifies with you.

O: Right. As we were leaving, we were walking to this residential intersection.

H: And she's just walking with you?

O: She's walking right behind me, and she doesn't even wonder what's happening. She's walking right behind me, and I know that she's there, and I know that she's following me, and as I'm coming to the corner, a police car, patrol car pulls up, and I hear them air the description of the girls they're looking for. I think what happened was, her mother was concerned about the weather—that it was too cold. So she went almost immediately there, and the girls never showed up. I think they looked for about an hour, then they called the police. So this police car pulls up and I hear the description over the air, and I am from here to this wall from them, and she's right there, and I made a left.

H: Were you wearing anything that would attract attention from the police?

O: She might have because she was wearing my jacket. I think I had torn up the clothes, the upper clothes. All she has on from the waist up is this big, you know, hooded sweat jacket with the little hands here. She's wearing that, some slacks, and tennis shoes. Well I'm thinking, give this up. That's why I made a left, and I'm thinking she's back there telling the police right now: hey this guy did this and that and my girlfriend is up there and all of the sudden, maybe I'm 30 yards away, I'm waiting for a "Hey you, stop," you know, and what do I hear, "Mister, Mister slow down. I can't keep up with you."

H: She walked right by them.

O: She walked right by the police car.

H: At that point you must have been very surprised.

O: Very. I expected a bullet in the back. I turned around and said come on let's go. So I held her hand, and when cars came by I just acted like she was my daughter, and she's going right along with it, and she didn't appear afraid of anything.

H: Do you think as you look back that maybe she was in shock?

O: It had to be something like that.

H: Did she talk with you as she walked?

O: Yeah. She saw her father. Her father and her mother were in a car. I remember it was a Chevy sedan. He was out looking for her. Passed by, and she said, "Oh there's my father, he must be looking for me." It was on the street. Another three seconds, five seconds...

H: They didn't see you.

O: No they didn't.

H: Twice you should have been apprehended. There should have been intervention, or there could have been. I am surprised that the police, when they saw you walking with this girl didn't at least stop to question you. There was no one else around.

O: She didn't act like she was having any problems. We finally made it to the place where I was living, and there I made her shower and dry her hair. In other words it was almost like, it was conscious effort to let this person look more adult, more like the ideal.

H: Was she saying anything to you?

O: I had told her I wouldn't hurt her anymore, and when we got in she said, "You said you weren't going to hurt me anymore."

H: And you had already burned her?

O: I think I had.

H: Okay, had you beaten her?

O: I had hit her.

H: You had oral sex with her?

O: Oral sex. She realizes there's not much she can do except do what I say.

H: She doesn't scream because she knows if she screams you'll beat her. What happens then?

O: I'm going to kill her. I suffocate her. I put a bag over her face and held a pillow over it.

H: How long did you leave the victim in your home?

O: Thirty-two hours from the time of death until I got the car. I was thinking, what am I going to do?

H: So there was not post-mortem acts or anything like trophy taking?

O: No, the only time that I ever did anything like that was my first victim, and I think this was probably characteristic of the first time... overkill. I was mad 'cause she was dead too soon.

H: You were mad because she was dead too soon. You couldn't get the payoff.

O: Yes. And I got mad and I kicked her and I beat her and I strung her up and was trying to get what I had wanted from this corpse. Of course it wasn't forthcoming and I had to dispose of her before finding another one. Getting back to what you had asked?

H: Then you took her in the car and dumped her?

O: Right.

H: How long did it take before they found anything? Who did they find first?

O: Linda. They found her probably an hour after we left. I wish I had been caught right away. But there were a lot of close calls. In fact there was somebody running nearby when we left that didn't see us leave.

H: And the second victim?

O: Mary. I like to put names with victims so they're not just a victim—they have a name. Mary was dumped in a mountain path.

H: How long before they found her?

O: Okay, I should say the first one, I killed her probably about 7:00 in the evening, and Mary died about eight hours later. About 3:00 in the morning. I have no way of knowing for sure.

H: You were with these victims for quite a period of time. Did you have any fear?

O: No. What develops is a sense of invulnerability with success. It was that sense of invulnerability. Now when the policeman was there I wasn't really scared, just kind of tense. The point I was making is that I had a vehicle, and even if I had not dumped that coat where I did, it was a coat that had a blood sample, and that girl had a very rare blood type, and the coat which belonged to the guy whose house I was sharing was a very unique coat. When they put it on the [TV] screen, he recognized it, and that was it. Before, I was very conscious about risk. And I was conscious here, I was just kind of stretching it a little.

H: So far as you could go.

O: Yes. I was gone within a week.

H: Okay, so within a week they apprehended you walking to the home of a relative.

O: I had left about three days, four days, afterwards and went to my cousin's home. By that time, the coat had been shown, they were on my trail, and I didn't know this. They just missed us at my cousin's house—the FBI.

H: When they approached you, did they have weapons drawn?

O: Yes. Everything, TV. "Down, you blankety-blank." And I am probably very fortunate that my cousin was there, although I sure regret having put him through that. He was instrumental in the confession as well. They more or less coerced me. You will speak or your cousin will go to prison for accomplice. He had nothing to do with it, but he knew that I was a fugitive in the kidnapping four years before.

The following interview statements reflect the thoughts and feelings of a select number of other serial killers. Each of these offenders was markedly distinct in personality, emotional stability, IQ, attitudes, and types of victims selected.

A. Offender has killed over 50 victims, many by poison or suffocation. He considers himself to be a nice, compassionate, caring person and is mean or cruel only when provoked. A homosexual, he remembers (since the age of five) a semi-happy childhood during which he was the victim of sexual abuse. The abuse lasted 13 years and involved a male neighbor and an uncle. As a child he was told his mother would be harmed if he did not submit to the sexual advances. Fearing for her safety, he complied. The sexual abuse, he feels, had nothing to do with the killings or his later involvement with homosexuality. He claims a strong belief in a forgiving God and expresses interest in the occult, although he denies that Satan influenced his actions. Some victims he killed as "acts of mercy," others died at his hands as a result of vengeance, fear, "justice," or anger. The offender claims remorse for some of the murders but would definitely repeat some of them again. He claims that although he was mentally disturbed during some of the killings, he no longer suffers from psychological problems. He portrays himself as a caring person who is at peace with himself and wants to help others avoid becoming murderers. If he can do this, he feels he will have accomplished something.

B. Offender has killed at least ten victims brutally, with extreme mutilation and trophy collecting. He portrays himself living a Dr. Jeykll/Mr. Hyde existence. He also describes a deep love/hate relationship with his mother. He killed out of frustration and his inability to communicate socially or sexually. The offender deeply feared failing in relationships with women. He felt that if he could just kill his mother, the need for murder would stop. He claims regret for not having sought out help earlier and thereby sparing several innocent lives. He feels that if he had had the courage, he could have sought help. He believes that if he were now free from prison that he would get married and have children.

C. Offender has killed 40–50 victims. Some of his victims were killed to cover up other crimes, but many were women who hitched a ride with him. He believed that women who hitchhiked were prostitutes. He carries a deep aversion to prostitutes because his mother was one. As a child he was subject to sexual exploitation and constant rejection by his mother. He finally killed her. After he killed several dozen victims, he claims God helped him have a change of heart. For him, the best way to avoid capture was to be constantly traveling. Now that he is on death row, he expresses remorse for the plight of his victims, including their families. He feels that his home life is primarily to blame for his criminal behavior. Both of his parents were usually drunk and showed no interest in him or the other siblings. He feels that a serial killer is someone who bases their life on that activity and that is exactly what he felt he did. A Christian, he firmly believes that he has been saved in God's eyes.

D. Offender has killed at least three victims and now resides in an institution for the criminally insane. He claims to have been under the influence of hallucinations that led to the murders. He claims remorse for killing his victims, especially his son, but that he forgot about the killing after it was done. For this offender it did not matter who his victims were. Inevitably he knew he was going to kill three million people, so it really did not matter where he started. In addition, the offender has a fascination with mutilating sexual organs and claims he will do so again if he ever gets an opportunity. He explains that his hallucinations continue to encourage him to kill. He believes the voice in his hallucinations is that of the devil, which possesses him.

Serial Murder: An International Perspective

Most Americans have heard of Jack the Ripper. What many Americans do not know, however, is that since Jack's debut there have been other "Rippers" in England. European countries have also had their share of multiple killers. For example, Harold Smith (1987) identified several noted serial killers in Europe, and Jenkins (1988) chronicled the activities of multiple killers in England between 1940 and 1985. Indeed, serial killings have appeared and been documented in most countries. Even the U.S.S.R., which used to underreport crime, has reported cases. In one instance a Soviet newspaper, *Sovetsky Sport*, reported that the director of a teenage sports club murdered several children and photographed their hanging corpses. The offender, Slivko of Nevinnomyssk, was executed for his crimes. The paper also noted that the crimes had occurred over a span of several years. Another Soviet publication reported the execution of a locksmith in Byelorussia for the murders of 33 female victims. France has experienced "Bluebeards" and "Rippers"; England, "Vampire Killers" and "Rippers"; Germany, "The Monster of Düsseldorf" and "The Ruhr Hunter"; Ecuador, "The Monster of the Andes."

The following chronological lists of serial killers outside the United States are only partial accounts of such offenders in other countries. They essentially comprise the more sensational and publicized cases.

There has yet to be any systematic comparison of serial killers in the United States with those of other countries. Much closer examination of homicide data in other countries is necessary if we are ever to produce reliable comparative data sets. Even then we are hampered by differential reporting patterns, definitional problems, and impediments to accessing pertinent data. Although such problems may never be adequately resolved, a number of general comparisons can be made between serial killers in the United States and 22 other countries.

Male Serial Killers in Countries Other Than the United States

YEAR(S)	NAME	NUMBER OF VICTIMS	COUNTRY
1430	Gilles de Rais	800+	France
1600	Sawney Beane	1500+	Scotland
1790–1840	Thuggee Buhram	931	India
1800	Andreas Bichel	50+	Bavaria
1820	William Burke	32	Scotland
1840	Billy Palmer	14	England
1861–1864	Joseph Phillipe	8–18	France
1865	Pierre Voirbo	11	France
1869	Jean Baptise Troppmann	8	France
1871–1872	Vincent Verzeni	12	Italy
1890	Alfred Deeming	20	Australia, England
1894–1897	Joseph Vacher	10–20	France
1898–1901	Ludwig Tessnow	30+	Germany
1901–1903	George Chapman	3+	England
1908–1936	Adolf Seefeld	12	Germany
1911–1915	George J. Smith	3	England
1913–1930	Peter Kurten	15+	Germany
1913–1920	George Karl Grossman	50+	Germany
1915–1922	Henri Desire Landru	11+	France
1918–1922	Fritz Haarman	30–40	England
1920–1923	Albert Edward Burrows	4	England
1924	Carl Denke	30+	Poland
1941–1946	Dr. Marcel Petiot	63	France
1942	Gordon F. Cummins	3	England
1942	Edward Joseph Leonski	?	Australia
1943	Bruno Ludke	85	Germany
1943–1953	John R. H. Christie	6+	England
1944–1949	John George Haigh	9	England
1945–1963	Teofilo Rojas	592+	Colombia
1946	Neville Heath	5+	England
1953–1963	Efrain Gonzales	117	Colombia
1958	Peter Manuel	9	Canada
1959	Wendell Lightborne	3+	England
1959–1976	Joachim Kroll	14+	W. Germany
1960–1964	Klaus Gossman	7	Germany
1960–1961	Michael Copeland	3	Germany, England
1961–1963	William MacDonald	?	Australia

(continued)

Male Serial Killers in Countries Other Than the United States *(continued)*

YEAR(S)	NAME	NUMBER OF VICTIMS	COUNTRY
1962	Lucian Staniak	20	Poland
1962–1966	Jurgen Bartsch	4	W. Germany
1962–1971	Graham Young	?	England
1963–1964	Ian Brady	3+	England
1964	Hans Van Zon	5	Holland
1965–1967	Raymond L. Morris	1+	England
1966–1976	Charles Sobhraj	10	England
1969–1984	Daniel Camargo Barbosa	71	Brazil
1971	Sjef Rijke	2+	Holland
1971	Fran Hooijaijers	5–250	Europe
1971–1983	Peter Sutcliffe	13	England
1973	Bruce Lee	26	England
1973–1975	Patrick David Mackay	5–7	England
1973–1981	Clifford Olson	11+	Canada
1974–1981	James Odo	3+	Canada
1977–1983	Dennis Nilsen	15–17	England
1977	Pedro Lopez	300+	Ecuador
1977	Al Marjek	3	Syria
1977–1980	Arnfinn Nesset	22–25	Norway
1980–1981	Robert E. Brown	9	Canada
1982	Barry Peter Prudom	?	England
1984–1985	Pawel Alojzy Tuchlin	9+	Poland
1984–1986	Thierry Paulin	14	France
1985	Angel Piaz Balbin	8	Peru
1986	Sohrab Aslam Khan	13	Pakistan
1987	"Locksmith"	33	U.S.S.R.

1. Many countries appear to have a similar problem of certain cases being defined as "super killers." This means that some offenders have claimed or have been accused of hundreds of murders. The problem with these numbers is that they are usually not verifiable. Many of the "super killers" lived in earlier centuries when documentation was practically nonexistent. In all likelihood, the large numbers are a product of sensationalism and exaggeration. For example, in the United States during the 1800s, Charles Gibb, John Murrell, H. H. Holmes, and June Toppan allegedly murdered collectively more than 900 people. In other countries, dating back as early as the 1400s and as late as the 1970s, 11 offenders, including Buhram of India; Susi Olah of Hungary; Gilles de Rais of France; Teofilo Rojas of Colombia; Pedro Lopez of Ecuador;

Female Serial Killers in Countries Other Than the United States

YEAR(S)	NAME	NUMBER OF VICTIMS	COUNTRY
1610–1614	Countess Elizabeth Bathory	600	Hungary
c. 1660s	Catherine la Voisin	1500+	France
c. 1660s	Madame de Montespan	1400+	France
1676	Marie de BrinVilliers	100+	France
1809	Anna Marie Zwanziger	3+	Bavaria
1811	Anna Marie Schonleben	3+	Germany
1828	Gesina Gottfried	20+	Germany
1830–1850	Helena Jegado	60+	England
1852–1871	Mary Ann Cotton	14–21	England
1890	Greta Beier	4	Germany
1908	Jeanne Weber	9+	France
1909–1929	Susi Olah	100+	Hungary
1924–1926	Antoinette Scieri	6	France
1936	Dorthea Waddingham	?	England
1953–1963	Maria de Jesus Gonzales	91+	Mexico
1953–1963	Delfina de Jesus Gonzales	91+	Mexico
1963–1964	Myra Hindley	3	England
1968	Mary Flora Bell	2	England
1983	Maria Velten	5	W. Germany

Countess Elizabeth Bathory of Hungary; Abbe Guibourg, Madame de Montespan, Catherine la Voisin, and Marie de BrinVilliers of France supposedly murdered over 6,400 victims!

2. Well-publicized cases in which females are the offenders appear to be much more common in foreign countries. Similar to female offenders in the United States, there does not appear to be a "Jack the Ripper" type of female offender in other countries. In cases where physical violence was used, women usually had at least one accomplice. Also, most female offenders who lived during earlier times resorted to poisons, as their female counterparts did in the United States.

3. Team killers, or those who killed with accomplices, appear to be much more common in the United States than in other countries. However, in-depth examination of cases in other countries may yet reveal many more team killer cases. For the present, those designated as team killers in other countries appear to kill twice as many victims each as their U.S. counterparts.

4. Team killers and solo killers, regardless of whether they were American or foreign, murdered approximately the same percentages of all victims.

5. U.S. killers appear to be much more mobile and travel more than foreign offenders do; those in other countries are much more likely to be classified as "local" killers. This may in part be due to proximity to population centers, language barriers, cultural diversities, or availability of transportation.

6. In the majority of cases, both U.S. and foreign offenders were strangers to their victims. Foreign killers also appear to target acquaintances as victims.

7. Torture, strangling, and stabbing/chopping as modes of death seem to be used in similar percentages of cases. Americans sometimes use guns to kill or torture their victims; however, foreign offenders appear to rarely use firearms.

Although many countries have recorded cases of serial killing, the majority of cases appear to come from industrialized nations. Of course, this may be misleading, because other countries may experience such crimes without widely publicizing the information. Certainly, much more research needs to be done before we can accurately compare and contrast serial killers around the world.

Unsolved Murder Cases

At the time of this writing a serial killer is roaming the streets of Los Angeles. The killer is going after "strawberries," or prostitutes who sell sex for drugs. So far, at least 12 women have been murdered. Regardless of the motive, offenders who want to kill young women can find easy targets among prostitutes. Dealing with strangers is their trade, and someone who decides to start killing prostitutes can go undetected for several years.

In July, 1982, a cyclist found the strangled body of 16-year-old Wendy Coffield. Seven years later Wendy has been joined by nearly 50 other female hitchhikers, transients, and prostitutes from the Seattle, Washington, area. These killings have been dubbed the "Green River" killings, because most of the victims have been located in or around the Green River area. A task force was created to focus specifically on apprehending the Green River killer. At times as many as 60 agents were investigating the case on any given day. Bodies kept surfacing, and police maintained their intense manhunt. The killings now appear to have stopped, and, with no leads, police are at a standstill in the investigation. Possibly the killer moved to another killing site or is in prison for other offenses. Perhaps he became ill or died. Unless the killer chooses to come forward, it is unlikely the case will ever be solved.

Another serial murder case occurred in the Boston area, where at least eight prostitutes were found dumped in woods along the interstate highways. Similar stories can be related about missing and murdered young women in Kansas City, Missouri (1988), and the Washington, D.C. area (1987). A small sampling of other unsolved cases includes: the Joliet, Illinois, murders of 1983, 15 victims; the 1976 killings in the Detroit area, seven victims; the 1974 "Los Angeles Slasher" case involving eight victims; the "Texas Strangler" case of 1968–1971 involving 11 victims; the 1967 Kenosha, Wisconsin, murders of seven victims; the 1956 Chicago serial killings of five people; and the 1935 "Mad Butcher of Cleveland" case that yielded 12 victims.

Women, of course, are not the only targets. The "Executioner" in Los Angeles (1986) killed at least nine male transients. Vagrants, like prostitutes, are accessible and vulnerable. Occasionally homosexuals, usually males, become the target of someone who has decided it is time to cleanse the earth of people they perceive as wicked. More often it becomes evident that such killers are themselves homosexuals. (However, this does not mean that homosexuals are given any more to violent pathologies than heterosexuals. Although there have been a number of homosexually related serial killings, those figures do not appear to be disproportionate to other types of serial killings.)

As discussed earlier, there does appear to be an increase in the number of people being killed in nursing homes and hospitals. Sophisticated drugs such as digoxin, pavulon, and potassium chloride are either difficult to detect or the procedures for testing for such drugs are not well established. At the Toronto Hospital for Sick Children in Ontario, Canada, dozens of infants were believed to have been killed with overdoses of the heart drug digoxin between 1980 and 1981. Authorities were never told until it was too late. By then evidence had been discarded, exhibits misplaced, bodies cremated, and files "cleaned up." One nurse, arrested for the crimes, was released because of lack of evidence. To date that case has yet to be resolved.

Perhaps murders are increasing in nursing homes and hospitals because of some of the following reasons:

1. Victims are accessible and vulnerable.

2. An offender can easily operate without detection because no one expects such crimes would or could ever occur in such a setting.

3. An offender has access to a variety of murder weapons that are then easily disposed of without detection.

4. Often autopsies are not performed when a death occurs under the care of an attending physician. People routinely die in hospitals, especially critical care units. Consequently there is rarely a need to be suspicious. Doctors can misdiagnose the actual cause of death. Congestive heart failure, for example, may be induced through a variety of causes.

5. Efforts are sometimes made by supervisors/administrators to edit reports that somebody is acting suspiciously or could be harming patients. Scandals of purported murders inevitably can adversely affect admission rates. Negative publicity in the minds of some administrators is to be avoided at all costs.

6. Finally, prosecuting those who are believed to be involved in the deaths of patients can be very difficult as a result of lost evidence, sensationalism, and legal procedures. For example, in August, 1975, FBI agents were called to the Ann Arbor Veterans Hospital to investigate 50 breathing failures spanning a six-week period. On June 16, 1976, a Detroit grand jury indicted nurses Filipina Narcisco and Lenora Perez with mass poisoning. In July, 1977, the two women were found guilty of injecting five patients with Pavulon, a drug that freezes the muscles necessary for breathing. A federal judge granted the pair another trial, citing misconduct by federal prosecutors that had denied the women a fair trial. Federal prosecutors then dropped the charges (*Detroit Free Press*, December 6, 1988).

Certainly these offenders who kill in hospitals and nursing homes do not fit the stereotype of the typical lust murderers who stalk and viciously attack young women. They are the quiet killers who go about dutifully performing their assigned tasks, and when the urge or opportunity arises, silently and dispassionately take the life of some unsuspecting, trusting patient. These offenders are usually not "Jack the Ripper" types nor do they attract media attention as do traveling serial killers. Hospital personnel in general are ill prepared to cope with their suspicions and the consequences of homicides. Sometimes, as in the case of Donald Harvey or Jane Toppan, the offender is simply asked to resign when suspicions surface, and the police are not involved. In turn, such offenders inevitably find other hospitals or nursing homes in which to work and kill again. Hospital workers are in demand, especially anyone with some skills or experience. References are seldom checked, and even then there generally is no formal documentation of reasons why a person left his or her previous employment.

When we take into account the fact that serial killers operate in nursing homes, hospitals, and private homes as well as in and around cities and in different states, it is not surprising that we are faced with what appears to be an increasing number of unsolved cases. According to media reports, the United States is being "inundated" with serial killers, most of whom are extremely difficult if not impossible to apprehend, and law enforcement and the criminal justice system is unable to effectively stop serial killers. However, such criticism of law enforcement may be premature if not inappropriate. Law enforcement may be doing a much better job than anyone realizes. For example, it is quite plausible that law enforcement personnel actually apprehend many would-be multiple homicide offenders for one or two murders, thus stopping them before they can commit more. On what can we base this assumption? We know that prison populations comprise an estimated 20%–30% of psychopathic or antisocial personality types. These types of offenders are considered to be the most dangerous because they are more prone to violent behavior. Certainly not all psychopaths are prone to violent behavior nor do all those in prison have the propensity to harm others, but many do. We also know that such offenders have the highest rates of recidivism for criminal behavior and time in prison. An argument could then be made that many psychopaths who have been apprehended would have killed if they had not been arrested. Most of them are caught as a result of their own blunders and the good investigative skills of the police.

Serial killers are not indestructible nor do they have special mystical powers. They are humans who have acquired certain skills and certain patterns of deviousness that permit some of them to elude police. Making an accurate determination of the number of active serial killers is virtually impossible. As discussed in the final chapter, police agencies have only recently begun to allocate resources specifically for the detection and apprehension of serial murderers. And when these murderers are apprehended, the courts are faced with the determination of appropriate sentencing of these offenders. Sentencing often fails to meet the demands of public outrage or provide necessary treatment facilities and programs for these violent offenders.

CHAPTER 10

Apprehension and Disposition of Serial Killers

Robert Keppel, a former detective investigating the Ted Bundy case, once remarked that apprehending serial killers is very difficult. "Police departments generally are not equipped or trained to apprehend serial killers. They are organized to catch burglars and robbers and to intervene in family fights" (Lindsey, 1984, p. 1). Several factors set the serial offender apart from typical domestic killers and other violent criminals. Serial killers can be highly mobile and traverse many law enforcement jurisdictions while still remaining in a relatively small area geographically. Offenders generally prefer strangers as victims and are usually careful to minimize the amount of evidence left at the crime scene. Consequently, months may go by before there is sufficient interagency communication to recognize a common pattern of homicides. Coordination of information can be even more difficult when offenders cross several state lines, committing murders along the way. Although there has been considerable criticism of law enforcement in tracking down serial killers, police have made concerted efforts in some cases to join forces and conduct multiagency investigations. In several cases task forces have been organized, including:

1. *The Michigan murders*—A multi-agency task force was set up by the Wastenow County prosecutor's office that included five different police agencies. Eventually the Michigan State police assumed the coordination efforts, and on August 1st, 1969, John Norman Collins was arrested in the murders of seven young females.

2. *The Atlanta child killings*—In July, 1980, under the direction of then commissioner Lee Brown, a task force of local police agencies was formed. In November, the FBI was ordered into the investigation and eventually assumed direction of the investigation. On June 21, 1981, Wayne B. Williams was arrested in the murder of Nathaniel Cater and suspected to be involved in the disappearances and deaths of 27 other victims.

3. *The Green River killings*—In 1982, a task force of police investigators was organized to track down the killer(s) of young female prostitutes, hitchhikers, and transients in the Seattle, Washington, area. Having

learned a great deal from mistakes made in an Atlanta investigation, the Green River task force was thought to be the best investigative team ever organized. However, even with sophisticated techniques for investigating, it was not until July of 1989, seven years later, that a suspect was arrested. He was eventually released for lack of evidence.

Public anxieties demand quick apprehension of a serial offender; however, conducting investigations requires an enormous amount of resources and agency coordination. Glover and Witham (1989) identified four issues in managing major cases:

1. *Media impact*—Long-term media coverage creates immense pressure on law enforcement. Police must nevertheless establish an acceptable working relationship with the press.
2. *Management of departmental resources*—Who will take charge of the investigation and maintain a coordinated flow of command?
3. *Multi-agency jurisdiction*—Coordinated investigations, reporting, and expenditure of resources need to be addressed.
4. *Unusual complexity of the case*—Numerous victims, locations, and modes of death can create problems in sorting out evidence, investigative leads, and so on (pp. 2–16).

Investigation Factors and Techniques

At the investigation level, Keppel (1989) examined the "solvability factors" involved in serial murder and found the most important ones to be:

1. Quality of police interviews with eye witnesses
2. Circumstances that lead to the initial stop of the murderer
3. Circumstances that established probable cause to search and seize physical evidence
4. Quality of the investigations at the crime scene(s)
5. Quality of the scientific analysis of the physical evidence (p. 4).

This last solvability factor often becomes critical in multiple homicide investigations because they can include an enormous amount of physical evidence taken from the crime scene(s), from the offender(s) and his or her possessions, and from victims and their possessions. Forensic science has become a valuable tool in linking suspects to the crime scenes and in identifying evidence. Regional labs, such as the Atlanta Crime Laboratory, are used to analyze physical evidence from crime scenes in many states. For example, in the Atlanta child murders, a great deal of hair fiber evidence was catalogued and eventually used to convict Wayne Williams. Other types of physical evidence inspection and analysis now performed in crime labs include:

1. Glass and soil fragments

2. Organic analysis such as elements, compounds, chromatography, spectrophotometry, and mass spectrometry

3. Inorganic analysis such as atomic absorption spectrophotometry and neutron activation analysis

4. Hair, fibers, and paint analysis including typing and identification

5. Drug analysis such as narcotics, stimulants, depressants, and hallucinogens

6. Toxicological analysis such as alcohol, drugs, poisons

7. Arson analysis including flammable residues and explosives

8. Serological analysis including blood, bloodstains, and semen

9. Fingerprinting analysis including classification, detection, and preservation of prints

10. Firearms and toolmarks including analysis of bullets, gunpowder residue, primer residue, serial number restoration, and so forth

11. Document and voice analysis such as handwriting comparisons, typewriting, alterations, erasures, obliterations, and voice examinations (Saferstein, 1987).

Profiling

Tracking the serial killer and the multitude of problems posed by such a task have led, in the past few years, to the development of psychological profiling. Swanson, Chamelin, and Territo (1984) define the intent and purpose of profiling:

> The purpose of the psychological assessment of a crime scene is to produce a profile, that is, to identify and interpret certain items of evidence at the crime scene which would be indicative of the personality type of the individual or individuals committing the crime. The goal of the profiler is to provide enough information to investigators to enable them to limit or better direct their investigations [pp. 700–701].

Profiling, although in its infancy, has received mixed reviews. Some professionals, such as Godwin (1978) and Levin and Fox (1985), have been skeptical of the utility of profiling. Other researchers express varying degrees of support for the success of psychological profiling development, including Egger (1985), Geberth (1983), Holmes (1990), and Ressler and his colleagues (1988). Psychological profiling has yet to function as a "magic wand" to solve serial killings, but it is still too early in its development to be considered a failure. Programs such as those developed around profiling often require several years of testing and refinement before we are able to evaluate them. For profiling to fulfill its potential, law enforcement personnel must be willing to collaborate with those in the academic and medical professions. For example, psychiatrists can be of particular value in profiling, provided law enforcement people are willing to accept and use their profiles. Liebert (1985), in evaluating the contributions of psychiatry to the investigation of serial murders, such as lust killings, stated:

> Acceptance that the Borderline or Narcissistic Personality Disorder, with severe sociopathic and sadistic trends, can commit murder as a substitute for normal erotic pleasure or even nonviolent perversion is the foundation for exploration of motivation in serial murders. With a mutually respectful desire to learn about the bizarre world of the lust murderer, the investigator and psychiatric consultant can enhance their sense of "type" for a suspect. The investigator is less likely to make a mistake in judging the grandiosity of pathological narcissism and the manipulativeness of sociopathy with "normalcy." The lust murderer can present a facade of relationships and effective, perhaps even superior, performance. Not infrequently, he will be in the bright-superior intelligence range and, therefore, potentially a skilled impostor [p. 197].

The following are two examples of profiling in action: In New York a police department submitted an unsolved case after months of intensive but futile investigation. A woman had been strangled and brutally beaten, her mutilated body left on the roof of the Bronx housing project where she had lived. FBI profilers suggested to police that they look for someone 25–35 years of age, white male, who lived or worked in the area, a high school dropout, living by himself or with one parent; very likely police had already interviewed him. A few months later police arrested a 32-year-old white male, a high school dropout living with his father on the fourth floor of the victim's building. Police had interviewed the son but then removed him from their suspect list because he had been confined to a mental hospital at the time of the murder. Further investigation revealed that patients at the hospital were able to come and go as they wished (Barnes, 1986).

In a second case, several young women had been killed in various states. As police began to gather data, agents began to notice similarities in the modus operandi. Victims tended to be found along major interstate highways and trucking routes. Eventually a truck driver was arrested in the murders.

Profiling can be very useful, but caution must be exercised to avoid constructing hasty or poorly grounded profiles that may lead investigators in wrong directions. This inevitably places a strain on resources, and, most important, additional lives may be lost.

Errors in the information transmitted to NCAVC [National Center for the Analysis of Violent Crime], mistaken assessments by the evaluation team, and other potential glitches mean profiles can and do go wrong. In one case, for example, a profile on a criminal suspect told investigators the man they were looking for came from a broken home, was a high school drop out, held a marginal job, hung out in "honky tonk" bars, and lived far from the scene of the crime. When the attacker was finally caught, it was learned the psychological assessment was 100% wrong. He had not come from a broken home, he had a college degree, held an executive position with a respected financial institution, did not use alcohol, and lived near the scene of the crime. With this possibility for error, the bureau warns investigators not to become so dependent on the evaluation that they neglect other leads or become biased to the point where they blindly follow only the clues which match the scenario described in the profiles report [Goodroe, 1987, p. 31].

Profiling must be used as only one tool that will complement crime scene investigations. The strength of profiling will come as a result of interagency and interdisciplinary cooperation.

National Center for the Analysis of Violent Crime (NCAVC)/Violent Criminal Apprehension Program (VICAP)

In 1984, the U.S. Department of Justice, composed of the Office of Justice Programs, the National Institute of Justice, and the Office of Juvenile Justice and Delinquency Prevention, along with the Federal Bureau of Investigation in conjunction with the Criminal Justice Center at Sam Houston State University in Huntsville, Texas, established the National Center for the Analysis of Violent Crime (NCAVC). This center serves as a clearinghouse and resource for law enforcement agencies involved in "unusual, bizarre and/or particularly vicious or repetitive violent crime" (Brooks et al., 1987). The NCAVC is composed of four core programs: Research and Development; Training; Profiling and Consultation; and the Violent Criminal Apprehension Program (VICAP).

VICAP is located in the Behavioral Science Unit in Quantico, Virginia, and serves as a national clearinghouse for reports involving solved or un-solved homicides, attempted homicides, abductions, missing persons where violence is suspected, and unidentified dead bodies involving homi-cides. In turn, VICAP provides law enforcement agencies "reporting similar pattern violent crimes with the information necessary to initiate a coordi-nated multi-agency investigation so that they may expeditiously identify and apprehend the offender(s) responsible for the crimes" (Brooks et al., 1987, p. 41). Once patterns are established by VICAP staff involving vic-timization, physical evidence, information about the suspect(s), modus operandi, and so on, then the multi-agency coordination is set into motion. Ressler and his colleagues (1988) summarized the actual step-by-step process provided by VICAP:

> When a new case is entered, the VICAP computer system simultaneously compares and contrasts over 100 selected modus operandi (MO) categories of that case with all other cases stored in the database. After overnight processing, a printed computer report is returned to the VICAP crime analyst handling the case. This report lists, in rank order, the top ten "matches" in the violent crime databank; that is, the ten cases that were most similar to the new case. This crime pattern analysis technique, called *template pattern matching*, was specifically designed for VICAP and programmed by the FBI Technical Services Division. The VICAP computer system also produces selected management information system reports which monitor case activity geographically, with hope that it will eventually trace the travels of serial violent criminals across the United States [p. 113].

In June of 1985, VICAP became operationalized, and within the first year several problems were recognized with the system. More sophisticated computer programs had to be installed to sufficiently manipulate and analyze the large amounts of data and properly develop case matching. In addition, VICAP received fewer cases than expected, and good understanding of cases from reported data was more difficult to achieve than anticipated (p. 118).

Certainly NCAVC and VICAP have the potential to move forward in the battle against violent and nonviolent criminals. While tracking serial killers is a top priority, other offender data is also being collected and analyzed. For example, Hazelwood and Burgess (1989) conducted research into serial rapists. However, to date, VICAP has been sharply criticized by the media as having yet to catch any criminals (Allen, 1988). One of the problems lies in the limited cooperation of other local and state police agencies. Considering there are over 17,000 law enforcement agencies in the United States, many of which operate on shoestring budgets, it is not surprising that the flow of information to the federally operated control center has been less than overwhelming. VICAP should be viewed as a long-term program that will eventually develop and meet its founders' expectations.

As Ressler and his colleagues (1988) point out, "VICAP's purpose was not to investigate cases but to analyze them" (p. 119). During the next several years NCAVC and VICAP will continue to improve the quality and sophistication of computer programs, reporting methods, and analytical procedures. One hopes that, in years to come, those who operate VICAP will expand their current definition of serial killing, which generally focuses on lust killers who move about the country. Serial killers who are place-specific, those who do not become sexually involved with victims, and female serial offenders all warrant recognition and appropriate inclusion in VICAP files. We may never have female lust killers in our society, but, as has been presented in this research, women simply choose other methods of murder and have proven they are capable of mass murders and serial killings. The VICAP program is a developing tool that police can use to assist them in their investigations. In the final analysis, it is the police/agents in the cities and towns throughout America who ultimately must track down and apprehend the serial killers.

Sentencing

Once a serial killer is apprehended, the disposition of the offender is often very time consuming. Some of the most notorious cases receive extended hearings and go through a morass of legal proceedings that help set them apart as special cases. In part, this is due to the complexity of the case as well as the fact that such crimes often attract prominent legal figures. Most of these cases end up costing the taxpayers millions of dollars, and many communities are becoming impatient with lengthy legal proceedings. Meanwhile the offender often assumes celebrity status, attracting reporters and television and radio stations throughout the country.

Many Americans are apprehensive about giving serial killers anything but a death sentence. However, not all states carry the death penalty, and sometimes (as in the case of Donald Harvey) offenders will enter into a plea bargain to avoid the sentence of death. Indeterminate sentencing, whereby the offender receives a range of years in prison, is occasionally passed down by the judge. In some cases offenders will serve their multiple convictions concurrently, which means, for example, that 180 years in prison for six murders actually becomes 30 years plus time off for good behavior. Some offenders are given life in prison with no possibility of parole. It is unlikely that a serial or mass murderer, once convicted and incarcerated, will ever be free again. Some offenders, such as Edmund Kemper and Charles Manson, do receive periodic parole hearings, but these hearings become little more than a legal formality. No parole board is likely to take the risk of releasing a convicted mass killer back into society.

Although offenders convicted of serial murders are not paroled, some other types of murderers are paroled. Those offenders presently in prison for violent crimes who, if paroled, will eventually go on to become serial offenders are often impossible to identify. We generally cannot incarcerate people for crimes they have yet to commit. The closest we have come to this is through the habitual offender classification, which involves a person who has been convicted of three or more felonies. Such offenders are considered to be likely candidates for committing future crimes and are given extended sentences. Selective incapacitation (incarcerating chronic offenders for longer periods of time than other offenders) may affect serial murder rates by unknowingly containing potential offenders. Court records are replete with the names of offenders incarcerated for murder(s) who served time and were then released into the community where they killed again and again.

In 1939, Louise Peete, convicted of murder, was paroled only to become involved in the murders of several more victims. A similar situation occurred with George Fitzsimmons, who was institutionalized for killing his parents. Upon his early release to his aunt and uncle, he took out insurance policies on them and then stabbed them to death. Frederick Wood had served 17 years in Clinton State Prison for second-degree murder. Following his release, he went on a killing spree, and, upon his next arrest, confessed to five more murders. Another killer, Richard Marquette, was paroled after 12 years for the mutilation murder of a woman. He went on to decapitate and mutilate at least two more women before he was apprehended a second time (Brian, 1986).

This does not mean that most people who commit murder and serve time in prison are likely to kill again after their release. It does suggest, however, that some violent offenders never should be released.

Capital Punishment

Many proponents of the death penalty argue that punishment for crimes should be gauged according to the seriousness of the criminal offense. The harshest penalty then should be reserved for the worst crimes. Modern classical thinkers also point out that capital punishment stands as the last resort to deter people from committing particularly heinous crimes. Obviously someone who is already serving a life sentence with no chance of parole has little to lose by killing a correctional officer or another inmate. However, certain offenders might be less inclined to kill witnesses if they knew a death sentence would likely be imposed. In addition, supporters of the death penalty believe that offenders such as serial killers are so dangerous to other human beings that executing them presents the safest way of protecting society. Others argue, from an economic perspective, that maintaining offenders in prison for life is inevitably much more expensive than executing them.

Victims' rights groups have flourished in the past several years. Some have become particularly outspoken regarding the demise of the usually forgotten victim. The courts are asked to consider, in several states, victim impact statements outlining the devastation of physical, emotional, and financial hardships the victim has suffered. Victims seek restitution, compensation, and a sense of justice. Frank Carrington (1978) observed in the introduction of his book, *Neither Cruel nor Unusual*:

> This book is written from the point of the proponents. It is not objective. It is a defense of the death penalty. In a prior book, *The Victims*, I took the position that it is high time that the rights of the victims of crime were recognized in our criminal justice system. No where is this more true than in the area of capital punishment. Richard Franklin Speck is today contentedly watching television in an Illinois penitentiary at the

taxpayers' expense. The eight students whom he murdered have been in their graves for ten years, all but forgotten [p. 14].

Efforts are being made by victim coalitions to strike a blow for victims' rights. It seems that the criminal has been afforded all the rights; these groups say that now it is time to create a sense of legal and moral balance. People experience a myriad of emotions once they become victims of crime or families of victims, especially murdered victims. Revenge, hatred, anger, depression, and anxiety become moving forces in victims' lives and have made stalwart retributionists out of some formerly indifferent people.

Opponents to the death penalty are just as vocal and adamant that state-sponsored executions must never be accepted as a course of punitive action. Indeed, it is argued that our moral progress is unalterably impeded by adopting capital punishment as a method of expressing social vengeance. Legal scholars, such as Charles Black, argue that arbitrary discretion is found in every case that leads to the chair (1974). In other words, given the same crime of murder not all offenders sentenced to death will stand the same chance of being executed. Such discretionary factors include race, gender, age, and IQ of the offender.

In the case of Paula Cooper, a black 15-year-old girl in Gary, Indiana, who stabbed an elderly white Bible teacher 33 times, great debates began, and national attention was focused on her death sentence. Even Pope Paul sent a message from Rome to intercede on her behalf. Eventually, in 1989, she was removed from death row by the Indiana Supreme Court. We have decided that people are just too young to be executed for crimes committed at 15. "When a nation does violence to human beings, by conducting wars or executing criminals, it incites its citizens to more criminal violence than they would otherwise commit...the state can make violence the coin of its own realm" (Wilkes, 1987, pp. 27–28).

Denis (1986) conducted interviews with some of the country's most outspoken and respected opponents to the death penalty. Psychiatrist Karl Menninger, philosopher Hugo Bedau, and sociologist Michael L. Radalet each point out various problems with a pro-capital-punishment stance, including the facts that it discriminates against minorities, that innocent people are sometimes mistakenly executed, that in our current "pick and choose" mentality there appears no rational reasoning in selecting those who should be put to death and those who should be allowed to live, and that executions constitute cruel and unusual punishment (Chapter 22). Jeffrey J. Daughtery, 33, was electrocuted in Florida State Prison in November of 1988. In his final statement he criticized the legal system by stating, "I hope with all my heart I will be the last sacrificial lamb of a system that is not just, and all these people know it is not just. The executions serve no purpose." Daughtery had been involved in the serial murders of four young women.

Black (1974) expounded on the construction of cruelty in capital punishment:

> When we turn from the two usual arguments in favor of capital
> punishment—retribution and deterrence—to the other side, we find,
> above all, that the cruelty of it is what its opponents hate—the cruelty of
> death, the cruelty of the manner of death, the cruelty of waiting for
> death, and the cruelty to the innocent persons attached by affection to
> the condemned—unless of course, he has no relatives and no friends, a
> fairly common condition on death row [p. 27].

In the matter of serial killers, it seems that people are overwhelmingly in
favor of execution. In a sense, it has become a numbers game: the more
victims an offender kills, the more people are willing to accept execution as
the "best" choice in sentencing. The more victims involved, the more intense
is the media coverage. It is not surprising then that since the early 60s, when
serial killers began to appear in larger numbers, the general public has been
increasingly turning a deaf ear to objections regarding capital punishment.
California, for example, which has experienced a proliferation of mass
murders, has a special provision for such offenders: in cases of multiple
homicides, offenders can be sentenced to death or life in prison without
eligibility of parole. Most states appear to use both of these sentences to
handle special cases of multiple killings. Consequently, most serial killers in
prison today will never have the opportunity to be free again.

Because of the relative rarity of serial murder cases and the accompanying publicity, there exists a much smaller risk of racial discrimination involving cases of capital punishment. Similarly, it would be extremely unlikely for
an innocent person to be executed for seven or eight murders. The issue of
intelligence and competency is negated by the fact that most serial offenders
are of at least normal, if not above-average, intelligence. Rarely are they
found to be insane or incompetent. Consequently, when we are faced with
the serial killings of dozens of children, even some people who generally
oppose capital punishment agree that exceptions are necessary.

Few people have many qualms about executing an offender who has
murdered 30 young women. However, one seldom finds such a display of
revelry as occurred when Ted Bundy was electrocuted. One proponent of
capital punishment for mass killers wrote the following verse:

TO A MASS MURDERER

You know the Judge can send you up
for your remaining years,
And so I send this card to you
to banish all your fears;
No life in prison awaits you, pal.
You won't be rotting there;
The legislators changed the law—
They're bringing back the Chair.
                    [*Anonymous*]

We execute in the name of justice, for revenge, for punishment, for protection, to reduce recidivism, and a host of other often emotional rea-

sons. Those reasons seem to become clearer when we are faced with a case of multiple homicide. Aside from the moral and philosophical issues surrounding the death sentence, if American society is going to use capital punishment then serial offenders, who are by far the most dangerous offenders, should be first to qualify for execution. If capital punishment is not to be used, then we must ensure that serial killers will remain securely confined.

The following statements were made by inmates of Pendleton, a maximum security prison in Indiana. Some of the offenders were serving time for single homicides, robberies, or drug-related crimes. They were asked the question: What should we do with serial killers? The inmates responded:

1. "I feel that a counseling and treatment program could be established if necessary. If this does not help, then maybe we should go back to electroshock treatments and start from the beginning."

2. "The question was raised, are serial murderers treatable? I believe that more experience is needed in both medical and psychology fields before the question can be truthfully answered. As it stands now, I am not in favor of capital punishment, but I don't believe in keeping a person locked up for life either. Maybe, just maybe, there is some way to make use of these people that will please both society and the trade unions. Maybe there are certain kinds of people, certain environments that they can safely be useful to. We should also answer the questions brought about by serial killing. Can their thoughts and feelings be changed?

   "When the questions are asked, we must stay away from socially acceptable answers and deal only with the realistic answers and act on them."

3. "I think the serial killers should be given the opportunity to live, but they should be given this opportunity in a cell locked up for the rest of their life. What I am saying is, lock them up and put the key in the river."

4. "A serial killer is a person with strong emotional instabilities. I am not saying they're not intelligent, but deranged in the sense of perception of rights and wrongs."

5. "These people perform the most hideous acts on human beings possible. I don't think they should ever be released back into society. A person that ever possesses or has possessed such behaviors, can never be trusted. I know you should try, but is it worth the expense of possibly more victims? I say, hell no."

6. "As far as what to do with them goes, I feel they should be studied. Researched for as long as it is deemed helpful to resolving the problems. Do you kill them after this? I should say no, but what good are they to society? I don't believe in capital punishment, but I am

leery of these types of persons. As long as it's affordable and feasible, they should be housed in institutions. But one day we will have to discover the way to cure them or in the end kill them."

7. "They are a menace to society. A touchy decision to make on what should be done. But research is my main idea through dealing with these types of individuals... study rather than execute."

There is much we could learn about serial killers by studying those now incarcerated. We have already grouped some sex offenders into special programs, often in state hospitals, where they can receive treatment and be studied at the same time.

By creating regional centers designed to accommodate limited numbers of serial offenders, both researchers and law enforcement alike could benefit. Such an arrangement, however, would require federal funding, consent of offenders, and extensive planning and interagency coordination. In the meantime, serial offenders can almost routinely expect a death sentence or life in prison without parole.

Treatment

In an effort to interview a serial offender who had murdered between 10 and 12 teenagers and children, I received a personal letter from the Warden attempting to explain why such a visit would be unwise. In part, the letter stated: "To permit such a visit would reinforce the inmate's notoriety. It does not assist nor encourage him to become a law-abiding individual and countermands our desire to ultimately integrate him into an open population setting within an institution" (author's files, Nov. 1988).

Implicit in this statement is the assertion that a serial killer can be viewed as a candidate for some form of rehabilitation, even if it is enough to allow him or her to integrate with other inmates. Also implicit is the notion that some form of therapy can assist the offender by increasing his or her willingness to be law abiding. One usually does not think of serial killers in these terms. Rather, it generally becomes the aim of many to have the offender executed or permanently incarcerated. No treatment strategies are discussed as part of the sentence. Once the offender enters prison he or she is, for all intents and purposes, forever removed from normal society. Prisons are not managed or operated in such a manner that they are able to provide specialized services.

Dr. Samuel Yochelson, a psychiatrist, served as project director for The Program for the Investigation of Criminal Behavior, funded by the National Institute of Health. Half of his subjects were psychiatric patients, and the remainder came from the courts and other agencies:

> To his consternation, he found that after several years of intensive
> treatment, in which they gained many insights, his criminal patients

were still committing crimes. However, the crimes were now more sophisticated, and the insights they gained were being used to excuse what they did. Insight became "incite." In following the lead of the therapists, the criminal discovered even more people against whom he was incited. The criminal became skillful in seizing upon any adversity in his life and blaming it for his criminality. Traditional therapy became just one more criminal enterprise. The efforts to help him were exploited by the criminal to make himself look good and to substantiate his view of himself and of the outside world [Samenow, 1978, p. 17].

Treatment, however, may provide researchers opportunities to explore facets of the murdering mind that have yet to be examined. Certainly the prognosis for rehabilitation is not good. It is unrealistic to believe that the psychological complexity of a repetitive killer might ever be completely dismantled.

Considerable work has been conducted in the area of sex-offender research providing some insight into "lust" killers and the prognosis of treatability. Dr. Liebert, who served as a consulting psychiatrist on the Green River task force, the Atlanta children's murder task force, and the "Ted" (Bundy) task force, Washington, noted:

The lust murderer has primitive personality abnormalities making him incapable of normal intimacy. . . . Lust murderers may be able to maintain effective facades as impostors, imitating normal people, but they are not normal enough to tolerate the intensive bonding demands to meaningful psychotherapy. . . . Lust murder represents the extreme sadomasochistic and sociopathic end of the Borderline-Narcissistic Personality Disorder Spectrum—consequently, the least treatable part of the spectrum [1985, p. 197].

Our society's continued frustration in dealing with dangerous sex offenders has lead to a growing ostracism of these people. In one case, a convicted child molester with an extended history of sexual assaults was ordered by the courts to post a large sign on his door that read "Dangerous Sex Offender—No Children Allowed." Unfortunately, although the intent may be good, such an approach will do little to deter someone who wishes to act out his or her deviant sexual fantasies.

Prevention

Maxfield (1989), in his examination of homicide categories, stated: "Certain types of homicides are as amenable to prevention as are the events and circumstances with which they are associated. . . . If propensity to commit violent crimes follows certain patterns, intervention at early stages may truncate a criminal career" (p. 29). His conclusions are based on drug-related homicides, street gangs, and conflict-related murders—but is it possible to create a prevention strategy for serial murder? Currently, we see little hope either of deterring the serial offender or of protecting the potential victim. However, members of various communities are singling out what they feel facilitates/stimulates serial offenders. Some groups have increased their war on pornography, alcohol, and drugs believing that curtailing such vices will inevitably reduce violent criminal behavior. Others are beginning to realize the vulnerability of certain people identified as potential victims. For example, the United States has over 15,000 nursing homes that provide a wide range of quality care. Patient care and safety is a growing concern as more cases of "mercy killing" and angel-of-death attacks begin to surface. Much improved legislation is necessary if we are to protect the elderly and sick.

We must also become more aware of people who create emergencies in order to be rescuers, such as those who work as firefighters and set fires or work as nurses and poison patients. Such people create the opportunities to live out their hero fantasies. They feel so inadequate that they are willing to jeopardize lives in order to be recognized. Although such people are relatively rare in professions like firefighting and nursing, it would seem advisable for such professions to implement sound psychological testing and screening of potential employees.

Of course, every person should use general caution in dealing with strangers and reduce his or her own vulnerability by decreasing unnecessary risk taking. Walking or jogging alone, hitchhiking, or giving rides to total strangers, allowing strangers into one's home—all these activities increase risk potential.

The issue of prevention is really twofold. On one hand, we are trying to detect, apprehend, and incarcerate serial offenders and figure out ways to protect ourselves; on the other hand, we want to identify strategies to prevent individuals from becoming serial killers. People sometimes ask: What is the single most important recommendation that should be made from what we currently know about serial murder and our efforts to deter the phenomenon? Our knowledge is limited, but from the available data, *reducing violence in the home appears to be the most significant action to affect the circle of violence outside our homes*. This would include reduction/eradication of all forms of child abuse, including neglect, both physical and emotional. It would include reduction/eradication of spouse abuse and a restabilization of the family unit. It would require less divorce and increased bonding between parents and children. It would require parents taking parenting much more seriously. Someone once said that no success can compensate for failure in the home and that the greatest work we will ever do will be within the walls of our own homes.

However, a solid, happy home does not guarantee the absence of later violence. If we can alter how people feel about themselves—increase their self-esteem—we might be able to alter how they will feel and respond to others. These recommendations have no particular novelty or originality and may appear idealistic, but they are nonetheless timely. It appears much easier to build hospitals to care for the tens of thousands who die every year of alcoholism, tobacco-related diseases, and diseases caused by pollutants than it does to address the more chronic social ills of our society. The roots of victimization run deeply into our social structure and will only go deeper if we continue to ignore the needs of the family.

Future Issues and Research

Several issues, focal concerns, and areas of research currently need attention as we explore the phenomenon of serial murder. Some specific needs are:

1. Increased interaction and involvement between academicians and law enforcement in the form of seminars and workshops.
2. Increased cooperation between law enforcement agencies to better establish increased flow of data regarding violent offenders.
3. Increased training of local and state law enforcement personnel regarding serial murder and profiling.
4. Increased empirical research into all facets of serial murder to establish a greater base of understanding about offenders and victims.
5. To debunk and challenge many of the myths and stereotypes that surround serial murderers and their victims.
6. To generate an acceptable operationalized definition of serial murder that will inevitably reduce confusion among governmental and private agencies.
7. To explore improving methodological issues in data collection and analysis of multiple homicide offenders.
8. To examine prevention strategies using a team of experts, including law enforcement; social services; medical, psychiatric, and academic personnel.
9. To create public awareness programs that filter information in a rational and responsible manner.
10. To allow for greater accessibility to serial killers through the establishment of special research programs and projects.
11. To establish projects funded by the federal government specifically for the advancement of multiple homicide research.

References

Abraham, S. (1984). *Children in the Cross Fire: The Tragedy of Parental Kidnaping*. New York: Atheneum.

Abrahamsen, D. (1973). *The Murdering Mind*. New York: Harper Colophon Books, Harper and Row.

—— (1985). *Confessions of Son of Sam*. New York: Columbia University Press.

Adler, F. (1975). *Sisters in Crime: The Rise of the New Female Criminal*. New York: McGraw-Hill.

Aichorn, A. (1934). *Wayward Youth*. New York: Viking Press.

Alexander, S. (1983). *Nutcracker: Money, Madness, Murder: A Family Album*. New York: Dell.

Allen, T. (1988, November 13). Portrait of a serial killer, *Statesman Journal*.

Allen, W. (1976). *Starkweather*. Boston: Houghton Mifflin.

Associated Press (1987, June 7). Mother faces trial in child's death, *Atlanta Journal and Constitution*.

Athens, L. H. (1980). *Violent Criminal Acts and Actors*. Cambridge, MA: Routledge & Kegan Paul.

Atlanta Journal and Constitution (1982–86). Box 103009, Atlanta, Georgia.

Bandura, A. (1973). *Aggression*. Englewood Cliffs, NJ: Prentice Hall.

—— (1974). Behavior theory and the models of man, *American Psychologist, 29*, 861–862.

Bandura, A., & R. H. Walters (1963). *Social Learning and Personality Development*. New York: Holt, Rinehart and Winston.

Bard, M. and D. Sangrey (1986). *The Crime Victim's Book* (2nd ed.). New York: Brunner Mazel.

Barnes, B. (1986). FBI specialist, *Atlanta Journal and Constitution*, 1,7a.

Bartol, C. R. & A. M. Bartol (1986). *Criminal Behavior: A Psychosocial Approach*. Englewood Cliffs, NJ: Prentice-Hall.

Baumann, E. (1987). When demons preyed, *Chicago Tribune*, October 12, 1–2.

Becker, H. (1963). *Outsiders: Studies in the Sociology of Deviance*. New York: Macmillan, 9.

Bensing, R. C., & O. Schroeder, Jr. (1960). *Homicide in an Urban Community.* Springfield, IL: Charles C Thomas.

Berkow, R. (1977). *The Merck Manual* (13th ed.). Rahway, NJ: Merck, Sharp and Dohme Research Laboratories Publications.

Berkowitz, L., & J. Macaulay (1971, June). The contagion of criminal violence, *Sociometry, 34*, 238–260.

The Holy Bible (1979). King James Version, Church of Jesus Christ of Latter-Day Saints, Salt Lake City: 1241–1271.

Bierer, J. (1976). Love-making—An act of murder, *The International Journal of Social Psychiatry, 22*(3), 197–199.

Black, C. (1974). Capital punishment, in *The Inevitability of Caprice and Mistake.* New York: Norton.

——— (1980). Objections to S. 1382, a bill to establish rational criteria for the imposition of capital punishment, *Crime and Delinquency, 26*, 441–53.

Blackburn, R. (1971). Personality types among abnormal homicides, *British Journal of Criminology, 11*.

Blau, J. R., & P. M. Blau (1982, February). The cost of inequality: Metropolitan structure and violent crime, *American Sociological Review, 47*, 114–29.

Boar, R., & N. Blundell (1983). *The World's Most Infamous Murders.* New York: Simon and Schuster.

Boston Globe (1988, January 21). U.S.: One in four children had a single parent, 11.

Brian, D. (1986). *Murderers Die.* New York: St. Martin's Press.

Briar, S., & I. Piliavin (1965). Delinquency, situational inducements and commitment to conformity, *Social Problems, 13*, 35–45.

Brodsky, S. L. (Ed.) 1973. *Psychologists in the Criminal Justice System.* Urbana, IL: University of Illinois Press.

Brooks, P. R., M. J. Devine, T. J. Green, B. L. Hart, & M. D. Moore (1987, June). Serial murder: A criminal justice response, *Police Chief*, 40–44.

Brophy, J. (1966). *The Meaning of Murder.* New York: Thomas Y. Crowell.

Brown, S. E. (1984). Social class, child maltreatment, and delinquent behavior, *Criminology, 22*(2), 259–278.

Brownmiller, S. (1975). *Against Our Will: Men, Women and Rape.* New York: Simon and Schuster.

Bruch, H. (1967). Mass murder: The Wagner case, *American Journal of Psychiatry, 124*(5), 693–698.

Bugliosi, V. (1974). *Helter Skelter.* New York: Norton.

Cameron, D., & E. Frazer (1987). *The Lust to Kill.* New York: New York University Press.

Capote, T. (1965). *In Cold Blood.* New York: Random House.

Caputi, J. (1987). *The Age of Sex Crime.* Bowling Green, OH: Bowling Green State University, Popular Press.

Carrington, F. (1978). *Neither Cruel nor Unusual*. Westport, CT: Arlington House.

Chapman, J. (1980). *Economic Realities and the Female Offender*. Lexington, MA: Lexington Books.

Charny, I. W. (1980). A contribution to the psychology of genocide: Sacrificing others to the death we fear ourselves, *Israel Yearbook on Human Rights, 90*, 90–108.

—— (1982). *How Can We Commit The Unthinkable?* Boulder, CO: Westview Press.

Cheney, M. (1976). *The Co-ed Killer*. New York: Walker and Company.

Cleckley, H. (1976). *The Mask of Sanity* (5th ed.). St. Louis: Mosby.

Clinard, M. B., & R. Quinney (1986). *Criminal Behavior Systems*. A Typology (2nd ed.). Anderson Publishing Co.

Cline, V. (1990). Privately published monograph, Department of Psychology, University of Utah, Salt Lake City, Utah.

Collins, G. (1987). Women who kill. *New York Times* Service.

Coons, P. M. (1988, January 5). LaRue D. Carter Memorial Hospital, personal memo to author.

Corder, B. F., B. C. Ball, T. M. Haizlip, et al. (1976). Adolescent parricide: A comparison with other adolescent murder, *American Journal of Psychiatry, 133,* 957–961.

Cullen, T. (1977). *The Mild Murderer*. Boston: Houghton Mifflin.

Daly, M., & M. Wilson (1988). *Homicide*. New York: Aldine Degruyter.

Danto, B. (1982). A psychiatric view of those who kill, in J. Bruhns, K. Bruhns, & H. Austin (Eds.), *The Human Side of Homicide*. New York: Columbia University Press, 3–20.

Dean, A. L., M. M. Malik, W. Richards, & S. A. Stringer (1986). Effects of parental maltreatment on children's conceptions of interpersonal relationships, *Developmental Psychology, 22*(5), 617–626.

Deming, R. (1977). *Women: The New Criminals*. Nashville: Thomas Nelson.

De River, J. P. (1949). *The Sexual Criminal*. Springfield, IL: Charles C Thomas.

Detroit Free Press (1988).

Dettlinger, C. (1983). *The List*. Atlanta: Philmay Enterprises.

De Young, M. (1982). *The Sexual Victimization of Children*. Jefferson, NC: McFarland, 125.

Doerner, W. G. (1975, May). A regional analysis of homicide rates in the United States, *Criminology, 13*, 90–101.

Dostoyevsky, F. (1962). *The House of the Dead*. London: Dent.

DSM-III R (Diagnostic and Statistical Manual of Mental Disorders, 3rd ed., revised) (1988). Washington, D.C.: American Psychiatric Association.

Dugdale, R. (1910). *The Jukes*. New York: Putnam.

Durham v. United States, 214 F. 2d 862 (D.C. Cir. 1954).

Egger, S. A. (1985). *Serial Murder and the Law Enforcement Response.* Unpublished Dissertation, College of Criminal Justice, Sam Houston State University, Huntsville, Texas.

—— (1986). *Utility of the Case Study Approach to Serial Murder Research.* Paper presented at the 1986 annual meetings of the American Society of Criminology, Atlanta, Georgia.

—— (1990) *Serial Murder: An Elusive Phenomenon.* New York: Praeger.

Eisler, R. (1951) *Man into Wolf.* New York: Greenwood Press.

Eitzen, D. S., & D. A. Timmer (1985). *Criminology.* New York: Wiley.

Ellis, A., & J. Gullo (1971). *Murder and Assassination.* New York: Lyle Stuart.

Estabrook, A. (1916). *The Jukes in 1915.* Washington, D.C.: Carnegie Institute of Washington.

Eth, S., & Pynoos, R. S. (1985). Developmental perspective on psychic trauma in childhood, in C. R. Figley (Ed.), *Trauma and Its Wake: The Study and Treatment of Post-Traumatic Stress Disorder.* New York: Brunner & Mazel, 36–52.

Eysenck, H. J. (1973). *The Inequality of Man.* San Diego, CA: Edits Publishers.

—— (1977). *Crime and Personality* (2nd ed.). London: Routledge & Kegan Paul.

Federal Bureau of Investigation (1984a). Crime in the U.S., *Uniform Crime Reports.* Washington, D.C.: U.S. Department of Justice, U.S. Government Printing Office.

—— (1984b). *Report to the Nation on Crime and Justice.* Washington, D.C.: FBI Statistical Department, United States Department of Justice.

—— (1988). Crime in the U.S., adapted from the *Uniform Crime Reports.* Washington, D.C.: U.S. Department of Justice, U.S. Government Printing Office.

Finkelhor, D. (1979). *Sexually Victimized Children.* New York: Free Press.

—— (1988). *Nursery Crimes.* Newbury Park: Sage.

Fortune, J. (1934). *The Story of Clyde Barrow and Bonnie Parker.* Dallas: The Ranger Press.

Fox, J. A., & J. Levin (1989). Satanism and mass murders, *Celebrity Plus,* 49–51.

Frank, G. (1966). *The Boston Strangler.* New York: The New American Library.

Franke, D. (1975). *The Torture Doctor.* New York: Hawthorn Books.

Frederick, C. (1981). *Violence and Disasters: Immediate and Long-Term Consequences.* Paper presented at Psychosocial Consequences of Violence Conference, The Hague, April 6–10.

Freeman, L. (1955). *Before I Kill More.* New York: Crown.

Freud, S. (1936). *The Problem of Anxiety.* New York: Norton.

—— (1961). *The Standard Edition of The Complete Psychological Works of Sigmund Freud,* J. Strachey (Ed.). London: Hogarth, Vols. 1–20.

Fromm, E. (1973). *The Anatomy of Human Destructiveness.* New York: Holt, Rinehart and Winston.

Gaddis, T. E., & J. O. Long (1970). *Killer: A Journal of Murder.* New York: Macmillan.

Gallagher, B. J., III (1987). *The Sociology of Mental Illness* (2nd ed.). Englewood Cliffs, NJ: Prentice-Hall.

Gastil, R. D. (1971, June). Homicide and a regional culture of violence, *American Sociological Review, 36,* 412–27.

Gaute, J. H. H., & R. O'Dell (1979). *The Murderer's Who's Who.* New York: Methuen.

Geberth, V. J. (1983). *Practical Homicide Investigation.* New York: Elsevier.

Gebhard, P. H. (1965). *Sex Offenders.* New York: Harper and Row, 856.

Gibson, W. B. (1965). *Murder, The Fine Art.* New York: Grosset and Dunlap.

Glaser, B. G., & A. Strauss. (1967). *The Discovery of Grounded Theory: Strategies for Qualitative Research.* Chicago: Aldine.

Glover, J. D., & D. C. Witham (1989). The Atlanta serial murders, *Policing, 5,*(1), 2–16.

Godwin, J. (1978). *Murder U.S.A.* New York: Random House.

Goffman, E. (1961). *Asylums.* Garden City, New York: Doubleday.

Golden, C., J. Moses Jr., J. Coffman, W. Miller, & F. Strider (1983). *Clinical Neuropsychology.* New York: Grune & Stratton.

Goodroe, C. (1987, July). Tracking the serial offender, *Law and Order,* 29–33.

Gray, G. (1986). Diet, crime and delinquency: A critique, *Nutrition Reviews, 44,* 89–94.

Graysmith, R. (1976). *Zodiac.* New York: Berkley Books.

Grombach, J. V. (1980). *The Great Liquidator.* New York: Doubleday.

Guttmacher, M. (1973). *The Mind of the Murderer* (Selected Libraries Reprint Series). New York: Arno Press.

Guze, S. B. (1976). *Criminality and Psychiatric Disorders.* New York: Oxford University Press.

Hafner, H., & W. Boker (1973). Mentally disordered violent offenders, *Social Psychiatry, 8,* 220–229.

Hagan, F. E. (1986). *Introduction to Criminology: Theories, Methods, and Criminal Behavior.* Chicago: Nelson-Hal.

Hahn, J. K., & H. C. McKenney (1972). *Legally Sane.* Chicago: Henry Regnery.

Haizlip T., B. F. Corder, & B. C. Ball (1964). The adolescent murderer, in C. R. Keith (Ed.), *The Violent Adolescent.* New York: Free Press.

Hale, E. (1983, April 18). Startling discoveries shed new light on enigma of multiple personality, *Chicago Tribune,* 1, 5.

Hare, R., & J. Jutai (1959). Criminal history of the male psychopath: Some preliminary data, in K. T. Van Dusen & S. A. Mednick (Eds.), *Perspective Studies of Crime and Delinquency,* 225–236. Boston: Kluwer-Nijhoff (1983).

Harris, T. (1987). *Red Dragon*. New York: Bantam.

Hazelwood, R. R., & A. W. Burgess (1987, September). An introduction to the serial rapist, *FBI Law Enforcement Bulletin*, 16–24.

—— (1989, February). The serial rapist: His characteristics and victims, *FBI Law Enforcement Bulletin*, 18–25.

Hazelwood, R. R., & J. Warren (1989, January). The serial rapist: His characteristics and victims, *FBI Law Enforcement Bulletin*, 10–17.

Heath, L. (1984, August). Impact of newspaper crime on fear of crime: A multimethodological investigation, *Journal of Personality and Social Psychology*.

Helpern, M., & B. Knight (1977). *Autopsy: The Memoirs of Milton Helpern, the World's Greatest Medical Detective*. New York: St. Martin's Press.

Henderson, S. K. (1939). *Psychopathic States*. New York: Norton.

Henn, F. A., M. Herjanic, & R. H. Vanderpearl (1976). Forensic Psychiatry: Diagnosis of criminal responsibility, *The Journal of Nervous and Mental Disease*, 162, 423–429.

Hewitt, J. D. (1988). The victim-offender relationship in homicide cases: 1960–1984, *The Journal of Criminal Justice*, 16(1), 27–38.

Hickey, E. (1985, March). *Serial Murderers: Profiles in Psychopathology*. Presented at the Annual Meeting of the Academy of Criminal Justice Sciences, Las Vegas, NV.

—— (1986, October). The female serial murderer, *Journal of Police and Criminal Psychology*, 2(2), 72–81.

—— (1990a). The etiology of victimization in serial murder, in *Serial Murder: An Elusive Phenomenon*. New York: Praeger, 53–71. Copyright by Steven A. Egger.

—— (1990b). Missing and murdered children in America, in *Helping Crime Victims: Research, Policy, and Practice*. Newbury Park, CA: Sage, 158–185. Copyright by Albert R. Roberts.

Hill, D., & W. Sargent (1943). A Case of matricide, *Lancet*, 244, 526–527.

Hill, D., & P. Williams (1967). *The Supernatural*. New York: Signet Books.

Hirschi, T. (1969). *Causes of Delinquency*, Berkeley, CA: University of California Press.

Hirst, W. (1982). The amnesic syndrome: Descriptions and explanations, *Psychological Bulletin*, 91, 435–460.

Hoffer, P. C., & N. E. H. Hull (1981). *Murdering Mothers: Infanticide in England and New England 1558–1803*. New York: New York University Press.

Hoffman-Bustamante, D. (1973). The nature of female criminality, *Issues in Criminology*, 8, 117–136.

Holmes, R. M. (1990). *Profiling Violent Crimes*. Newbury Park, CA: Sage.

Holmes, R. M., & J. DeBurger (1988). *Serial Murder*. Newbury Park, CA: Sage.

Horney, J. (1978). Menstrual cycles and criminal responsibility, *Law and Human Nature*, 2, 25–36.

Howard, C. (1979). *Zebra: The True Account of the 179 Days of Terror in San Francisco.* New York: Richard Marek.

Inciardi, J. A., & A. E. Pottieger (Eds.) (1978). *Violent Crime: Historical and Contemporary Issues* (Vol. 5). Newbury Park, CA: Sage.

Inglis, R. (1978). *Sins of Fathers: A Study of the Physical and Emotional Abuse of Children.* New York: St. Martin's Press.

Jaffe, P., D. Wolfe, S. Wilson, & L. Zak (1986). Similarities in behavior and social maladjustment among child victims and witnesses to family violence, *American Journal of Orthopsychiatry, 56,* 142–46.

James, P. D., & T. A. Critchley (1986). *The Maul and the Pear Tree.* New York: Mysterious Press.

Jenkins, P. (1988). Myth and murder: The serial killer panic of 1983–85, *Criminal Justice Research Bulletin, 3*(11), 1–7.

Jones, A. (1980). *Women Who Kill.* New York: Holt, Rinehart and Winston.

Jones v. United States, 103 S. Ct. 3043 1983.

Kadish, S. H., & M. G. Paulsen (1981). *Criminal Law and Its Processes,* 215–16.

Kahaner, L. (1988). *Cults That Kill: Probing the Underworld of Occult Crime.* New York: Warner Books.

Kahn, M. (1971). Murderers who plead insanity: A descriptive factor-analytic study of personality, social, and history variables, *Genetic Psychology Monographs, 84.*

Karmen, A. (1990). *Crime Victims* (2nd ed.). Pacific Grove, CA: Brooks/Cole.

Karpman, B. (1954). *The Sexual Offender and His Offenses.* New York: Julian Press.

Katz, J. (1988). *Seductions of Crime: Moral and Sensual Attractions in Doing Evil.* New York: Basic Books.

Keppel, R. D. (1989). *Serial Murder: Future Implications for Police Investigations.* Cincinnati, OH: Anderson.

Kerman, S. L. (1962). *The Newgate Calendar.* New York: Capricorn Books.

Keyes, D. (1986). *Unveiling Claudia: A True Story of Serial Murder.* New York: Bantam Books.

Keyes, E. (1976). *The Michigan Murders.* New York: Simon and Schuster.

Kirshner, L. (1973). Dissociative Reactions: A historical review and clinical study, *Acta Psychiatrica Scandanavica, 49,* 698–711.

Kramer, E., & A. Iager (1984). The use of art in assessment of psychotic disorders: Changing perspectives, *Arts in Psychotherapy, 11*(3), 197–201.

Langlois, J. L. (1985). *Belle Gunnes.* Bloomington, IN: Indiana University Press.

Larson, O. N. (Ed.) (1968). *Violence and the Mass Media.* New York: Harper & Row.

LaVey, A. (1969). *The Satanic Bible.* New York: Avon.

Lee, R. A. (1988, July/August). A motive for murder, *Police Times,* 6.

Leith, R. (1983). *The Prostitute Murders.* New York: Pinnacle Books.

Lemert, E. (1951). *Social Pathology.* New York: McGraw-Hill.

Lester, D. (1979). The violent offender, in Hans Touch (Ed.), *Psychology of Crime and Criminal Justice*, 301. New York: Holt, Rinehart and Winston, citing the National Commission on the Causes and Prevention of Violence; to Establish Justice, to Ensure Domestic Tranquillity, Washington D.C.: U.S. Government Printing Office, 1969.

—— (1986). *The Murderer and His Murder.* New York: Ams Press.

Lester, D., & G. Lester (1975). *Crimes of Passion: Murder and the Murderer.* Chicago: Nelson Hall.

Levin, J., & J. A. Fox (1985). *Mass Murder: The Growing Menace.* New York: Plenum Press.

Lewis, D. O., B. S. Moy, L. D. Jackson, R. Aaronson, N. Restifo, S. Serra, & A. Simos (1985, October). Biopsychosocial characteristics of children who later murder: A prospective study, *American Journal of Psychiatry, 142,* 10.

Leyton, E. (1986a). *Hunting Humans.* Toronto: McClelland and Stewart Limited.

—— (1986b). *Compulsive Killers: The Story of Modern Multiple Murder.* New York: New York University Press.

Liebert, J. A. (1985, December). Contributions of psychiatric consultation in the investigation of serial murder, *The International Journal of Offender Therapy and Cooperative Criminology, 29*(3), 187–200.

Lifton, R. (1982, November). Medicalized killing in Auschwitz, *Psychiatry, 45*(4), 283–297.

Lindsey, R. (1984, January). Killers who roam the U.S., *New York Times, 21,* 1, 7.

Linedecker, C. L. (1980). *The Man Who Killed Boys.* New York: St. Martin's Press.

—— (1987) *Thrill Killers.* New York: Paperjacks.

Livsey, C. (1980). *The Manson Women.* New York: Richard Marek.

Lombroso, C., & Ferrero, G. (1916). *The Female Offender.* New York: Appleton.

Lombroso-Ferrero, G. (1972). *Criminal Man According to the Classification of Cesare Lombroso.* Montclair, NJ: Patterson Smith, 100.

Lunde, D. T. (1976), *Murder and Madness.* San Francisco: San Francisco Book Company.

Malmquist, C. P. (1971). Premonitory signs of homicidal aggression in juveniles, *American Journal Psychiatry, 128,* 461–465.

Marron, K. (1988). *Ritual Abuse.* Toronto: McClelland-Bantam.

Marsh, F. H., & J. Katz (Eds.) (1985). *Biology, Crime, and Ethics: A Study of Biological Explanations for Criminal Behavior.* Cincinnati, OH: Anderson.

Marwick, M. (1970). *Witchcraft and Sorcery.* Baltimore: Penguin Books.

Masters, B. (1986). *Killing for Company.* London: Coronet.

Masters, R. E. L., & E. Lea (1963). *Sex Crimes in History.* New York: Matrix House.

Matza, D. (1964). *Delinquency and Drift*. New York: Wiley.

Maxfield, M. G. (1989, November). Circumstances in supplementary homicide reports: Variety and validity, *Criminology, 27*(4), 671–695.

May, R. (1980). *Sex and Fantasy*. New York: Norton, 140.

McCarthy, J. B. (1978). Narcissism and the self in homicidal adolescents, *American Journal Psychoanal, 38;* 19–29.

McDonald, R. R. (1986). *Black Widow*. New York: St. Martin's Press.

McDonald, W. (1970). *The Victim: A Social Psychological Study of Criminal Victimization*. Unpublished doctoral dissertation. Ann Arbor, MI: University Microfilms.

McLeod, M. (1984). Women against men: An examination of domestic violence based on an analysis of official data and national victimization data. *Justice Quarterly,* 1, 171–193.

Mednick, S., & J. Volavka (1980). Biology and crime, in N. Morris & M. Tonry (Eds.), *Crime and Justice*. Chicago: University of Chicago Press, 85–159.

Mednick, S., G. William, & B. Hutchings (1983). Genetic influences in criminal behavior: Evidence from an adoption cohort, in K. Teilmann, V. Dusen, & S. Mednick, (Eds.), *Perspective Studies of Crime and Delinquency*. Boston: Kluver-Nijhoff, 39–57.

Megargee, E. I., & M. J. Bohn, Jr. (1979). *Classifying Criminal Offenders*. Newbury Park, CA: Sage.

Messner, S., and K. Tardiff (1986). Economic inequality and levels of homicide: An analysis of urban neighborhoods, *Criminology, 24,* 297–317.

Michaud, S. G., & H. Aynesworth (1983). *The Only Living Witness: A True Account of Homicidal Insanity*. New York: Linden Press/Simon & Schuster.

Miller, A. (1984). *For Your Own Good*. New York: Farrar, Straus, and Giroux.

Miller, D., & J. Looney. (1974). The prediction of adolescent homicide: Episodic dyscontrol and dehumanization. *American Journal of Psychoanalysis, 34*(3): 187–98.

M'Naughten (1843). 10 Clark & Fin. 200, 210, 8 Eng. Rep 718, 722.

Model Penal Code (1952). 401.

Monahan, J., & Geis, G. (1976). Controlling "dangerous people," *Annals of the American Academy of Political and Social Science, 423,* 142–151.

Monahan, J., & H. Steadman (1984, September). *Crime and Mental Disorder*. Washington, D.C.: National Institute of Justice Research in Brief.

Money, J. (1976). Influence of hormones on psychosexual differentiation, *Medical Aspects of Nutrition, 30,* 165.

Moser, D., & J. Cohen (1967). *The Pied Piper of Tucson*. New York: The New American Library.

Muncie Star (1988, March 11).

Murder: No Apparent Motive (1980). HBO Undercover Series.

Nash, J. R. (1973). *Bloodletters and Badmen.* New York: M. Evans and Company.

—— (1980). *Murder America.* New York: Simon & Schuster.

—— (1981a). *Almanac of World Crime.* New York: Anchor Press-Doubleday.

—— (1981b). *Look for the Woman.* New York: M. Evans and Company.

—— (1984). *Crime Chronology.* New York: Facts on File.

Nettler, G. (1982). *Killing One Another.* Cincinnati, Ohio: Anderson.

Neustatter, L. W. (1957). *The Mind of the Murderer.* London: Christopher Johnson.

Newsweek (1985, October 7). How many missing kids?, 30–35.

—— (1985, December 16). Wisconsin: The hunt for the emotional rapist, 30.

Ninety-eighth Congress. (1984). Hearing before the subcommittee on the judiciary United States Senate, first session on patterns of murders committed by one person, in large numbers with no apparent rhyme, reason or motivation, July 12, 1983. Washington, D. C.: Serial No. J-98-52, U.S. Government Printing· Office.

Norris, J. (1988). *Serial Killers.* New York: Doubleday.

Nunberg, H. (1955). *Principles of Psychoanalysis.* New York: International Universities Press.

O'Brien, D. (1985). *Two of a Kind: The Hillside Stranglers.* New York: New American Library.

Olsen, J. (1972). *Son: A Psychopath and His Victims.* New York: Dell.

—— (1974). *The Man with The Candy.* New York: Simon and Schuster.

Ott, J. (1984). The effects of light and radiation on human health and behavior, in L. J. Hippchen (Ed.), *Ecologic-Biochemical Approaches.* New York: Van Nostrand Reinhold, 105–183.

Pearson, E. (1936). *More Studies in Murder.* London: Arco Publishers.

Peck, M. S. (1983). *People of the Lie.* New York: Simon and Schuster.

Perdue, W., & D. Lester (1974). Temperamentally suited to kill: The personality of murderers, *Corrective and Social Psychiatry and Journal of Behavioral Technology, Methods, and Theory, 20.*

Peyton, D. (1984, December 16). Henry Lucas was a killer at age 14, *West Virginia Herald-Dispatch,* A5.

Pfeffer, C. (1980). Psychiatric hospital treatment of assaultive homicidal children, *American Journal Psychotherapy, 2,* 197–207.

Piers, M. W. (1978). *Infanticide.* New York: Norton.

Podolsky, E. (1964). The chemistry of murder, *Pakistan Medical Journal, 15,* 9–14.

Pokorny, A. D. (1965, December). A comparison of homicides in two cities, *Journal of Criminal Law, Criminology and Police Science, 56,* 479–87.

Pollak, O. (1950). *The Criminality of Women.* Philadelphia: University of Pennsylvania Press.

Posner, G. L., & J. Ware (1986). *Mengele.* New York: Dell.

Prentky, R. A., A. W. Burgess, & D. L. Carter (1986). Victim responses by rapist type: An empirical and clinical analysis. *Journal of Interpersonal Violence, 1,* 73–98.

Prince, M. (1908). *Dissociation of Personality.* New York: Longmans, Green.

Quimby, M. J. (1969). *The Devil's Emissaries.* New York: Barnes and Company.

Rada, R. (1983). Plasma androgens in violent and non-violent sex offenders, *Bulletin of the American Academy of Psychiatry and the Law, 11,* 149–58.

Rada, R. T., D. R. Laws, & R. Kellner (1976). Plasma testosterone levels in the rapist, *Psychosomatic Medicine, 38,* 257–68.

Reckless, W. (1967). *The Crime Problem.* New York: Appleton Century Crofts.

Reinhardt, J. M. (1960). *The Murderer's Trail of Charles Starkweather.* Springfield, IL: Charles C Thomas.

—— (1962). *The Psychology of Strange Killers.* Springfield, IL: Charles C Thomas.

Reiss, A., Jr. (1980). Victim proneness in repeat victimization by type of crime, in S. Fineberg & A. Reiss, Jr. (Eds.), *Indicators of Crime and Criminal Justice: Quantitative Studies,* 41–54. Washington, D.C.: U.S. Department of Justice.

Rennie, Y. (1978). *The Search for Criminal Man: A Conceptual History of the Dangerous Offender.* Toronto: Lexington Books.

Resnick, P. (1969). Child murders by parents. *American Journal of Psychiatry, 126,* 325–34.

—— (1970). Murder of the newborn: A psychiatric view of neonaticide, *American Journal of Psychiatry, 126,* 58–63.

Ressler, R. K. (Ed.) (1985). Violent crimes, *FBI Law Enforcement Bulletin, 54,* 1–31.

Ressler, R. K., A. W. Burgess, & J. E. Douglas (1988). *Sexual Homicide.* Lexington, MA: Lexington Books.

Ressler, R. K., et al. (1985) *FBI Law Enforcement Bulletin, 54,* 1–43.

Revitch, E. (1965). Sex murderer and the potential sex murderer, *Diseases of the Nervous System, 26,* 640–648.

Revitch, E., & L. B. Schlesinger (1981). *Psychopathology of Homicide.* Springfield, IL: Charles C Thomas.

Robins, L. N. (1966). *Deviant Children Grow Up.* Baltimore: Williams & Wilkins.

Rosenblatt, E., & C. Greenland (1974). Female crimes of violence, *Canadian Journal of Criminology and Corrections, 16,* 173–180.

Rowe, D. (1986). Genetic and environmental components of antisocial behavior: A study of 265 twin pairs, *Criminology, 24,* 513–32.

Rowe, D., & D. W. Osgood. (1984). Heredity and sociological theories of delinquency: A reconsideration, *American Sociological Review, 49,* 526–40.

Rubin, R. (1987). The neuroendocrinology and neurochemistry of antisocial behavior, in S. Mednick, T. Moffitt, & S. Stack, (Eds.), *The Causes of Crime: New Biological Approaches*. Cambridge, England: Cambridge University Press, 239–62.

Rule, A. (1980). *The Stranger Beside Me*. New York: New American Library.

—— (Stack, A.) (1983) *Lust Killer*. New York: New American Library.

—— (Stack, A.) (1984). *The I-5 Killer*. New York: New American Library.

—— (1988). *The Want-Ad Killer*. New York: New American Library.

Saferstein, R. (1987). *Criminalistics: An Introduction to Forensic Science* (3rd ed.). Englewood Cliffs, NJ: Prentice-Hall.

Samenow, S. E. (1978, September/October). The criminal personality: New concepts and new procedures for change, *The Humanist*, 16–19.

—— (1984). *Inside the Criminal Mind*. New York: Time Books.

Sampson, R. (1987). Personal violence by strangers: An extension and test of the opportunity model of predatory victimization, *Journal of Criminal Law and Criminology, 78*, 327–56.

Schacht, T. E. (1985). DSM-III and the politics of truth, *American Psychologist, 40*, 513–521.

Schreiber, F. R. (1973). *Sybil*. New York: Warner Books.

—— (1983). *The Shoemaker*. New York: Simon and Schuster.

Schur, E. M. (1972). *Labeling Deviant Behavior*. New York: Harper and Row, 21.

—— (1984). *Labeling Women Deviant: Gender, Stigma, and Social Control*. New York: Random House.

Schwarz, T. (1981). *The Hillside Strangler: A Murderer's Mind*. New York: Doubleday.

Scully, D., & J. Marolla (1985). Riding the bull at Gilley's: Convicted rapists describe the rewards of rape. *Social Problems, 32*, 251–63.

Sendi, I. B., & P. G. Blomgren (1975). A comparative study of predictive criteria in the predisposition of homicidal adolescents, *American Journal of Psychiatry, 132*, 423–427.

Sifakis, C. (1982). *The Encyclopedia of American Crime*. New York: Facts on File.

Simons, R. (1983, March). No ghosts for killer Gacy, *Toronto Star*.

Sizemore, C. (1982, August 25). Conversation Hour. Annual Meeting of the American Psychological Association, Washington, D.C.

Smith, H. E. (1987, January). Serial killers, *C. J. International, 3*(1), 1–2.

Smith, S. (1965). The adolesent murderer: A psychodynamic interpretation, *Archives of General Psychiatry, 13*, 310–319.

Sparrow, G. (1970). *Women Who Murder*. New York: Abelard-Schuman.

Spitzer, R. L. (1985). DSM-III and the politics-science dichotomy syndrome, *American Psychologist, 40*, 522–526.

Stanley, A. (1983, November 14). Catching a new breed of killer, *Time Magazine*, reported by David S. Jackson.

Steffensmeier, D. J., & M. J. Cobb (1981, October). Sex differences in urban arrest patterns, 1934–1979, *Social Problems, 29,* 37–50.

Stoller, R. F. (1975). *Perversion.* New York: Pantheon Books, 128.

Strauss, M. A., & L. Baron (1983). *Sexual Stratification, Pornography, and Rape.* Durham, NH: Family Research Laboratory, University of New Hampshire.

Suinn, R. M. (1984). *Fundamentals of Abnormal Psychology.* Chicago: Nelson-Hall.

Swanson, C. R., N. C. Chamelin, & L. Territo (1984). *Criminal Investigation.* New York: Random House.

Sykes, G. (1976). *The Concise Oxford Dictionary* (6th ed.). Oxford: Clarendon Press.

Sykes, G., & D. Matza (1957). Techniques of neutralization: A theory of delinquency, *American Sociological Review, 22,* 664–770.

Tanay, E. (1976). *The Murderers.* Indianapolis: Bobbs-Merrill.

Terry, G., & M. Malone (1987). The Bobby Joe Long serial murder case: A study in cooperation, *F.B.I. Law Enforcement Bulletin,* November, 12–18; December, 7–13.

Thigpen, C., & H. Cleckley (1957). *The Three Faces of Eve.* New York: McGraw-Hill.

Thomas, W. I. (1907). *Sex and Society.* Boston: Little, Brown.

——— (1923). *The Unadjusted Girl.* New York: Harper and Row.

Thompson, G. N. (1953). *The Psychopathic Delinquent and Criminal.* Springfield, IL: Charles C Thomas.

Thompson, T. (1979). *Serpentine.* New York: Dell.

Turner, F. J. (Ed.) (1984). *Adult Psychopathology.* New York: Free Press Winston.

United States v. Brawner, 471 F.2d 969 (D.C. Cir. 1972).

U.S. Department of Justice (1988). National Center for Missing and Exploited Children, Office of Juvenile Justice and Delinquency Prevention, Washington, D.C.

——— (1989a, January). Stranger abduction homicides of children, *Juvenile Justice Bulletin.* Washington, D.C.: Office of Juvenile Justice and Delinquency Prevention, Government Printing Office.

——— (1989b). *Missing and Exploited Children: Progress in the 80s.* Washington, D.C.: Office of Juvenile Justice and Delinquency Prevention, Government Printing Office.

Virkkunen, M. (1986). Reactive hypoglycemic tendency among habitually violent offenders, *Nutrition Reviews Supplement, 44,* 94–103.

Vitek v. Jones, 445 U.S. 480, 100 S. Ct. 1254 (1980).

The Washington Post (1988, May 26). When moms kill their infants.

Webster-Stratton, C. (1985). Comparison of abusive and nonabusive families with conduct-disordered children, *American Journal of Orthopsychiatry, 55,* 59–69.

Weisheit, R. A. (1984a). Female homicide offenders: Trends over time in an institutionalized population, *Justice Quarterly, 1*(4), 471–489.

——— (1984b). Women and crime: issues and perspectives, *Sex Roles, 11,* 7/8.

——— (1986). When mothers kill their children, *Social Science Journal, 23*(4), 439–448.

Wilbur, C. (1978). Clinical considerations in the evaluation and treatment of multiple personality (lecture delivered at Multiple Personality Conference, Friends Hospital, Philadelphia).

Wilkes, J. (1987, June). Murder in mind, *Psychology Today,* 27–32.

Wille, W. (1974). *Citizens Who Commit Murder.* St. Louis: Warren Greene.

Wilson, C., & D. Seaman (1985). *Encyclopedia of Modern Murder 1962–1982.* New York: Putnam's.

Wilson, J. Q., & R. J. Herrnstein (1985). *Crime and Human Nature.* New York: Simon and Schuster.

Winn, S., & D. Merrill (1980). *Ted Bundy: The Killer Next Door.* New York: Bantam.

Wolfe, D. A., P. Jaffe, S. K. Wilson, & L. Zak (1985). Children of battered women: The relation of child behavior to family violence and maternal stress, *Journal of Consulting and Clinical Psychology, 53*(5) 657–665.

Wolfgang, M. E., (1958). *Patterns in Criminal Homicide.* Philadelphia: University of Pennsylvania Press.

——— (1967). Criminal homicide and the subculture of violence, *Studies in Homicide.* New York: Harper and Row.

Wooden, K. (1984). *Child Lures.* Shelburne, VT: National Coalition for Children's Justice, Child Lures, Inc.

Yallop, D. (1982). *Deliver Us from Evil,* New York: Coward, McCann and Geoghegan.

Zitrin, A., A. Hardesty, E. Burdock, & A. Drossman (1975). Crime and violence among mental patients, *Scientific Proceedings of the 128th Annual Meeting of the American Psychiatric Association, Abstracts, 142,* 140–141.

Index

Witham, D., 228
Wolfe, D., 58
Wolfgang, M., 80–81, 87, 110
Women's liberation movement, 121
Wood, F., 234
Wooden, K., 97
Woodfield, R., 1, 37, 80, 130

XYY, 36, 65

Yochelson, S., 238

Zitrin, A., 41
Zodiac killer, 5